DEDICATION

For Janett -
Who loved books.
May your spirit fly high, my friend.

For Beth -
The champion of ship identifying.
You nailed it.

For Karen -
Because you loved them and wanted more.

And my Matthew
Because of what you are.
The beginning and the end of my world.
I love you

Dear Reader,

Thank you for selecting book 1 in the Mission Cove series.

The Summer of Us Part I was featured in the One Hot Summer anthology. I have added content in Part I. However, if you had read the previous short story and are anxious to find out what is next for Linc and Sunny, you may navigate to Part II.

Be sure to sign up for my <u>newsletter</u> for up to date information on new releases, exclusive content and sales.

Always fun - never spam!

xoxo,
Melanie

PART I

1

LINC

"What?" I frowned in confusion. "A job? I already have something for the summer. Why do I need a different job?"

My father's cold eyes studied me over his thick-rimmed glasses. "Because I said so, Lincoln."

"But, Father..."

"You aren't spending it fucking around, drinking with your friends, sleeping the summer away, and spending my money. You're going to work."

I gaped at him. "When the hell have I ever done those things? I spent the last three summers volunteering at the local animal shelter."

He scowled. "Watch your tone. Walking dogs and feeding cats teaches you nothing."

"It teaches me responsibility and to care for other creatures."

He waved his hand. "It's making you soft. I need to toughen you up."

I wanted to argue with him and tell him how wrong he was, but I knew there was no point. Franklin Thomas didn't do feelings. Or care about anything. Animals were on the earth to feed him and for him to place bets on at the occasional horse race. You didn't love them.

According to him, it was better never to love anything. Including me.

"You'll be working at the summer camp. My company is sponsoring it this year, and I want a Thomas there representing me. You'll be assisting the head of the camp with whatever he requires you to do."

I held back my groan. I didn't want to work at the camp. I wanted to be at the shelter—learning and soaking up as much knowledge as I could.

"Father, I want to be a vet. I told you this before, many times. Volunteering at the shelter will look good on my resume in a few years."

He shook his head. "We've discussed this, and I told you no. You'll be joining the firm. Forget that stupid dream. Your mother put that idea in your head when you were a kid—one of her many idiotic thoughts—and it's time you grow out of it."

I curled my hands into fists at my sides. I hated the way he spoke of my mother. As if she meant nothing. When, in fact, it was the opposite. She had meant everything to me and had been the bright spot in my world.

That died when she did, and my life was never the same again. My already distant father became cold and unfeeling. His entire world revolved around one thing—money. Happiness didn't matter. I didn't matter—a fact that he made perfectly clear.

I tried one more time. "Father, please—"

He stood, slamming his fists onto his desk. "There will be no arguments, or it's all gone, Lincoln. The car, your allowance, *any* freedom I allow you—everything."

I knew he was serious.

"When do I start?"

"You report day after tomorrow. I've decided you can stay there, but you come back every Sunday to report in. You keep your eyes open and your nose clean. Camp ends mid-August. If you do a good job, there'll be a reward."

I frowned. My father never gave rewards. "Sir?" I asked.

He smiled—one of his cold, unreal smiles that unnerved me. "I won't shut down that fucking animal shelter you like so much. Fuck this up, and I'm pulling the lease."

I turned and left, not wanting him to see my disgust. I headed out the door and hurried down the path to the cliff that overlooked the water below. I sat on the edge, drawing my knees up to my chest and resting my arms on them.

I knew my father owned the building the shelter was in. Hell, he owned most of the buildings and businesses in town. Not that anyone knew it. His maze of numbered companies kept that hidden. Rents went up, people lost their homes and businesses, and he sat back, not caring, enjoying the sick, twisted game he played with people's lives. Laughing at the fact that it was him pulling the strings so often, moving people around like pieces on a chessboard. To most people, my father was a well-respected businessman. He owned several companies in various towns, along with a lot of real estate, including some huge holdings in Toronto. He sat on the chamber of commerce board, the council, and was tight with the mayor and the police here in Mission Cove. He duped them all.

I despised him.

I had been looking forward to spending the whole summer at the shelter. Caring for the animals, picking the brains of the vets who volunteered their time there. I had hoped to convince one of them to let me volunteer at their clinic so I could learn more. It would have looked great on my application to veterinary school. It was hard to get into, and I would need all the help I could get.

Except my father had just crushed those dreams, hadn't he? The same way he crushed everything else I hoped for. Everything I loved.

I knew it looked like I was the kid who had it all. I drove a new car, wore nice clothes, and I always had money in my pocket. My grades were good, and I was well-thought-of by my teachers and peers alike.

They all saw what I allowed them to see.

None of them saw the emptiness of the huge house I lived in. The meals I ate alone since my father couldn't be bothered to sit down with me. No one knew of the holidays I spent by myself, the forgotten birthdays, or the constant criticism I lived with. They didn't know the strict rules my father enforced on me—or the punishments I suffered if I broke them. Franklin Thomas demanded perfection in everything I did, and when I fell short, he liked to show his displeasure.

With his fists.

I had a small social circle, very few friends, and a life I hated.

Except for one thing.

A secret I kept hidden from everyone, loathing the fact that I had to, but needing to do so to protect her. To protect us.

The image of rich brown eyes and long, soft curls the color of the sunset filtered through my mind.

Sunny Jenson.

The first girl I had ever liked—had liked for as long as I could remember. When my mother was alive, she thought it was the sweetest thing and encouraged it. My father knew nothing about it.

Sunny was my best friend in grade school, my sidekick in junior high, and now so much more. It happened naturally, without fanfare or thought. People were used to seeing us together. I knew they talked, but I didn't care. All I cared about was her.

I walked her home one night after a school function, knowing she didn't like the dark. We stopped at the park, and she sat down on a swing.

"Push me!"

I settled my hands on her hips and shoved her forward, stepping aside to let her go as high as she wanted. She laughed in the darkness, soaring up and back, slowly letting the momentum die and returning

to the sand where I waited. I reached out and gripped the metal chains,
halting her movements.

"Fun?" I teased.

She grinned, her eyes shining in the moonlight. Suddenly, I
noticed things I had never seen before. The swell of her tits, the way
her hair tumbled over them. How soft her skin looked. How much I
wanted to touch it. Our eyes met and held, and before I knew what I
was doing, I bent down and kissed her. Fumbling, awkward, and
perfect. When I pulled back, she smiled.

"Be my girl," I begged.

She wrapped her hand around my neck. "I already am, Linc. I
already am."

Sunny Jenson became my own personal ray of sunlight. I was her
protector, her best friend, and the boy head over heels for her.

She was a five-foot-nothing dynamo with eyes like melted chocolate. Tiny and delicate, she looked as if a strong wind could blow her
over. But my girl was as tough as nails. Smart, funny, and sweet.

I had been looking forward to being at the shelter, which was
around the corner from the diner where she usually worked all
summer, in addition to her shifts at the grocery store.

My father detested her—anyone like her. Anything good and
right, he looked at with derision and loathing, and with his announce-
ment, he had just stolen that bit of happiness.

I wanted to talk to her, to call her and vent my frustrations.
Hearing her gentle voice would help calm me down, but I couldn't do
that.

Sunny came from the wrong side of the small town where we lived.
Her mother worked as a maid at the large hotel on the edge of the city
limits. Owned, of course, by my father. A lot of the care of her two
younger sisters fell on Sunny, and she adored them. Between school,
her two jobs, caring for her sisters, and her volunteering at the shelter, it
was hard for us to find time together, but we managed. Money was
tight for her, and Sunny didn't come with the trappings that other girls

her age did. There was no expensive clothing. She didn't wear makeup. She rode her bike, took the bus, or walked everywhere she went, and she didn't own a cell phone. Every penny she made went toward saving for university tuition and helping her mother.

I wanted to get her a cell phone, but my father tracked all my bills, and I couldn't risk him finding out about her. He would end it and make life hell for her mother. I wouldn't do that to her or her family. Sunny wasn't someone he would ever approve of. She wasn't the "right" kind of people.

I remembered the day he walked into my room, without knocking or caring he was interrupting me. He tossed a box of condoms onto my dresser.

"You're fifteen. I'm sure you know how to use your dick. Wrap it. I don't want any other mistakes ruining my life." He paused in the doorway. *"Dip your wick wherever you want, but don't bring them here and don't get attached. I have plans, and you're going to fucking carry them out."*

I looked at him, struck silent in shock.

"I saw you walking with that girl. The waitress. She isn't part of your future, Lincoln. Fuck her and forget her. I don't want to find out you've been seeing her. If I do, you know the consequences."

Then he walked out. Typical of my father. He told me how to live every day. What to think, who I should like. How I should act. He never let me forget how my mother's pregnancy changed his life. I was the reason for everything that went wrong. How I robbed him of her attention and time. How her shifting focus angered him. How if I hadn't come along, she might have been a good wife instead of his finding her constantly lacking. He even found a reason to blame me for the aneurysm that took her from me.

It inconvenienced him.

My mother's family had been well-off, but her parents' will, and then hers, made it impossible for my father to get his hands on the money. Another reason he hated me.

I wished, more than once, I could get access to the trust fund to help out Sunny and get away from my father. But it wasn't available to me until I was nineteen.

Two more years.

Two years and I would walk away from this town and the man who made my life miserable. He thought I would work for him. Do his dirty work. However, I had other plans that I kept to myself.

Once I had that trust fund, I was gone. Wherever Sunny wanted to go, I would take her. Her mother and sisters as well. Whereas my father thought of people like the Jensons as trash, they were nothing but kind to me. Sunny's mom always welcomed me to their small house with a hug and kiss on the cheek, clucked about me being too thin and that I needed to eat. Her fussing warmed something long dormant in my chest. I tried to help out in small ways—repair broken things or carry out the garbage. Sunny's two younger sisters, Emily and Hayley, treated me like a big brother. They loved hugs and cuddles and smiled in delight at the chocolate bars or cookies I would bring. I loved spending time there. The house was run-down, small, sparse, and on the wrong side of town, but it was a home. Unlike the huge, vacant rooms of my house, their place was filled with love. I could be myself there, and it was okay. They expected nothing and asked for nothing but for me to be Linc. And I accepted them.

Sunny's dad had caused a scandal by walking out on them when she was young and abandoning them completely. He lived openly with a hairdresser, who had deserted her husband, until a couple of months later when they were killed in a head-on collision with a semi on the highway. With no life insurance and no money, Sunny's mom had to move the family to a smaller place, went to work cleaning offices, leaving Sunny to look after her much younger sisters. Eventually, they moved in with her grandmother to help with expenses. The scandal passed, but Sunny's mom never got over it. She stopped cleaning offices and went to work at the hotel when it opened. She kept her head down and raised her kids, ignoring the whispers and stares, proving herself to be above them all. I thought she was fucking amazing.

Once I had that money, we'd all start a life together that didn't include Mission Cove, my father, or the gossips.

One where I didn't have to hide or pretend. Where Sunny, her mom, and sisters could start fresh.

I stood and looked down at the water, the waves breaking against the rocks, deciding to go into town. I felt like some ice cream.

If Sunny happened to be behind the counter at the diner, that would be even better.

2

LINC

My father's car was gone when I went back to the house. I was glad I didn't have to see him again. I grabbed my keys and drove into town. Our large, rambling house was set on the hill overlooking the small town my father ruled—a gaudy, shiny symbol of his wealth and status.

I went to the diner, sitting patiently in the corner booth no one liked. It was somewhat hidden and closer to the kitchen, the smell of the grease from the fryer lingering in the air. The old air conditioner that hung over the front door didn't have the force it needed to reach this far into the room, so it was warmer than the rest of the place and the booth was usually empty.

Lucky me.

From my vantage point, I watched Sunny in the diner, filling coffee, scooping ice cream, always smiling and friendly.

She was so pretty. Her hair was caught up in a high ponytail, the bright strawberry-blond gleaming under the artificial light. Despite her lack of height, you noticed her. Her smile and laughter, the kindness she treated everyone with.

She approached my booth, a mischievous grin pulling up one corner of her mouth and her eyes dancing.

"Hey, Lincoln. Didn't expect to see you in here today."

I winked. "Sunny-girl. I was hungry." I eyed the way her uniform stretched over her high, tight tits and the short skirt showed off her tanned legs. I wasn't hungry for food, and she knew that.

She set down the menu and glanced behind her. The diner wasn't overly busy at the moment, mostly a few locals gathered around, sipping coffee, and gossiping. There was no one sitting close, so she leaned in and kissed me swiftly, then sat across from me.

"Hi," she whispered.

"Hi."

"Are you okay?" She frowned. "Was your dad at you again?"

I passed a hand over my face. "How can you tell?"

"You always get those lines on your forehead when you're upset. And your dad always upsets you."

"I'm fine."

She bent closer, her eyes troubled. "Did he-did he hurt you?"

"No."

The bell over the door chimed, and she stood. "I'll be back. I get my break in ten minutes, and we'll talk."

My thoughts drifted to the last time my father and I'd had words.

His fist slammed into my ribs, stopping my breath and causing agonizing pain to ripple through my body. He knew exactly how to hit. To cause me pain without permanent damage, and where to hit so that no one could see.

"I told you to drop the fucking tart. She has no place in your life."

I was on my knees, gasping for air, my mind racing.

I had fucked up and bought Sunny flowers on my credit card. She'd been having a bad day, and I wanted to do something to make her smile. I'd even had them delivered, remembering she had told me once she'd never been sent flowers.

My father saw the charge on the card and traced it.

And now I was taking the punishment.

He grabbed my hair and lifted my head. The anger on his face was frightening.

"Drop her, or I will drive her out of town. Her entire family. Got it? Some gold digger who has convinced you she likes you for anything except my money isn't going to fuck up my plans."

Another punch landed, and I was out cold. When I woke up, I was alone.

It was Sunny who saw the bruises. Sunny who made me tell her what happened. She listened with a horrified expression and decided we needed to break up.

"I'm not worth that," she sobbed. "Someone needs to stop him."

I held her arms, refusing to let her go. "No one can stop him, Sunny. I'm not giving you up. But I'm afraid," I admitted. "Afraid of what he'd do to you." I sucked in some air. "Don't leave me, Sunny. Don't make me go back to being alone again."

She threw her arms around my neck. "I don't want to."

"We'll have to be more careful. I can't risk you."

She sniffled, and I held her face in my hands.

"One day, we won't have to hide. I promise."

Her kiss said it all.

Since then, we'd been so cautious that at times it felt as if we were strangers barely acknowledging each other in town. We sought out private moments, hiding in deserted places. I lived for the hours when we were alone together.

She returned, carrying a strawberry shake and a piece of pie which I knew were for me. I shook off my dark thoughts. I wasn't allowed ice cream or sweets at home, so I always got them when I was with her. She set them in front of me and returned a moment later with a sandwich and coffee for herself.

"Tell me," she said between bites.

I told her what occurred. Instead of her looking disappointed, however, I was surprised when her eyes lit up.

"Did you hear what I said? I won't be at the shelter this summer. I'll barely see you." I let my fork fall to the plate. "I was hanging on to this. Looking forward to it, and now he's fucked it all."

"Language," she chided.

I ignored her. "He somehow constantly finds a way to make me fucking miserable."

"Well, he failed this time."

"Care to explain that logic to me? I was going to be right around the corner at the shelter. I could come in here every day and see you since he would be in the city. Now, I'm going to be stuck five miles away at the damn camp."

She hunched forward, her smile never fading. If anything, it got brighter. After another glance over her shoulder, she slid her hand toward mine, entwining our fingers. "I have my own news."

I squeezed her hand. "Tell me."

"I'm working at the camp too."

I lifted my eyebrows in surprise. "What?"

She nodded, looking excited. "I'm going to be working in the kitchen."

"What about your sisters? Who will watch them?"

She smiled, although her eyes were sad. "My grandmother's estate was finally settled. She didn't have much, but there was a little money left over when it was done." I waited for her to continue, squeezing her fingers in comfort. Her grandmother had been a special person to Sunny, and when she died a year ago, it had hit her hard. Sunny still became emotional when talking about her.

"So," she continued, "my mom and I talked, and she decided she was going to send the girls to summer camp. She wants them to have a good summer after the last couple of years. She knew how much I wanted to work there, and she spoke with Gerry—the guy who runs it. It turned out he was looking for another body, so I went and saw him, and I got the job. Harry said I'd still have a job in the fall part time again." She peeked over her shoulder. "Things aren't great here, and he can't really afford me full time this year. His daughter is taking more shifts to help out, and the grocery store hours are being cut back too, so I really needed this to happen."

"Why didn't you say anything?"

"Because you would want to help or give me money, and I don't need that from you, Linc. I just need you to be Linc. My mom and I would have figured something out." Then she grinned. "But look how it's all worked out!"

Her smile was infectious, and I felt my own grow. "So, you'll be there too?" I asked, feeling the weight of my father's words lifting away.

She lifted her eyebrows in amusement. "Six weeks away from this town and all the people here? Without a doubt."

Still, I felt a flash of hurt. "You were going to take the job, and you didn't tell me?"

She laughed, shaking her head. "I was going to talk to you about it. But when I spoke with Gerry the other day, he said he was getting an assistant. He mentioned the name Lincoln, and I knew there couldn't be two of you around with that name. Plus, he said your father's company was sponsoring the camp this year, so I was sure. I said yes right away. I figured you'd be coming and going, but at least we'd see each other in the daytime."

"No, my father says I'm staying there." I barked out a low laugh that was bitter. "I guess he figured it was less he had to see of me, while still keeping tabs on what I was doing."

Sunny smiled, looking guilty. "Is it wrong I'm excited at the thought of sharing a cabin with girls my age and not my sisters?" Then she giggled. It was one of my most favorite sounds in the world. "And now I know you'll be there *all* the time? This is perfect."

A glimmer of excitement hit my belly, and I grinned. "Yeah. He wants me home every Sunday to 'report in,' as he calls it, but other than that, I'm free." It had been the one good piece of news he had given me when he informed me how I would be spending my summer.

"See?" Sunny smiled, the expression lighting her entire face. "It's actually great."

I hunched over the table. "I wish I could kiss you."

"Tonight. Our spot."

Our spot.

The deserted camping ground not far from where Sunny lived. Easy for her to get to, and a place no one would ever look for me. We'd walk through the woods and sit at the water's edge, by a tiny cove. The area was too small to be a party place and the ground was rocky, but it was sheltered by the rough cliff walls and secluded. It was a spot Sunny had discovered and loved. No one ever went there, so it became ours. Our own little paradise. Our favorite thing was to build a small fire and sit and talk for hours. On rainy or cold nights, we'd sit in my car. We could be us there with no one watching.

I winked. "Looking forward to it."

3

LINC

I pulled away from Sunny's mouth, my breathing hard. The same with my dick. It was always hard when we were close.

The day had turned cloudy, the skies dark and the rain intermittent. My car was a warm, private place, and we were taking full advantage of it.

Sunny's eyes were clouded with desire, her lips swollen from mine. She followed my movements, her face staying close.

"More, baby."

I groaned. Making out with her was, by far, my favorite thing to do. But we hadn't gone much further. The back seat of my Honda wasn't overly roomy, and I didn't want our first time to be rushed and cliché. There was a lot of touching, groping, fondling, and kissing, but nothing else.

"I can't," I moaned as her tongue traced a path up my neck. "Sunny, you have to stop."

I shouted as she ran her hand down my torso and pressed her hand to my cock that was straining against my jeans.

"I could make you feel good. Let me."

She'd been demanding more every time we were together. I couldn't resist her. I didn't want to resist her.

"Only if you let me too."

Straddling my thighs, she was every fantasy I had ever had, hovering over me. The sunroof allowed the dim moonlight to filter into the back of the car as the clouds lifted. Sunny's hair was mussed from my hands, falling in masses of messy waves down her back. Her loose T-shirt hung off her shoulders, the strap of her camisole pushed away by my eager hands. I loved her soft skin. How it tasted under my tongue. Felt under my touch. I wanted to feel all of it. All of her.

She bit her lip, then nodded. I pulled her back to my mouth.

In seconds, we were a mass of fingers and lips. Her tongue on mine was sweet and soft. The sound of my zipper being pulled down was loud in the car—the metal teeth opening, her fingers fumbling on the button, and then the feel of her hand wrapped around my dick. I groaned at the sensation. It was so different from my own hand. Smoother, more hesitant.

Better.

She began to stroke me. Gently.

"Harder, Sunny." I wrapped my hand around hers. "Like this," I whispered, my cock jumping as she worked me. "Yes. Like that."

Our mouths fused together again. Bravely, I ran my hand up the back of her leg, slipping it between her thighs and finding the sweet secret they hid. I dipped my finger inside her, finding her slick and ready.

"Fuck, baby, you're so soft. So wet."

"I always am for you."

Her words made me harder. Her hand around my dick made me frantic. The feel of her on my fingers made me want more. All of her.

But for now, I would settle for this. I knew we were both virgins. Learning each other for the first time. I wanted to make it good for her.

Her hand wrapped around my cock ensured it would be good for me.

The car filled with low gasps and moans. The windows began to steam up. I stroked and teased, finding her clit and rolling it, listening to her reactions and trying to respond to them. I sank one finger inside her, still playing with her clit. She gasped and stroked me faster, rocking against my hand. Our lips met in long, wet kisses, our tongues stroking and teasing. She moved faster. Gripped me harder. My balls began to tighten, and I buried my head in her shoulder.

"Not gonna last," I managed to grit out.

She gasped suddenly, arching over me, her body taut. I swear I saw stars as my own orgasm shot through me, and I came all over her hand, thrusting hard and not caring.

She collapsed on top of me, her warm weight welcome. I wrapped my arms around her, holding her close.

"Holy fuck," I gasped.

She slapped my chest. "Language."

I pushed her heavy hair away from her face. "I didn't expect that."

She lifted her head, meeting my gaze. "Me either, but it felt right." She grinned. "In fact, it felt fucking awesome."

I burst out laughing at her curse. She rarely ever swore, and if she did, it was something mild like hell or damn. Hearing her say fuck was sexy. In fact, it got me hard again. Her lying on top of me didn't help.

She glanced at me, arching an eyebrow. I shrugged.

"What do you expect? I'm seventeen, and you just gave me the best orgasm I've ever had. Of course, I want more."

"More than my hand?"

"I know we're not ready for that. But whatever you want to give me, I'll take."

She smiled, tracing my jaw with her finger. "Just think, Linc. We have all summer. A whole summer of this. Of us."

I grabbed her, kissing her hard. "Yeah. All summer."

I braced my foot against the bottom of the deck and pulled at the rotted stump. It finally gave way, and I fell back into the dirt with a groan. I pushed the offending mass of roots and wood off me and stood, dusty, hot, and happier than I had felt in ages. I pulled off my shirt and wiped my face.

A throat clearing made me look up. Gerry Braun stood, his arms folded over his chest, studying me. I had been at the camp for three days and worked my ass off. This was no cushy assistant's job. This was a do-whatever-has-to-be-done job, and although I was sure my father thought he was punishing me, I loved it.

Gerry approached, holding out a bottle of water. I accepted and downed it in long swallows, then pushed the sweaty hair off my forehead.

Silently, he handed me a brown bag, and I looked inside, grateful to see a thick sandwich and an apple. I sat down on the steps and began eating. Gerry sat next to me, placing another bottle of water on the steps beside me.

"Stay hydrated."

I grunted around a mouthful of ham. His wife was a stellar cook, and I was going to enjoy eating this summer. If all my work was like this, I would burn it off fast and my father would never know.

"I'm almost done here, then I'll replace those rotted boards of the dock." I wadded up the wax paper and pulled out the apple, taking a huge bite.

Gerry turned and faced me. "I owe you an apology, kid."

I swallowed before answering him. "Sorry, sir?"

He chuckled gruffly, shaking his head. He pushed back his ball cap and wiped his forehead.

"The camp's been struggling the last couple years. When your father made the offer to sponsor it and give us some money, I was suspicious." He side-eyed me. "I know he wants this land."

I didn't deny it. My father had ordered me to keep my eyes open and "find the weaknesses" at the camp.

"I want to find out what he needs, what makes him vulnerable, and make him an offer he can't refuse," he instructed. *"Find it and tell me."*

My father's words hadn't surprised me. He didn't do anything out of generosity, so I knew he would have a hidden agenda for having me here. Aside from creating space between Sunny and me.

I shrugged. "I don't plan on helping him with that goal, sir."

He nudged my shoulder. "Knock it off with the *sir* shit. It's Gerry."

I finished my apple. "Okay, Gerry." I relaxed back against the step, and he mimicked my action.

"I thought you were going to be a lazy, rich little SOB. A brat I was going to have to babysit who would spend the summer lying on the dock and bothering my counselors."

I started to laugh. "I don't blame you."

"You're all right, kid. You're a hard worker." He admitted. "The list I gave you were things I haven't been able or wanted to do myself. Hard, messy shit that, frankly, should have taken you a week, if not more. You've knocked it out in three days, and not once have you complained."

I looked around. "What's to complain about? I get to work outside, your wife's cooking is incredible, and I can eat all I want. I can swim in the lake or the pool and go to sleep when I feel like it." I couldn't help but tease him. "Although a bed would be more welcome than a cot in the office."

He stared at me for a moment. "You sound as if you're tired of being told what to do, kid."

"I am. I like it here. I work and get rewarded."

He cleared his throat. "Yeah, about that. Your father insisted I direct deposit your pay to an account he gave me."

I wasn't surprised. I had to account for every dollar I spent. Every week, I handed over my journal of expenses and receipts. My father would top up the cash I was allowed to have on hand and then give me back my credit card. I never had more than a hundred dollars in my pocket or less than twenty. It wasn't that he felt I should have the money, but he kept up the image of being a good father and provider. That he cared for his son's well-being and looked after him. He also refused to have his son look anything but well-off. It was all a sham, but I liked to spend his money. It was the one retribution I had.

Thank god my father thought I was an airhead who smoked dope (no such thing as a receipt for weed), got the munchies (explained all the bills from the diner and grocery store when I visited Sunny), and bought a lot of condoms (an easy cover for treats I got for the girls at the drugstore). Whatever extra I could skim went to much better use than sitting in his bank account. I slipped tens and fives into Sunny's wallet and dropped twenties into drawers at her mother's. I was sure they were onto me, but they let it alone. I think they knew how important it was to me to help look after them. They looked after me in return.

The bottom line was that my father didn't give a flying fuck if I screwed half the town and liked weed. As long as I didn't get caught, or get some girl pregnant, and I stayed away from him, it was fine. If he knew the cash went to help Sunny, however, the punishment would be severe. I had experienced that already.

"Nothing you can do, Gerry. My father is my father."

He'd dropped me here himself, not even turning off the engine as I got out, duffel bag in hand. I wasn't allowed my car for the summer. I had been late getting home from my night with Sunny, disturbed him coming in, and he was displeased with my explanation of where I had been. My ribs still felt the ache from his displeasure, and then he took away my car.

"Find a way to the house Sunday or else," were his last words.

Gerry tilted his head, studying me. "I think there's a story, and I think you're too private to share. But this is what I'm gonna do. I lowballed your father and told him this job paid way less than it does. So, every week, I'm gonna give you the difference. What you do with it is up to you."

I blinked.

"And the room off the office? There's a bed there and a private shower. It's yours for the summer, kid." He stood and brushed off his legs. "I'm wondering—is your father sending a car for you? I saw him drop you off and leave, but I know you have to see him on Sundays."

I shook my head, now embarrassed. "No, sir, ah, Gerry. I'll get up early and walk."

"Five miles?"

I shrugged. "Good exercise."

He shook his head. "Follow me."

He led me to one of the outbuildings and opened the door. A two-person scooter sat inside, helmet on the handles. It was old, somewhat rusty, and needed a good wash. I looked at Gerry, who was watching me.

"You know anything about engines?"

"A little. A friend of mine is a grease monkey, and I help him sometimes."

He handed me a set of keys. "Tune it up and fill it with gas. You can use it on Sundays and your other morning off." He winked. "I didn't fail to notice the way a certain girl's dark eyes lit up when she heard your name, or the way you casually asked to see the list of counselors and their days off. Or how, interestingly enough, your two half days matched hers."

I ducked my head with a grin.

He paused on his way out of the shed. "Be sure to wear a helmet. The registration and ownership are in the little bag. Anything else you need, kid?"

I couldn't help asking. "Another sandwich would be great."

He grinned. "Get it yourself, kid. The missus loves to see you eat."

I watched him walk away, feeling overwhelmed. I wasn't used to kindness, aside from Sunny and her family. Most people treated me with kid gloves because of who my father was. Some disliked me because of it, and others ignored me. Indifference and hostility were the main reactions when people heard my name. I was used to it.

But I had earned Gerry's respect. I wanted to continue to earn it.

I rolled the door closed and went to finish my chores.

But first, I was going to stop and get another sandwich.

4

LINC

The next four weeks were, without a doubt, the happiest of my
life. The days were busy and crazy—filled with kids, work, and
lots of play.

And Sunny.

I got to see her anytime I wanted. She always had a treat waiting
for me in the kitchen when I would drop in. We sat together at meals,
her sisters occupied with their new friends. Emily and Hayley were
thrilled to see me when they arrived and sought me out for hugs
almost daily, but other than that, they were busy and happy. It was
good to see.

Sunny was relaxed and smiled all the time. We knew very few
people at the camp since a lot of them came in from other towns to
work here. The couple of people we recognized couldn't be bothered
with either of us, so we were actually free. My father had no spies
here, and no one reporting to him. He never contacted me, and other
than the two times I went to see him, he seemed to care less about
what I was doing.

As far as he was concerned, I was out of his hair, away from
Sunny, and doing what he wanted. I purposely let him think I was

miserable, talking about the menial work, and complaining about all the kids and roughing it.

I was sure he was delighted with my supposed misery. I drove Sunny to her house and dropped both her and the scooter off before walking to my father's. I was hot and sweaty when I arrived, but he seemed unconcerned about the idea that I had walked the full five miles, instead ordering me to take a shower, then asked me what I had found out. He wasn't happy with my lack of information and told me to dig harder, then dismissed me. The next week, it was the same thing, although his anger was more evident. He took my cell phone and dropped it into his desk drawer.

He stood. *"You're wasting my time. Don't come back until you have something I can use. Find something."* He waited until I was at the doorway and called out, *"Don't make me angry."* His threat was clear, but at that point, I didn't care.

I left, not planning on returning until camp was over, and already making plans to spend the free days with Sunny. I had nothing to say to him, and I wouldn't help him take Gerry's camp away from him, so I wouldn't return. He was going to hit me no matter what I said to him, so I would enjoy my time away from him and take my punishment later.

On the way back to camp, we stopped at another small town, and I bought two pay-as-you-go cell phones. I couldn't do that where I lived—there was no place to get them. Now we each had a phone, and once I got home, even if I got my other one back, Sunny and I could stay in touch and my father would never know. The money Gerry was giving me each week would cover the cost for a long time.

The best times were the evenings. Once the kids were in bed and the camp was quiet. Often we walked along the water's edge or sat, hidden in Sunny's favorite spot. Two large weeping willows soared above the other trees, standing about twenty feet apart and set way back from the water, almost on their own as if they'd been planned. When the breeze blew hard enough, their branches lifted and touched, and Sunny insisted they were soul mates reaching for each other. I teased her about her romantic notion, but secretly I liked it. I carved my name and date into the base of one tree, and hers into the other. She cried when I told her our souls would now touch for eternity too.

She also let me touch her tits even longer that night, so it was a win-win situation for me.

But most nights, Sunny found her way into my room, and we spent the time talking and exploring each other.

I was addicted to her. The taste of her mouth. The feel of her skin. I couldn't get enough of her.

Like now.

She moaned as I slid my hands under her shirt, cupping her tits. They fascinated me. I ran my thumb over her nipple, feeling the bud harden under my touch.

"Please," I begged, tugging on her shirt. Every time we were alone, we went a little further. Pushed our boundaries. Tonight, I wanted to see her.

She sat up, gathered her bravado, and pulled her T-shirt over her head. She looked down, her plain cotton bra white against the golden color of her skin from the sun. For a moment, she looked sad, and I cupped her cheek.

"What?"

"I wish this was prettier," she whispered, touching the strap on her shoulder.

I shook my head. "I don't need that prettier. You're the prettiest thing in the world. Nothing can compete."

She gazed up at me. "You're so perfect."

I snorted. "I'm hardly perfect. Ask my father."

"No," she insisted, rising up on her knees. "You are to me. You're my world, Linc. I trust you more than anyone."

"Show me."

She reached behind herself, unclasping her bra. It slipped from her shoulders, fully exposing her to me. I stared in awe at her tits. Full, round, with tempting pink nipples that taunted me. My hand was shaking as I reached out, tracing one finger around her areola, then stroked her nipple with my thumb. When she moaned and arched her back, I bent forward and took her nipple in my mouth. She gasped, burying her fingers in my hair as I sucked and kissed, groaning at the taste and feel of her. Sunshine, summer heat, and my girl.

In seconds, she was under me on my narrow bed. I licked and sucked, held her full tits in my hands, squeezed and stroked. Even having starred in every disgusting, teenage hormonal fantasy I ever had, they were better than I imagined. Sunny moaned softly, arched, and breathed my name. She tugged on my T-shirt, and without asking, I sat up and tore it off, flinging it somewhere behind me.

She traced my torso, her fingers lingering on my abs. "You're so cut," she murmured. "So sexy."

I looked down, liking how her hand looked against the darker skin on my body. All the manual labor I was doing was making me strong. Fit. In better shape than the gym ever did for me. I wondered at times when I saw myself if I would be able to fight back now. If my father would realize his fists no longer had the power they once did.

If I could break the cycle.

If he didn't have the ability to physically hurt, I could claim my life as my own. I could live with his nasty words, since I didn't care about his opinion.

Buoyed by the thoughts, I kissed Sunny. "I have other hard things, too."

She hummed, running her hand over the bulge in my shorts. "Can I see too?"

I swallowed. "God, yes."

I lay down, lifting my hips and yanking down my shorts. My cock sprang free, hard and already leaking precome. She traced one finger down my length, making me shiver.

"I've never seen one before yours," she admitted.

A flash of possessiveness went through me. "Mine is the only one you'll ever see."

She grinned, a tiny dimple showing beside her eye. "Is that so? I guess I had better get acquainted with him."

Then she took me in her mouth.

I was on a high the next day, my smile never leaving my face. I'd had my first blow job. I thought it was amazing—the feel of Sunny's mouth and hands on me. The way her lips wrapped around my dick was a sight I would never forget. I came far too fast, but she assured me it meant she did a good job. I planned on making it last longer next time. It felt too good to let go that quick, but she'd shocked me, and the sensations were overwhelming. She let me use my fingers to make her come afterward, but I was determined to reciprocate as soon as I could. The horn announcing all counselors had to be in their bunks for bed check had put a stop to our experimenting.

I lifted some bales of hay around the fire pit, shifting and arranging them for tonight's cookout and songfest. The kids loved it, and I had to admit that although I was too old to be part of a sing-along, I did hum a little under my breath.

"Hey, kid."

I turned to see Gerry approaching. "Hey," I replied.

"I need to send you to Dalewood."

I brushed off my hands. Dalewood was a large town about ten miles away from the camp in the other direction. "Okay."

"The delivery truck broke down, so the missus needs her orders picked up." He clapped me on the shoulder. "You can take the camp van and someone to help you."

"I'm good."

He grinned. "I thought a pretty strawberry-blond girl in the kitchen might enjoy a drive and lunch out."

Just like that, my day got even better.

"Yeah, maybe I could do with some help."

He smirked. "Thought so. Sam will finish this. You shower and head to the kitchen. Cindy will give you all the instructions."

"Done."

I hurried back to the office and jumped in the shower, then headed to the kitchen, my hair still wet. It was bustling as always, but Sunny was with Cindy, who was handing her a list. Cindy's eyes crinkled as she looked at me.

"There's my boy." She smiled, handing me the keys. "Sunny has a list. There are four stops. The most important one is the butcher. Save it until last. He'll pack it in the coolers Gerry put in the back since our van isn't refrigerated. Everything else is ordered and waiting for you."

"Okay."

"Drive safe, and I need you back by four."

I glanced at the clock. It was close to ten. "We'll be back in plenty of time."

"Walton's Grill has great burgers. Have lunch before you come back. Look around. It's a pretty little town." She paused with a wink. "Great place to get lost in."

I couldn't help stepping forward and pressing a kiss to her plump cheek. She treated me the way Sunny's mom did—with affection and love. She did the same to everyone at the camp, but for me, it meant more.

"Thanks, Cindy. You're the best."

"Get on with you," she chuckled and pushed me away. "Fill the tank up at Larson's. They keep a tab for us, and he knows you're heading there today."

"Okay."

The drive in was fun. It was a bonus having Sunny with me, talking and playful. Both of us free and happy. She was shier than normal at first, but once I teased her a little, she relaxed.

"Do you know what tomorrow is?" I asked.

"Um, Saturday?"

I chuckled. "Yep. And ten months to the day since I first kissed you."

Her smile told me she knew exactly what the date was that I referred to.

"Yeah."

"And we're both off after seven and free until lunch Sunday. No bells to interrupt us." As long as you signed out the night before your morning off, you were excused from the bed check, although you had to be back on the grounds by one, unless you had permission. I glanced at her, then back to the road. "My room?"

She glanced out the window, her cheeks flushed. She reached for my hand. "Yeah."

I grinned the rest of the way into Dalewood.

In town, we went through the list, filling the van. I checked our progress and smiled. "Only the butcher left. Why don't we walk a bit and have lunch?"

Sunny grinned, looking around. "I'd like that."

It was an amazing feeling to walk with her, being able to hold her hand or sling my arm over her shoulders. We wandered and looked. I bought a couple new T-shirts since I seemed to be destroying the ones I had, and Sunny ducked into a woman's store for a while, telling me to stay outside. I peeked in and saw her by a rack of lingerie, then scuttled to the bench she'd left me on.

I didn't want to ruin her surprise, but I knew I was gonna like it. I looked down the street and stood, strolling to the window that caught my eye. I studied the display, then looked over my shoulder to make sure she wasn't back outside yet, and ducked into the small shop.

I emerged five minutes later, my own surprise hidden in my pocket. As I approached the bench, Sunny came out of the shop, tucking a small pink bag into her purse.

I pretended not to notice. We could both keep our secrets for now.

I held out my hand. "Lunch?"

She rose up on her toes and kissed me. Caught in the moment of happiness, I lifted her in my arms, so her feet dangled in midair, and kissed her back. Firm, possessive, exactly the way I knew she liked it now. It was a kiss filled with joy and elation. One caught in sunlight and life, and born of knowing the girl I held was the girl I would love for the rest of my life. The thought settled into my head, no shock or surprise occurring, only an ease within my chest.

Sunny would be my life. Where she was would be my home. And I planned on telling her tomorrow.

I put her on her feet with a grin. "Ready for lunch?"

A black car went by, the windows tinted. It was slow in moving past us, and the sight of it made my stomach clench, but I didn't recognize the driver, and there would be no reason for my father to be in this town. He worked in the opposite direction, and it was rare he went anywhere during the week except the office. His underlings did the legwork. He made the decisions and the money. I shook off the dread that rolled over me. I was being paranoid. I wasn't used to being happy or carefree. It was simply a coincidence, and lots of people drove dark sedans like that one. I refused to let the ghost of him dampen this day.

I wrapped my hand around hers, dismissing my dark thoughts. "Let's go."

5

SUNNY

I was a bundle of nerves all day on Saturday. I knew what tonight meant. What was going to happen. I was ready, and I wanted to give myself to Linc, but still, I was anxious.

Linc was the first boy to kiss me. To touch me. He was my first everything. He was shy and sweet, and we had sat together on our first day of school years ago. He shared his crayons with me. Mine were from the dollar store—all my mother could afford—but his were the large, expensive box containing a rainbow of colors. He let me use the magenta and teal ones, and when I got home that night, he had put them in my box, keeping two of my cheap ones for himself—the orange and yellow, the two worst colors I had.

I fell in love with him right then.

We were the best of friends in grade school. When his mom died, he became quiet and withdrawn at school and with other people, but with me, he seemed happier. We grew closer but only remained friends. I was afraid to push beyond that, happy to at least have him in my life. I knew his father would never approve of me. The few times I saw him, his gaze flickered over me as if I were a piece of dirt beneath his expensive shoes. In town, he was a "big deal," as my mom called him, but not well-liked. Feared, was more like it. I knew Linc feared him. I saw the bruises to prove it, but he refused to tell anyone.

He said it would make matters worse, and he made me promise not to say a thing to anyone. I promised him, because I loved him.

The day he kissed me and changed my life forever was one of my best days. By then, we were confidants, both of us anxious to leave this small town and start life fresh with no baggage. The feel of his mouth on mine, hesitant and gentle, changed everything. He became more.

We became more, and I knew I would follow him to the ends of the earth.

My mother and sisters adored him.

His father loathed me. I was horrified to find out he'd beaten Linc more than once, telling him to stay away from me. I was aghast at the lengths Linc went to in order to defy him. I hated sneaking around, keeping my face neutral and friendly if I saw him in town. At school, people were used to seeing us together, and we both worked hard to make sure they thought of us as friends—nothing more. I lived in fear of someone finding out and Linc taking more punishment.

I despised his father. He was a horrid, cruel man. Linc was nothing like him. He was protective, sweet, and kind. He tried to look after not only me, but my mom and sisters, which made me love him more.

I pictured our life together once we were able to get away from this town and the influence of his father. Linc assured me more than once, when he was nineteen, it would happen. He said he had money from his mother he could get to at that point, and we had to hold on until then.

I would wait for him for as long as it took.

"Sunny!" Cindy's voice broke into my thoughts. "The timer's going off, girl. Get your biscuits out before they burn."

I shook my head and pulled out the tray of biscuits. They were puffy, golden brown, and smelled delicious. I brushed the tops of them with honey butter, thinking how much Linc would enjoy them. Biscuits with butter and jam were his favorites.

As if he knew, he appeared in the doorway, taking my breath away.

The boy I loved was slowly turning into a man. He was tall, his shoulders beginning to widen. All the work he was doing made his chest broader and his muscles tight. His light-brown hair was golden from his days in the sun, and his blue eyes were bright in his face as he smiled at me. His teeth were straight and white against the brown of his tan. He looked sexy, his T-shirt tighter than before and his shorts hanging low on his hips.

I felt my cheeks grow warm as I thought of the way I had gripped his hips as I sucked his dick.

He had loved it.

Cindy laughed behind me. "How is it you always know when the biscuits are ready?"

He sauntered in, his gait relaxed, his eyes lit with mischief. He had both hands behind his back as he approached, his smile getting bigger.

"I don't know what you're talking about," he denied, pulling his hands out in front of him and holding out two small bunches of wild flowers. "I happened to be walking by with flowers for my two favorite girls."

Cindy scoffed. "Little rake, you are." She nudged me. "Go on, then. Get your boy a biscuit and jam." She accepted the flowers from Linc. "Make it two. He looks hungry."

I chuckled and slipped two onto a plate, slicing them open and adding butter and jam. I handed Linc the plate, taking my bunch of flowers with a smile.

He winked and came closer forward. "I am hungry. For biscuits —" he glanced to make sure Cindy was out of earshot "—and you." Then he took the plate and kissed me quickly, leaving me longing for more.

The biscuits disappeared in fast mouthfuls. He sighed. "Promise me you'll make these for me every weekend for the rest of our lives."

My heart stuttered at his words.

Our lives. I was going to get to spend my entire life with this boy.

"Yes."

"Out of the kitchen now, you!" Cindy shooed him away. "We have lunch and dinner to get done."

I laughed as she handed him another biscuit. "Be gone with you."

He left, throwing me a wink and a kiss.

She smiled. "He's got it bad for you, girl. I remember love like that. Young, passionate, and all-encompassing." She chortled. "Then real life sets in. Enjoy it while you can."

I couldn't respond. I was too busy basking in it.

In him.

I didn't go in for dinner. Instead, I ate in the kitchen and finished my tasks. I couldn't go into the dining room. It was too loud, with too many people. I was sure anyone looking at me would know what was going to happen later. I couldn't sit next to Linc and act casual. Every time I saw him today, I felt his stare. His intense gaze locked on me.

So, like a coward, I hid.

When I was done, I slipped out the back and went to my cabin, which was deserted. I had looked forward to sharing it with girls my age but found them standoffish. I was the new girl in their midst—and not welcome. I kept to myself, preferring to spend time with Linc or visit Emily and Hayley. My roommates never bothered to ask where I was, and we chose to respect one another's boundaries.

I grabbed a fast shower, the cool water welcome on the heat of my skin. I shaved and shampooed, the whole time my stomach in knots.

Linc had told me he was a virgin as well. He'd promised he'd waited for me the same way I had waited for him and we'd discover it all together.

But what if I was awful at it?

What if it hurt as much as I had heard girls whisper in school? I had seen the size of his cock, and considering how small I was compared to him, I had no idea how I would fit that inside me.

I was still fretting when a soft knock on the cabin door made me look up. Linc was framed in the doorway, leaning on his shoulder, regarding me with a gentle expression.

"Hey."

"May I come in?"

"Oh, yeah. Sure. Of course," I babbled.

He stepped in. "I missed you at dinner."

"Oh, well, ah, I had stuff. You know...I had to get ready, for, ah, later. Yeah, later."

Wordlessly, he held out his hand. I swallowed the nervous lump in my throat and walked to him, placing my hand in his.

He leaned down, pressing a kiss to my forehead. "Later is whatever we want it to be, Sunny. No pressure. I just want you and me alone." He dropped another kiss to my skin. "I'll wait for you. I'll always wait for you."

My nerves dissipated with his quiet declaration. I had to laugh at myself. It was *Linc*. My Linc. He would never do anything to hurt me.

I glanced up, lifting my shoulder. "Sorry, I'm being silly."

He shook his head. "No. You're being you." He smiled. "And I adore everything about you. Silly or not."

Our gazes held and I relaxed, all my worries gone. He tucked a strand of hair behind my ear. "How about a walk? We can sit by the fire with everyone if you want after?"

"The walk sounds nice." I picked up the bag I carried with me. It was full this time. "Maybe we could drop this off first?"

With a tender look, he took it from my hand. "Yeah, Sunny. We can do that."

We walked along the shore, hearing the campers around the fire in the distance. The water swirled around our feet. Linc had his hand wrapped around mine, protective and warm. We sat on the rocks, watching the sun begin its descent in the distance, casting burnished rays on the water.

Linc lifted a strand of my hair. "Sunsets remind me of your hair. The muted reds and gold."

I laughed quietly. "Being romantic, Linc?"

He chuckled. "Trying."

"Shut your eyes."

He did as I asked, and I fastened the thick, black, woven leather cuff I had seen in a secondhand shop while waiting for him to get one of the orders we were picking up. I had polished the silver clasp and cleaned the leather. I thought he would like how it looked.

"Okay," I whispered.

He opened his eyes, looking at his wrist. He turned and admired the clasp. "I fucking love it. I'll always wear it."

I grinned in delight at his reaction, cuss word and all.

He winked, then slipped a small box into my hand. "My turn."

I opened the box, a delicate necklace cushioned on black velvet making me gasp.

"It's not much," he whispered. "But I bought it with my own money, not his. Someday, I'll buy you something better. It says what I can't, though." He huffed out a long breath of air. "My heart is yours, Sunny."

I traced the two hearts woven together, the silver catching the last of the light.

I looked up at him, tears glimmering in my eyes. "I don't need something better, Linc. This is perfect."

"Yeah?"

"Yeah." I turned, lifting my hair. "Put it on me?"

He slipped it around my neck, making me giggle as he cursed, trying to get it to catch. Finally, he brushed a kiss to the juncture of my neck. "Done."

I faced him and slipped my hands around his neck. "Thank you."

He kissed me, his lips tender against mine. I pulled him closer, sliding my tongue along his bottom lip, loving how he groaned and opened for me, slanting his mouth, and moving his tongue with mine in lazy strokes. I whimpered as his hand slid up my rib cage, cupping my breast and circling my nipple. He loved breasts. My breasts in particular, he informed me, although he referred to them as tits. I loved him touching them.

The kiss intensified, becoming hot, wet, and passionate. He pulled me onto his lap, delving his hand under my shirt and stroking my back. I felt his erection pressing on me, and suddenly, I wasn't scared anymore. There was only him. Me. Us. I wanted him.

"Your room," I pleaded. "Now."

He stood, taking me with him. I giggled as he began walking toward the trees.

"Put me down."

"No. I know a shortcut, and those little legs of yours are not going to be able to keep up. Hold tight, Sunny-girl."

So, I did.

H is room was dim and quiet. He lit a candle on his small dresser then turned to me, his chest moving with his rapid breaths, his eyes dark with lust.

"Are you sure?"

I gripped the bottom of my shirt and yanked it over my head, then pushed down my shorts before I could get cold feet. I stood before him in the lacy bra and underwear I had bought the day before. They were pink and sheer, and I found them on sale, so I could afford them. I wanted to look pretty for this. For him.

He stepped forward, tracing a finger over the lace, my nipple hardening under his touch.

"This is pretty." He glanced up. "But nowhere near as beautiful as the girl wearing it."

I launched myself at him. In seconds, we were on his bed, all tongues, fingers, and lips. His mouth licked and bit at my skin as his hands roamed everywhere. Touching, stroking, caressing me until I was nothing but a mass of need. I yanked off his shirt, pushing his shorts down his hips with my feet. He had my pretty lingerie on the floor in seconds, his mouth on my breasts, lapping and sucking until I thought I would go mad.

Skin to skin with him, I relished the way our bodies fit together. He felt like a protective blanket draped over me, holding his weight on his elbows as he kissed me. We explored each other. I discovered he was ticklish and whimpered every time I stroked the sensitive skin of his pelvis. He learned every time he brushed his fingers up my thigh, I shivered. He held my feet, kissing the arch, then slowly making his way up my leg. I grabbed his shoulder as he reached my apex, nerves once again kicking in, and I tried to shut my legs.

"I've never... No one has ever..." My voice trailed off at his gentle gaze.

"Me either, but I want to try. Please?"

I relaxed, letting him in. He trailed his fingers over me, teasing my clit with his finger. I shut my eyes at the wave of pleasure. I felt his tongue slide along my folds, and I cried out at the intense sensation. He met my eyes, his gaze narrowed.

"Tell me it's okay."

"It's more than okay," I gasped.

"Good. Because I think it's fucking awesome." He lowered his head, learning and finding what I liked. What he liked. My legs began to tremble, an orgasm close.

"Lincoln," I begged. "Oh god, Linc."

My body tensed and I came, whimpering his name and gripping

the thick blanket on his bed with one hand, my other buried in his hair, never wanting him to stop.

He pulled back, a satisfied smirk on his face. He kissed the inside of my leg, resting his hands on my thighs, stroking them gently. "Okay, Sunny?"

I cupped his face, loving how he nuzzled into my hand. He was always so affectionate, and the thought that he'd had to go so long without any made me hold him tighter. "Yeah. More than okay."

He winked, his eyes growing round as I grabbed a condom off the small table beside his bed.

"Are you sure?"

I slipped the package into his hand.

"Yes."

The rest of the evening was a blur. Fragments of memories I held close after he walked me back to my cabin late into the night, kissing me long and sweet before I slipped inside.

The feel of him on top of me. The sensation of him carefully pressing inside me. Sinking in inch by inch until we were flush—our bodies so tightly meshed together, it was as if we were one. He kissed away my tears at the pinch of pain, waiting until I nodded before he started to move. We were awkward and unsure, then we found our rhythm. His movements became smoother, his body flowing into mine. He didn't last long, but it didn't matter. I was already sated, and the feel of him inside me was incredible.

"I'll do better next time," he promised.

I kissed him. We kissed for hours, it seemed. Until he was hard and inside me again. This time, we both found our release, and he lay beside me, a proud smile making him adorable and irresistible.

"I'll see you tomorrow," I murmured against his mouth.

"It is tomorrow. Come back with me now."

I shook my head. "I don't want one of the girls reporting I was out all night. I'll be back in a few hours."

He pouted but kissed and released me. He traced a finger over the necklace and smiled.

"See you soon."

He waited until I walked in, then disappeared into the darkness.

U nable to sleep, no matter how hard I tried, I made my way to his room as the sun was rising. The door to the office was ajar, and I frowned as I entered the dim space.

"Linc?"

There was no answer, and I headed to his door down the hall. I froze in the doorway, confused.

His bed was made, his duffel bag gone. The entire room was empty aside from the one glass candle that sat on the top of the dresser. I picked it up and held it in my hand. The curled end of the wick was the only thing that assured me last night was real.

For some reason, I investigated the small bathroom. His toothbrush and shaving stuff had disappeared.

In fact, it looked as if Linc had disappeared.

A noise behind me made me spin around. "Linc, I was..." My voice trailed off at the sight of Gerry in the doorway.

"Where is he?" I asked, my voice trembling.

"He left a couple of hours ago. His father came to get him. He said it was an emergency."

"Did he-did he leave anything?"

He handed me an envelope. "I found all this. Sorry, Sunny."

I couldn't speak, holding the thick envelope to my chest. Gerry left and I stumbled to the bed, tearing at the flap, knowing the explanation Linc left me inside of it would help calm the anxiety I was feeling.

Three things fell from the envelope. The cell phone that matched mine dropped into my lap, smashed to pieces, and my unease grew. A strip of the leather cuff I had given him followed next. I held up the frayed piece, confused. It had obviously been yanked off, and I wondered where the rest of it was. The last thing was an uneven, crumpled, torn piece of notepaper with Linc's writing, dark and deeply imprinted into the fibers.

I'm sorry.
forget about me.

6

LINC

TEN YEARS LATER

I adjusted my tie, frowning in the mirror as my hands shook. It was ridiculous to be nervous. Today was the last item to be checked off the list, and then my past would be locked away where it should be. The past.

I sat down at the island in my kitchen and picked up my coffee.

"Can I get you anything, Lincoln? A bagel or perhaps something more substantial?"

"No thanks, Mrs. Ellis. Coffee is fine." I smiled at my house-keeper. She was still new and getting to know the place and me. "I rarely eat breakfast."

She clucked, wiping down the counter. "At least you eat the meals I leave you—sometimes."

I chuckled and held out my cup for a refill, then headed into my office. I looked out the window at the city below me, a strange ache in my chest pushing at me.

I glanced at my watch, knowing I had to go, and dreading it.

But it was time.

The last time I would ever face the memory of my father.

The streets were still quiet when I pulled my car into Mission Cove. I was early, my lawyer not arriving until ten, and without conscious thought, I drove to the east end of town, pulling up in front of a place that used to feel like home.

The small house was gone now, replaced as most of those in the neighborhood were, with newer, larger homes. Mission Cove had prospered in the past three years, and I had made sure all areas were developed. My father would roll over in his grave if he knew how his money was being used.

That thought alone was the one thing that brought a tight smile to my face.

I kept driving.

The deserted campground was now a playground for children, with a picnic area for families. It was well maintained, with safe equipment and a pool for the hot summers. It had been aptly named The Sunny Place. I blinked at the onslaught of emotions that threatened to engulf me as memories I kept locked away attempted to break through. I shook my head and pulled away, knowing the entire day was going to be the same.

One sad, aching reminder of all I had lost.

In town, the streets were clean, a few stores already open and getting ready for the day. Tourist season hadn't hit yet, but as always, there would be some travelers around. Most of the old businesses were gone, replaced by newer ones. But the diner was still there, although it had been upgraded and modernized. The local dry cleaner was already open, the windows clean and bright. They had added a self-serve laundromat, which I was certain was very busy in the tourist season. It was a good addition. Around the corner, the animal shelter had a newer, larger building, completely subsidized by an anonymous donor. They never had to worry about it being shut down again.

I parked the car and glanced up at the overhanging vista. My father's house still stood on the hill, overlooking the town. The sun bounced off the windows, reflecting the light in a thousand directions —the only light that house ever had to it. That would change soon.

I climbed out of the car to take a stroll, unable to sit any longer. I slid sunglasses on to my face, not that I was worried about being recognized. The boy who left this town ten years ago was unrecognizable now.

My light hair had darkened, and I wore it longer than I used to, the back hitting the collar of my suit jacket. I had filled out completely, thanks, first, to the summer camp, then the two years at the "private school" where I'd lived. The gym, working out, and my ongoing plans for revenge were the only ways I had to cope with the isolation I endured, and I made full use of it. Now my shoulders were wide, my muscles tight and strong, and I walked with my head high, no longer hiding. All my suits were custom made to fit my shoulders, and I wore them like a cloak. Dressed in them, I was powerful and untouchable. No longer the scared, beaten boy—son of Franklin Thomas—but my own man. Lincoln Webber.

I had rejected everything that was my father and taken on my mother's maiden name, changing it as soon as I could once I returned to Canada.

Today was the final step in dismantling my father's legacy.

I walked along once-familiar streets, looking in windows and pleased with the changes I could see. Changes I had instigated that would benefit this town. Memories surrounded me at every turn, and I gave up trying to fight them off.

It wasn't a surprise that *she* was everywhere. All my good memories were tied to her—this entire town was tied to her. Her ghost followed me with each step, whispering memories in my ear. I paused at the corner and raked a hand through my hair, wondering if this was a mistake. I should have let my lawyer handle it all, but I had wanted to do this.

I inhaled, a sweet smell wafting through the air hitting me. Across the street was a bakery—new since I'd lived here. The door was open, the scent of fresh baking inviting. I read the sign with a smile. *Biscuits and Buns*. My stomach rumbled, and I headed in the direction of the tempting smell. I would grab a snack then head up to the house.

I stepped in, the aroma intensifying. There was one thing that smelled that good. Biscuits. I hadn't had one in years, but the scent alone was enough to bring back the most bittersweet of memories.

Sunny baking. Looking happy as she handed me a plate of warm biscuits soaked in butter and laden with jam. Her grandmother had taught her how to make them, and they were my favorite thing to eat. I shut my eyes as the feelings the memory stirred began to overwhelm me.

A throat clearing broke through my scattered brain.

"May I help you?"

My eyes flew open, and I stared at the mirage in front of me.

It had to be a mirage, right? I had been thinking of her so much that morning, it couldn't possibly be real.

But there, standing behind the counter, was Sunny. Her hair was still as bright, her beautiful eyes dark, setting off the ivory color of her skin. The girl was gone, replaced by a woman so lovely, it made my chest ache.

She frowned and spoke again in a voice I would recognize until my last breath. "Are you all right? Can I help you?"

I stepped closer, trying to find my voice. She tilted her head, studying me, wary. Up close, I could see more changes. Her eyes, once so bright and alive, were dimmer. Sad. Her hair was swept into a thick coil at the back of her neck—Sunny always hated to wear her hair up. She was as tiny as I recalled, and there was a coolness to her manner she'd never projected before. Reserved and formal.

Her brow furrowed as she looked at me. She began to worry her lip the way I remembered her doing. Her breathing picked up, whether in fear of the stranger in front of her, or some long-forgotten recollection of the boy I was to her surfacing—I didn't know.

I pulled off my glasses and met her confused stare. Her eyes widened in shock as we locked gazes. Years fell away, and the warmth of her stare that always filled me up hit me all over again. I was seventeen, staring at the girl I was in love with.

The girl I still loved, now a woman, a virtual stranger, who could still bring me to my knees with a glance.

"L-Linc?"

I sighed at the way my name sounded on her lips. How the letters sounded when she said them.

"Sunny," I replied, my voice low.

Then her expression changed. Bewilderment and anger brought her shoulders up and a scowl to her face.

"What are you doing here?" she snapped.

I cleared my throat. "Ah, some family business."

She barked out a dry laugh. "Family business. Yes, I know all about your *family* business. What are you doing in my shop?"

Her anger wasn't unexpected, but I had never heard Sunny's voice be so cold.

"When did you move back here?" I replied.

"How do you know I ever left?" she shot back.

I leaned on the counter, incredulous. "I looked for you. You had disappeared."

Her eyes widened, but before she could retort, a young girl came through the door at the back.

"The last batch is done, boss. You want me to start on some cookies?"

Sunny moved back. It was then I realized how close we had moved toward the other. I rose to my full height, stepping away from the counter.

"Yes, Shannon. Let's do the ginger ones today."

Shannon eyed me curiously, then smiled at Sunny, before disappearing through the door. "On it, boss."

We stared at each other.

"As much as I'd love to go down memory lane with you," Sunny informed me, her voice icy and filled with sarcasm, "I have a business to run. Do you want anything, or did you come in here to bring more upheaval into my life?"

I blinked. "I smelled biscuits."

She barked out another laugh. Even that sound was foreign. I recalled her sweet, low laughter. Her lighthearted giggle. This was neither of those.

She reached below the counter and grabbed two biscuits, shoving them in a bag. "There."

"I was going to—"

She cut me off. "No. You're going to take the biscuits and get the hell out of my shop and my life, Linc."

"Sunny, I want to talk. I need to—"

Again, she cut me off. "I said no. You had plenty of time to talk while I pined away for you. I no longer care what you need."

"But I—"

"Get out, or I'll have you arrested for trespassing."

I stared at the angry, cold woman in front of me. This wasn't Sunny. Not the Sunny I remembered. Then again, I wasn't the same boy.

"All right, I'll go. But I'm coming back. I'll see you soon."

Her eyes narrowed. "I've heard that before. I guess we already know that won't be happening."

Then she turned on her heel and walked away.

S he was on my mind all day, no longer a ghost, but a living, breathing woman. Beautiful. Sad. Angry.

Here. Right here in Mission Cove. I had looked for her years ago, unable to locate her, finally deciding to let her go and move on. Concentrate on my plan and make sure my father no longer had the power to hurt people. I knocked over the pieces in his intricate game of chess, taking his queen and leaving him with no moves left.

The day I received the call that he'd had a massive heart attack in his office and died had produced one emotion: relief. I didn't go to see him. There was no funeral. Only a simple statement in the paper and I had his ashes shipped to me.

I found great satisfaction in driving them to the local dump and tossing them into a pile of rotting garbage.

His soul was rotten, and that was where he belonged.

I shook my head, clearing my morbid thoughts. I glanced at the two boxes of possessions I was taking with me. Small mementos I had found in searching the house all day. Things my father would have overlooked since they were sentimental, and he would have had no idea they could mean something to me. Two of the boxes were items that belonged to my mother that were hidden in the basement, the cardboard covered in dust and forgotten. The other a few photos and various things I'd picked up as I walked around.

"Are you sure that is all?" my lawyer, Ned Jenkins, asked. "Some of the things in the house are incredibly valuable, Lincoln."

"I'm sure. Send all the books to the library. They can sell the first editions and use the rest. Open the place up. Biggest garage sale in the history of Mission's Cove. All the money goes to the town."

"The place will be swamped."

I lifted a shoulder. "I've hired the right people. It'll be handled. Once it's done, the house comes down."

"And what will you do with the land?"

"I'm still thinking on it. But the symbol of this place, the power my father had over this town, needs to go."

"I understand. I'll finish drawing up the papers and getting the permits. I should have most of them tomorrow. Anything else you need?"

"No."

"I'll be in touch."

He left, the sound of his car fading away, leaving me alone in the house I hated as a child, loathed as a teen, and now planned on destroying as an adult.

I sat at my father's desk, looking around the room. His seat of power—now crumbled to dust.

The same as his body.

Appropriate.

I opened the drawers, all empty now, the personal effects long removed. As I gripped the drawer front, I felt the edge of something with my finger, and I opened the drawer again, curious.

A key was fitted into the wood, and I pulled it out, studying it. It was nondescript and dull, and I had no idea what it was for. I stared at it, nonplussed. Why would my father have a key hidden in this drawer?

I pushed back the chair, studying the desk. On impulse, I pulled out the drawer and studied it, then glanced at the desk. The drawer was shorter than the desk by at least nine inches. Using my phone for light, I peered into the dark recess, shocked when metal glinted back at me. A hidden lockbox. My father had a hidden lockbox.

Reaching inside, I grasped the metal box and slid it out.

It sat on top of the desk, innocent-looking, yet somehow, I knew the contents held inside would prove to be anything but.

With a shaking hand, I inserted the key and opened the lid. I stared down at the items inside.

I picked up a book, flipping open the cover. It was a journal belonging to my mother from when she was younger. There were various envelopes, letters, documents, and files. I was mystified as to why these were all locked away.

I gasped as I saw the two piles of envelopes that lay at the bottom.

Rage built, anger crashing over me as I recognized my own writing.

"That *fucking* bastard," I hissed.

A movement in the doorway caused me to look up. Sunny stood, observing me, her arms crossed, anger holding her head high, her shoulders tight.

My own emotions were so heightened, I drew on her anger. Welcomed it with my own.

Found myself hardening at the sight of the beauty that her anger brought out in her. She was a fucking vision in her outrage. I dropped the items I was holding and crossed the room.

"Come to brave the monster in his den, Sunny?" I asked. "Get me in private so you can tell me what you think of me? What you think I did to you all those years ago?"

"I know what you did to me, Lincoln," she replied, her eyes flashing.

Her use of my full name made me angrier. "No. You think you do, but you don't."

"How dare you show up today, walk back into my life as if the last ten years didn't happen?"

I stalked closer, so we were inches apart. I wanted to push her past the breaking point. I wanted to break through the rigid shell she had around herself and find Sunny. To make her see Linc.

"I go anywhere I please, sweetheart. You might not realize it, but I own the building your shop is in." I pointed toward the window. "I own every goddamn place in the town, just like my father did."

"Is that a threat, Lincoln? Is that what happened to you? You became your father?"

"Maybe I did," I lied. "Maybe whatever thoughts you have of me now are right. Maybe I am a bastard like he was."

"The boy I loved wasn't a bastard."

"But he fucked you and left, isn't that how you see it?"

Her slap echoed in the room, my head snapping back from the force. We stared at each other, locked in a wordless war. I smiled grimly.

"How appropriate you hit me here, in this room. This is where he always beat me. Right here." I crossed the room to the center of the rug. "He'd start here—usually with a punch in the ribs, or kidneys if my back was turned. Once he had me down, he'd add a few more punches or use his feet. Those hurt, you know? Usually it was because I had been with you or couldn't account for every penny I'd spent. Again, usually because I made sure I left money in your house to help your family. Or he'd beat me because of my arrogance in thinking I deserved to make a decision for myself. Or sometimes because he fucking *liked it*. It made *him* feel better, and god forbid Franklin Thomas ever not feel *good*." By the end, I was shouting. I strode back to her, all my anger boiling over. "So, do it, Sunny. Hit me. Hit me until you feel better. One of us might as well."

Our eyes met—enraged, crazed blue clashing with bewildered, shocked brown. Silence hung between us, the only sounds my panting breaths and Sunny's muffled sobs, her hand covering her mouth as tears leaked down her cheeks.

Wait.

Why was she crying?

"Sunny?"

"I-I... Oh god, *Linc*."

The next thing I knew, her arms were around my neck and her lips on mine. Shock rendered me still for a moment, then every sense in my body came alive. I dragged her tight to my chest, kissing her like a starving man who had been offered the feast of a lifetime.

It was nothing like the kisses we had shared in the past. It was redemption and grief. Longing and need. Passion and hate. Love and hurt. Forgiveness and healing.

I lifted her off her feet, wrapping her in my arms. She was no longer a tiny, waiflike girl. She was a lovely woman with curves that fit in my hands as if they were made for me and me alone.

Because they were.

However much pain we had to go through, whatever secrets and scars we had to rip open to get back to finding us, I was determined it would happen. I wasn't losing her again.

7

LINC

"I'm sorry," she pleaded after our mouths separated. "Linc, I'm so sorry."

"Shh, Sunny. It's fine. I deserved that slap."

"I've never hit anyone," she hiccuped. "I can't believe I did that."

"Hey," I murmured, waiting until she met my gaze, her eyes sad and red-rimmed. "It's fine, baby. Considering how much you work with your hands, you're not very strong. It didn't even hurt."

Her lips quirked at my words, but she laid her hand on my cheek in a tender gesture. I leaned into her caress, the memories of her touch making me feel more alive than I had in years.

"Where did you go?" she whispered. "Why did you leave me?"

I set her down on her feet and took her hand, leading her to the small sofa in the corner. "My father." I frowned as I let the memory of that night come back. "I was on such a high after our night together, I went for a walk after taking you to your cabin. I sat on the dock for a while, thinking. Of you. Of us. What I wanted to do when we got home. Our future."

"I couldn't sleep either."

I smiled, lifting her hand to my mouth and kissing it. Her skin was still soft, although she had small calluses on her fingertips and palm from her constant work. I stroked them, feeling her life on her skin.

"When I went back to my room, my father was there, waiting. He had seen us that day in town, Sunny. He was furious. More than I had ever seen him. He told me to pack up and that we were leaving. I argued and told him off, but he pulled three documents from his pocket and gave them to me."

"What were they?"

"One was an eviction notice and condemnation of your grandmother's house. The second was the directive to fire your mother from her job. The third..." I swallowed. "The third was a letter to child services saying your mother was abusive and unfit and Hayley and Emily needed to be removed from a condemned house and placed in foster care."

Her eyes grew round.

"He had them all in his pocket, Sunny. The bank, the hotel, even social services. They were all false accusations, but they would have happened. He told me if I came with him, the directives would be destroyed. If not, your life—your entire family's lives—would be shattered. He told me he would also shut the shelter and make sure your reputation became so tarnished, you would have to leave town anyway." I sighed heavily. "I had no choice. I had to protect you. I thought I would somehow figure something out. I agreed right away."

"You disappeared."

I barked out a gruff laugh. "Yes, I did. He sent me to a school, a prison more like it, in Europe. I had no phone, no access to the outside world, no friends, and no way to get out. He isolated me."

I got up to walk, because I couldn't sit down. "He left me there for two years. He thought it would break me, but I fought back. I listened and learned. I worked out and built up my body so he couldn't hurt me again."

"You never contacted me."

"I left you a note."

She frowned. "It said you were sorry and to forget you. Your smashed cell phone and a piece of your cuff were all I had."

He dug into his pocket, holding up the rest of the cuff I had given him. Well-worn and cracked, the clasp missing, all that was left, the tattered pieces of leather. "My father caught me writing the letter. I planned to put it under my pillow and take the phone so I could call you. The note said I was sorry, but to be patient and I would get to you somehow. I said I loved you and not to forget me or what we had shared. I wasn't expecting the uppercut he hit me with, and I was out cold when he dragged me to the car. He obviously tore it up to suit his own agenda and smashed the phone." He huffed. "When I came to, I was still in the car, en route to the airport. I was gone before the camp opened the next morning."

"Oh, Linc," she whispered.

"I tried to get in touch with you. I wrote you every day for three months. I finally figured out the letters weren't reaching you, and I bribed another kid who had freer access than me to take my letters to town and send it. He had his return info on it, and it came back, saying Unknown-Moved."

"Your father made it impossible for us to stay. He didn't do any of the things he threatened, but he made life hard for my mom. She lost shifts and her work was called subpar in her file. Rumors were flying about how I had stalked you—even following you to the camp when you tried to get away from me. Emily and Hayley were being picked on. The whole town was talking about us." She closed her eyes. "My mom's cousin out east told us we could move there and he would help. We basically left everything behind unless it was sentimental and walked away. He had a place in a small town in the Maritimes, and we settled there. The girls went to school, Mom found a job, and I tried to pick up the pieces of my life. He even adopted us, and we took his last name—Hilbert." A small smile crossed her face. "We called him Uncle Pete, and he loved that. We all needed the fresh start. You couldn't find me because Uncle Pete had the records sealed in case your father looked for us."

That explained why I couldn't find her. "I changed my name too. I didn't want anything of my father's. I'm Lincoln Webber now."

"It suits you."

"It does. I'm my mother's son. I want nothing of my father—including his name."

Silence pulsed in the room until she spoke, her confession whispered into the air.

"I missed you every day."

"My memories of you, *of us*, were what got me through it," I admitted.

She lifted her head and pulled on a chain around her neck. The pendant I had given her, now dull, dangled from the necklace. I was shocked to see it, my heart bursting at the thought of what it meant. She had cared all this time. The same way I had cared for her.

"You still wear it?"

"I never took it off. It was the one thing I had that was still real. Well, that and this." She pulled out a set of keys, held together with a strip of leather I recognized. I took them from her and touched the leather, thinking of her expression when I'd snapped the cuff onto my wrist, swearing never to take it off. Another promise I failed to keep because of that bastard.

"Why did you come back?" I asked.

She looked sad. "My mom grew up here. She missed it." She swallowed, her gaze on her hands. "Uncle Pete died. Then she got sick, Linc. She wanted to come back. We had seen the news that your father died, and it had been so long, we figured most people would have forgotten us. The girls were busy and happy, getting ready for university, and I wasn't attached to anything or anyone out east, so I brought her back." Her voice became thick. "She died last year."

"Sunny," I murmured and dragged her back into my arms. She came easily, fitting against me. "I am so sorry," I said, kissing her crown, my eyes damp. "Your mom was always good to me."

"She liked you. Even after everything, she always insisted there was more to the story than we knew."

"I'm glad she thought enough of me to think that."

"What happened, Linc? Why did you come back?"

"My father brought me back after I turned nineteen. He thought I was broken, that I would toe the line. He didn't expect me to have done my homework and to beat him at his own game."

She frowned, confused.

"It was all about money, Sunny. The money my mother left me. My father always led me to believe there was just a little money waiting for me when I turned nineteen. Nothing of significance. But I had seen the paperwork. He had left it out once in error. There were millions, and the way it was invested, it kept growing. He planned on me signing it over to him, and then he'd get rid of me. Some job somewhere where I'd be none the wiser and he wouldn't care what I did, or who I did it with. He could keep an eye on me but be rid of me at the same time. He really thought I was that stupid and that broken. But I knew about the money, and the years I spent in that place taught me a few things. I found out ways to get around the stipulations that kept me locked down, with the help of a few friends. As soon as I was back, I contacted my mother's lawyer, and we were ready. I met with my father just to watch the expression on his face when he realized I knew."

I stood and paced. "I walked away from him and started my own company. Just like him, I kept myself hidden, but I did the opposite of what he had done all those years."

"What do you mean?"

I perched on the edge of the desk. "I started buying up properties here in town and gifting them to people he'd been screwing for so long. I used every resource I had and killed every deal he tried to make. News of his double-crossing started to spread. Word leaked out —I made sure of it. I bought every run-down home there was in this town and rebuilt them, employing the people he put out of work. I made rents in the new places lower, and people flocked to them. His places were empty. I picked them up for a song and did it again. I used every dirty trick he had ever utilized to take away the two things that ever mattered to him. Power and money. Without power, the money dwindled until he was struggling and starting to lose everything he had. He died before it happened. I took over the estate and tripled the wealth."

"The park," she stated, already knowing the answer.

"Yes, that was for you."

Her eyes glimmered, and we shared a smile.

"Did he know?" she asked quietly. "That it was you?"

"Yeah, he did. The rest of the world, no. But him? Yes." I studied her. "In some ways, I'm like him, Sunny. I systematically set out to take him down and made him pay for every horrible thing he did. The people he hurt. How he treated my mother. His misuse of power. His hatred of me."

"That doesn't make you like him," she replied. "That makes you human. And your endeavors helped people."

I looked out over the town below. "I hope it did. It was the one thing that kept me going after I lost you."

She stood and crossed over to me. I pulled her into my arms, holding her close.

"Are you still lost, Sunny?"

"I don't know," she admitted. "So much time, so many mistakes, and so much hurt has happened."

"But you're here," I insisted. "You came to me."

"To tell you off."

"But you stayed," I added, my voice low. "You're still with me."

She said nothing, her head resting on my shoulder.

"We would have to take it slow," she said finally. "I have to learn who you are now, Linc, and you have to get to know me. I'm not the same girl you lost ten years ago. I don't know how you went from the boy you were to the man you are today."

"I know." I reached behind me into the box and held out the stacks of envelopes. "You could start by reading these."

She took them, confused. "What are they?"

"The letters I wrote you. My father obviously had them waylaid.

I don't know why he kept them, unless he planned on using them to hurt me at some point."

She took them from my hands. "There are a lot."

"I wrote you every day. Some days, it was the only way I could cope. It felt as if I was talking to you."

Tears sprang to her eyes. "Are we too damaged for this, Linc?"

"No. We made it through all this shit for a reason." I cupped the back of her neck. "Let *us* be the reason, Sunny."

She bit her lip, the gesture familiar and comforting. "Slow," she repeated. "It would have to be slow."

"I'm good with slow."

She stepped back. "I'm going to leave. I need to think, and I have some reading to do."

I stood. "I'm ready to get out of here." I slammed the lid shut on the metal container and slid it back into place. I'd figure out what to do with the contents later. Right now, my head was spinning.

"What are you doing with this place?"

"It's being emptied, then I'm having it destroyed. I want to keep nothing of his, and I want no reminder of him in this town."

"And the land?"

"I'll decide that later."

Outside, I loaded two boxes into my car. I looked around. "Did you walk here?"

"Yes."

"Can I drive you down?"

"Okay."

"And can I see you tomorrow?"

She smiled. "I guess you're on a roll, Linc."

I smiled as I slid into the driver's seat. I pulled away from the house that had been another kind of prison to me.

I didn't look back.

I was at the shop before it opened the next morning. I had barely slept all night, thinking of Sunny. I had kissed her when I dropped her off. A long, gentle kiss that promised more. I would let her set the pace. I made sure we had each other's phone numbers and even texted her a few times to check in. By her fast responses, I knew she was feeling the same anxiety. The last time I'd kissed her good-night, we'd been torn apart. Morning couldn't come fast enough for me. I paced my hotel room, apprehensive, worried, and unable to settle. I couldn't shut off my mind or my thoughts. I hadn't planned on staying past one night and after that, never planned on setting foot in Mission Cove again. But now, those plans, it seemed, were discarded.

She came to the door, rolling her eyes. "I'm not even open yet."

"But I can come in, right? I smelled biscuits."

"Of course you did."

I stepped inside, leaning down and brushing a kiss to her cheek. "Hi."

She turned and kissed my mouth. It was far too brief for my liking. "Hi."

"You okay today?"

She nodded.

"You look tired," I murmured, tracing a finger under her eye.

"I read some of your letters."

"Just some?"

"They were difficult to read. I had to stop." She hesitated, and I saw the look of pain in her eyes. "They upset me. Knowing what you went through. That you were alone and scared."

"I'm here now. I was tougher than he thought. I was fighting to get back to you. To restart my life."

She paused, frowning. "You always wanted to be a vet. You loved animals."

I shrugged. "My life went in a different direction. I still volunteer when I have time. I love animals, and I support a large number of charities that help them."

"Like the shelter here?"

"Yes, like the shelter here. And other places. My father took that dream away from me as well, Sunny. He robbed me of everything I loved all those years ago."

"He robbed us both."

"Yes, he did."

She looked as if she wanted to say more. But I wanted today to be about us. Now.

"Um, biscuits?" I prompted. "Hungry here."

"Right," she replied, wiping her eyes and straightening her shoulders. "Savory or sweet?"

"Ah, both?"

"Sit down."

I watched her from the spot I chose in the corner. She moved gracefully, confident with herself. I tried not to stare, but she was so beautiful. Even years later, there was an air of sweetness around her.

She placed a plate in front of me, piled high, and a small pot of jam alongside it. "Milk?" she asked.

I tried not to be too pleased that she remembered I always liked milk with biscuits. I shook my head. "Cappuccino, please."

"You never liked coffee."

I shrugged. "I learned."

Without a word, she turned, and a few moments later, a steamy bowl of froth was set in front of me. "Thank you." I looked up. "These are as incredible as I remember."

Her smile was bright, her voice teasing. "I guess after making about a million fucking dozen, they should be."

My biscuit froze partway to my mouth. "You don't swear."

She smirked, then turned and walked away. "I learned," she called over her shoulder.

I chuckled as I ate my biscuit.

Learning. That was what we had to do. Relearn each other. Move forward from the past.

Could we do that? Could we be Linc and Sunny again?

THE SUMMER OF US

She slid into the seat across from me, sipping a cup of coffee. She looked out the window.

"It's almost summer," she mused. "It'll be busy here again."

I reached across the table for her hand. She let me take it, and I liked how mine engulfed hers, folding over her small palm protectively.

"Will you try with me, Sunny? Can we use the summer to get back to where we were?"

She shook her head, and my heart sank.

"I don't want to go back to where we were, Linc. It was too tumultuous and scary. Can't we just be Linc and Sunny now? Two people who have met and want to get to know each other?"

"Let the past go, you mean?"

She looked down at our hands. "The past shaped us, made us who we are. It will always be a part of us, but I would rather face the future looking forward." She smiled. "I know we still have a lot to talk about, and deal with, but I would like to try."

"With me?" I asked, hopeful.

"With you."

"Another summer of us, then?"

Her reply was all I needed to hear.

"I'd like to think of it as the start of us. A lifetime, instead of a season."

There was so much I wanted to say. Thoughts and dreams I wanted to share with her. Memories I needed to talk about and clear from my head. But with her words, I knew I could. We would find our way, and with time, we'd heal and move forward.

Together.

I hunched over the table and brought her mouth to mine.

"I can live with that."

She smiled as I kissed her.

And I was finally home.

PART II

8

LINC

I watched Sunny all morning, observing her over the screen of my laptop. She was cordial and welcoming, greeting customers by name, already preparing their orders when they walked in. I recognized a few people by her greetings but felt no pull to stand and reacquaint myself with anyone. I had never been close to a lot of people growing up, school mates included. I was polite and friendly, but distant. Mostly due to the fact that my father's influence was too great, and simply due to the fact that most other kids found me strange. They had no idea of the rules or pressure put upon me by my father, so it was easier for them to shrug off my behavior as different. And everyone knew how kids felt about different. They shied away from it, especially if it meant going against the majority. I had been a lonely kid, except for Sunny. She had been in my life so long, when we were apart, the pain was a physical pull.

As I sat in her shop, the sun streaming in the window, the scent of baking permeating the air, and her within my sight, that pain was now a low, dull ache. I didn't know what the future held for us, but I knew I wanted to find out.

She approached the table, another plate in hand. A thick sandwich sat on the simple china, and she held a glass of lemonade in her other hand. She slid them both beside my computer and sat across from me.

"Do you plan on sitting at this table all day?" she asked with a mischievous twinkle in her eyes. "I do have a no-loitering policy."

I pursed my lips, studying her. She had always been a pretty girl, her unique coloring making her stand out. But the girl was gone—replaced by a captivating, beautiful woman. Her strawberry-blond hair had darkened to a soft auburn, the glints of red catching the sunlight as she moved her head. Her once wide, innocent brown eyes were intelligent and warm, but they held a depth of sadness that I hated to see. Most people wouldn't notice because they weren't looking hard enough.

But I was looking.

Sunny was still tiny, but her frame was muscular, her arms defined, her shoulders held straight, and her curves more pronounced. She was incredibly sexy. Her hair was swept up, exposing her delicate neck, the soft-looking skin inviting. I recalled kissing that neck, tasting her at the juncture where her neck sloped into her shoulders.

I hoped to taste her there again.

My glance fell to her hands that rested on the table. Small, with thin fingers. Her nails were short but neat, manicured, and buffed. She was never able to grow them, even as a teenager, and she was always jealous of the girls with long nails, filed to a point and painted bright colors. I was glad to see although she could afford manicures now, she kept them natural. It suited her.

"Linc?"

I lifted my gaze. She stared back at me, her smile growing. "Do you want to take a picture?" she teased.

Without blinking, I lifted my phone and snapped a picture of her. My fast reaction caught her off guard, and the picture captured her startled but amused expression.

"Happy now?"

"Yes."

She pushed the plate my way. "If you're going to sit there all afternoon and glower at my customers over the top of your computer, eat some lunch."

"I'm not glowering, I'm observing. I like watching you in your environment."

She rolled her eyes. "You glower."

"Maybe when your male customers stay too long."

"Whatever, Linc. You've had a lot of admiring glances your way as well."

"I only see you."

She smiled. "You're crazy."

I held up my phone. "Dammit, Sunny, you're gorgeous," I muttered. "How can you not see that?"

She blushed, ignoring my words. "Eat your lunch."

I looked at the sandwich. "No biscuit?"

"Not everything has a biscuit, Linc."

"It should."

"We make the bread too."

I sighed dramatically and gave in. "Fine. I'll suffer."

"You've eaten six biscuits today. Surely, that is enough."

"In your opinion. I have ten years to make up for."

"You haven't had a biscuit in ten years?"

"No. They reminded me of you. It was too painful. At the place I was at, the food was bland. Nutritious, I was informed, but bland. When I got back, I gorged myself on everything I missed while I was away, but I couldn't touch biscuits."

Sadness flashed over her features. I hated to see it—we'd both been sad enough. So, I winked. "Just saying, Sunny-girl. I have a lot of time to make up for. Keep the biscuits coming."

"No one has called me that in ten years." She smiled, although her eyes remained sad. "I'm not a girl anymore, Linc."

I studied her briefly, then wrapped my hand around hers. "You'll always be the girl I fell in love with, Sunny. You will always be *my* girl."

Her breath caught and she stood. "I have to get back to work. Are you planning on occupying a table all day?"

I nodded. "Feel free to add rent to the tab."

She walked away, peeking over her shoulder. "Bank on it, Webber."

I liked how my chosen last name sounded coming from her lips. It gave me a thrill and made me smile. I watched her disappear through the kitchen door. Had I said too much? Had hearing the word love frightened her? It flew out of my mouth without conscious thought. Ten years hadn't changed my feelings for her. No amount of time would. I had met women—amazing, smart, beautiful women over the years, and never once had any of them even interested me beyond a date or two. I tried but they were never *her*. Now that she was back in my life, they never would be.

Sunny Jenson stole my heart the day she gazed wide-eyed and longingly at my box of crayons, asking in her soft little voice if she could "bowwow" the pretty purple one to color her dragon. I had handed her the box, letting her have any color she wanted. Her smile had been so bright, it eclipsed the sun itself, and since that day, I had lived to see that smile.

That was never going to change.

I knew I was going to have to prove myself to her all over again, but I was determined to do so. I could only hope she was as anxious for that to happen as I was.

A few moments later, the kitchen door opened, giving me a full view of Sunny working at a large table. I heard her tell Shannon to leave it open, which afforded me a clear line of vision to look at her. Every so often, I would lift my eyes to meet hers, and I realized she was checking on me as often as I checked on her.

I thought that, perhaps, I had my answer.

I rubbed the back of my neck, massaging at the stiff muscles. Sitting at a table, drinking too much coffee, and hunched over my laptop was not great for my posture—or my shoulders. Still, I was loath to leave—even to go to the hotel I had booked to stay at. My original plans had been to stay only one night, but I had extended my stay at the hotel. It was new, on the outskirts of town, and in no way associated with my father or me. Neutral territory with no memories attached to it. It wasn't at all like the luxurious places I was used to staying these days, but it was fine. It was small but the room spotless and the bed comfortable. It didn't help me sleep last night, but I doubted anything would have helped.

I'd contacted my assistant this morning with instructions to go to my place and pack a bag for me. I knew my housekeeper would have done so, but Abby had been with me a long time, and she knew exactly what I would want packed and brought. While she was here, we could also sit and discuss my schedule for the next while, since I hoped I would be here for some time.

One of the perks of being my own boss was that I answered to no one but myself.

I knew I couldn't hang out in Sunny's restaurant every day, but for now, that was where I planned to be.

The place became quiet as the afternoon wore on. The small staff she employed stayed busy, cleaning and prepping for the following day. About three o'clock, a man strolled in, carrying an armful of linens. He set it on the counter, leaning on the glass, looking comfortable in the shop. His face was familiar, but I couldn't quite place it. I bristled when Sunny came from the kitchen, greeting him warmly, kissing him on the cheek, and chatting to him. Their posture was relaxed and easy, suggesting a level of intimacy between them. My annoyance grew as I watched him lay his hand on her arm as they shared a private joke.

The rational part of my brain knew I had no claim on Sunny. That for the past ten years we had lived separate lives. I was under no illusions that she had been pining away for me and had shut herself off from the world. She was too beautiful and vibrant.

However, the caveman part of me wanted to walk over and grab the stranger's hand and yank it off her arm. Stand beside her and pull her close.

Claim her.

Which would probably end up with me on the floor after she kneed me in the balls. I had a feeling Sunny wouldn't take my gesture very well.

So, I sat and glared, hating the stranger. Hating the time that had separated us. Hating my father even more—something I didn't think was possible.

Then Sunny looked my way, smiled, and gestured for me to come over. I unfurled myself from the table, my legs protesting as I stood. I crossed the floor of the shop, wondering why the stranger was grinning so widely and why Sunny seemed so happy.

Before I could stop myself, I moved beside her and wrapped my arm around her waist, tugging her close. "You gestured?" I teased, pressing a kiss to her head while holding the stranger's gaze, letting him know who she belonged to.

Apparently, the caveman had won.

If anything, his grin became wider. He reached out his hand, pumping mine hard.

"Linc Thomas. You sorry son of a bitch. Never thought I'd see you again."

"Webber," I corrected him automatically. I hated hearing my name associated with my father's in any way. "Lincoln Webber."

He nodded. "Webber, then."

His voice was familiar. I narrowed my eyes, taking in his brown hair and light blue eyes. The small scar beside the right one. I recognized it because I gave him the cut that caused the scar. We were playing soccer, and I fell, my cleat catching the corner of his eye. There was a lot of blood, and he punched me, giving me a split lip. We were both ejected from the game.

Recognition hit me, and a smile cracked my lips.

"Michael Hall. What the hell are you doing here?"

Michael had been one of the few people I had liked at school. I'd considered him a friend—at least as much as I'd considered anyone outside Sunny a friend. We weren't close, but we respected each other and were in a lot of the same classes and sporting events. He knew about Sunny and me, his girlfriend someone Sunny trusted and had confided in, but he never let on about us. He allowed us our privacy, seeming to understand the reason for it.

He was always easygoing, cheerful, and more than once showed what a good guy he was by walking Sunny home when my father interfered with our plans, or even letting me know if she needed me. He had worked at the dry cleaner next door to the diner, and one memory stood out for me of his thoughtfulness.

I had been sitting in my usual booth at the diner, eating, talking with Sunny during her breaks, when the bell over the door jangled. It was getting late, and the diner was mostly empty, so I was surprised when Michael rushed in, heading straight toward me.

"Your dad is looking for you. I heard him asking people if they had seen you." He glanced toward Sunny. *"He's in a foul mood, Linc. You might not want him finding you here."*

I stood. "Shit."

"Go out the back door. Leave your stuff. I'll pretend it's mine, and I'll cover you and make sure Sunny gets home. Go."

Sunny gripped the cloth she was holding. "Go," she urged.

I ran through the kitchen and out the back door. I didn't stop running until I got to the house. I tore up the stairs and flung myself in bed, remembering to pull off my shirt that smelled of the diner before diving under the covers.

I heard the sound of my father's car, then the front door opening, and his voice bellowing my name as he came up the stairs. My bedroom door flew open so hard it hit the wall, and I pretended to be jolted out of a deep sleep and sat up, startled.

"What the hell?"

My father crossed the room, anger pouring off his body. "Where have you been?"

"Here." I managed a yawn and scratched my head, hoping to look sleepy and that he couldn't hear my accelerated heartbeat. "What's going on?"

He leaned down, his breath laced with scotch. "I heard you didn't make captain of the soccer team. I told you to make it happen."

"I told you I'm not good enough." The truth was I hated playing soccer and only did it to pacify him. I was glad to be passed up.

He narrowed his eyes. "If I tell you to do something, you make it happen."

"I tried. Jason is a better player. A better leader. I can't compete with his ability." I pointed out. "It was the coach's decision. Not mine."

"I'm taking your car away for a month. You can fucking walk. In fact, you had better run. I want ten pounds off you. And you're grounded for the next two weeks."

I bit back my retort. My car, I could live without. The grounding was harder to handle, although given his schedule, I could slip out at times if I wanted. It was better than being punished by his fists.

"You'll be captain next year, or there will be consequences."

I knew better than to argue with him. I had gotten off lightly this time.

But I should have known better. My father straightened and I relaxed. Then he punched me in the stomach so hard, I began heaving immediately. I hadn't even seen it coming. The milk shake I had drunk at the diner came up, spewing white all over my bed.

He eyed me with disdain. "Clean it up. Leave your car keys on my desk in the morning." He paused at the door. "And your little slut of a waitress was hanging all over some asswipe in the diner. Didn't take her long to set her sights on someone else." His tone was mocking. "Not that you're much of a catch either. Without my money, you're nothing."

Then he walked out.

I kept my arm around my stomach as I got up, knowing that if Michael hadn't warned me and my father had found me in the diner, I would have been in far worse pain. I hated the thought that Sunny obviously played up Michael being there, but I knew she had done it to take the heat off of me.

I wasn't sure why Michael had stepped in and helped, but I had never forgotten his empathy.

I grasped his hand, returning his grip. "How are you?"

"Good, Linc. I'm good. What are you doing in town?" His gaze moved to Sunny then back to me. "Or should I leave that well enough alone?"

Sunny's cheeks turned a soft shade of pink. I had to chuckle at his words. "Came to settle the last of my father's estate. I had planned on being here one day, but things, ah, changed."

He grinned. "Is that a fact? Well, Sunny, I think I need a coffee and a muffin. Linc and I have some catching up to do."

She scooped up the pile of linens from the counter. "What about you Linc? Are you coffeed out?"

I smirked at her—she had no idea. "Nope. Coffee and a couple more biscuits, please."

Michael and I moved to my table, and I shut off my laptop, slipping it into my bag. Sunny slid a tray onto the table containing a pot of coffee and two plates holding muffins and biscuits. I caught her hand. "Thank you."

She smiled and bent down, brushing a kiss to my forehead, then headed back to the kitchen. Her tender gesture did something to my chest. I hadn't been touched with gentleness since the day I was forced to leave her. I squeezed her hand in silent appreciation. She shut the door this time, leaving Michael and me alone in the shop.

"Should I extend condolences about your father?" he asked.

"Absolutely not. The only thing I felt when he died was relief."

He nodded, sipping his coffee. "Nasty son of a bitch, he was. The things he did to this town were bad enough, but the way he took his anger out on you was unacceptable."

I rested my elbows on the table. "How did you know, Michael? I never spoke about it. I thought I hid it well. You were kind to me, even though we weren't really friends. Close ones anyway."

He took a muffin off the plate, unpeeling the wrapper and breaking it in half. He took a large bite, chewing it slowly. "We weren't close, no, but I understood why. I understood *you*."

"Sorry?"

He finished the first half of his muffin and wiped his fingers. "My god, that woman can bake."

I had to agree. I took a biscuit, already buttered with a thick layer of jam on top, and bit into it. I would always think of Sunny when I ate one of these.

He sat back, gazing over my shoulder. "We moved here when I was young. My father was a mean, sorry drunk, and he liked to use his fists on me and my mother. She planned and saved, and one day, we were able to run. We came here—a small town where we could start again."

"Your father never found you?"

He shrugged. "He might have tried, but a couple of weeks after we left, he got so drunk, he fell down the stairs. He never woke up. A friend of my mom's knew where we were and let her know. She got the life insurance and total freedom to live her life again and not look over her shoulder all the time."

"I'm sorry for what you went through."

He lifted a shoulder. "The point is I recognized what was happening to you, Linc. I saw the signs. When your mom died, you changed. The happy kid I knew disappeared, and a frightened, stand-offish person replaced him. I tried to let you know I understood, but I got it when you refused to get close to anyone but Sunny. Your father was a force unto himself and, frankly, scary. Still, when I could, I tried to let you know you had a friend."

"Like the day in the diner."

He met my gaze, both of us thinking of that day. "Your father was so angry, and I knew if he found you hanging with Sunny, hell was going to rain down on you. I heard him, more than once, talk about his plans for you and that they didn't include some low-level waitress."

I was surprised at his words, and it must have shown on my face.

"I was a clerk in the dry cleaners and the drug store. A nothing to your father. Invisible. He would be on his phone talking, and I could hear him. He never even noticed me most of the time." He barked out a laugh. "Unless he wanted his dry cleaning carried to his car, then he'd snap his fingers and tell me to get it done. But that was the only time he ever spoke to or took notice of me. I can guarantee if I passed him on the street, he'd have no clue who I was."

"Yeah, he was like that."

"So, I understood your wariness, Linc. I know a lot of kids thought you were a snob and too good for them, but I knew you were just trying to survive." He met my gaze. "And protect Sunny."

"I was." I sucked in a long breath. "Thank you for being a friend, even when I wasn't."

"You were okay. You kept to yourself, but you were never a jerk." He paused. "Until you left her."

I rubbed my eyes. "I know how it looked."

"Your father?" he guessed.

"Yeah." I laughed bitterly. "My father."

Then I did something I never thought I would do. I told the truth about where I had been and what I had done. He listened in silence, whistling low when I finished.

"Wow. He was some piece of work."

I acknowledged his words with a nod. I felt exhausted after telling him. Drained. But I was done hiding. I was also done talking about myself.

"What about you, Michael? What has life been like for you?"

For the first time, I saw a cloud of sadness pass over face, and his smile faded.

"I'm still here," he stated.

"Here, as in Mission Cove? Or the world in general?" I asked.

He scrubbed his face. "Both, I suppose. There were a few years I wanted to leave Mission Cove, but the bottom line was, despite your father and his underhanded ways, I loved this town." His voice dropped. "I loved Molly Jones, too."

I remembered they had dated all through high school. "And now?"

He was quiet for a moment, filling his cup, then taking a long sip. "She got pregnant the last year of school. We got married."

I kept silent, knowing there was more to his story.

"It was hard to give up on my dreams. I wanted to go to university —into business management. But I had a family I needed to look after."

"It must have been difficult."

"At times. But my son, Jesse, and my wife made up for it. Then a few years later, we had a daughter." He hesitated, his eyes blinking rapidly. "My mom died not long after Jenny was born."

"I'm sorry, Michael."

He cleared his throat. "Not long after that, I was able to buy the dry-cleaning business from Old Man Tate. Molly got a job at the day care, and things were going good for us. Some unknown benefactor gave a bunch of people in town the chance to buy their buildings outright—dirt cheap." He cocked his head, studying me. "Happened after your father died. Know anything about that?"

I shook my head, trying to look surprised and puzzled. That had given me a lot of pleasure. Giving back to the people my father had stolen from for years, but I intended to keep it anonymous.

"Interesting turn of events," I mused.

He looked skeptical. "Isn't it just?"

"So, you bought the building?" I asked, already knowing the answer.

"I couldn't refuse at the price and terms it was being offered for. Luckily, people still need dry cleaning and laundry done, so we stayed busy. Not as busy as I need at times, but I get by."

I sensed there was more. "Good. So, things are going well for you."

"They *were*. Then Molly got sick."

The way he stated it, I knew Molly hadn't survived.

"Michael, I'm sorry to hear that."

This time, he didn't try to hide his emotions. "Breast cancer. She fought so hard, but in the end, it won."

"How long ago?"

He wiped away the tears under his eyes. "Almost two years."

"So now you're a single dad, running a business and looking after your family."

"Yeah. But I have great friends—" he indicated the kitchen with a jerk of his head "—including Sunny. She and Molly got closer after you were gone, and I know how much Sunny misses her as well. She's been a great help, and my kids love her. I have other people, and they help out too." He studied me in silence. "The town has changed, Linc. It's a great place—better than you remember it. Thanks to the unknown benefactor, the community has become tight. We're prospering."

"Good." I cleared my throat of the lump that had grown as Michael spoke. He had lost so much in his life, and I wanted to do something to help him. I would have to figure out what I could do.

"Do you have pictures of your kids?"

A genuine smile crossed his face, and he spent the next ten minutes showing me the pictures he had on his phone. Baby and toddler pictures. Family photos. Jesse and Jenny growing up. Michael and Molly, young on their wedding day and maturing over the years. One of Molly and the kids, her illness evident, but the smile on her face still bright and filled with love.

"That was about three weeks before she died," he explained. "She spent as much time with the kids as she could."

I handed him back the phone. "I'm sure they miss her. I'm sure you do as well."

"Every second of every day."

"Your kids are lucky to have you."

He scrubbed a hand over his face. "I try to be the dad I need to be for them. A mom too." He smiled ruefully. "I don't think I'll ever get the hair thing right for Jenny, but god knows I try." He mimicked making a ponytail in the air. "I never seem to get it in the right place, and my hair clips fall out." He grinned. "Luckily, Sunny's place is across the street, and she often steps in and helps."

I felt unease drip into my chest. Did Michael have feelings for Sunny? He spoke of her with great affection.

How close, I wondered, was she to his family?

To him?

Sunny had a life. An entire life I knew nothing about. Ten years of memories I wasn't a part of.

Had my arrival back in town, in her life, been a mistake? Was I robbing someone else of their happiness by trying to seek my own? I opened my mouth to ask when my phone beeped, and I glanced at the screen. Seeing the message, I stood.

"Sorry, Michael—" I grabbed my messenger bag "—I have to get going. I have someone I need to meet at the house." I extended my hand. "Good to see you. We'll catch up more later."

"Yeah, later, for sure. We need to catch up."

I glanced at the kitchen door. I could hear Sunny talking on the phone, her voice confident and sure as she spoke slowly and clearly, making sure her point was made. I hesitated.

"I'll tell Sunny you had to go."

Given our history, I didn't want to leave without telling her. I had no reason to think Michael wouldn't tell her, but still, I didn't like it.

"I should tell her myself."

The kitchen door opened and Shannon came through, carrying a stack of gleaming trays. I approached her with a smile. "Can I interrupt Sunny?"

She grimaced. "I wouldn't. She's on a rampage with a supplier."

"Okay. Tell her Linc had to go to a meeting up the hill. Ask her to call me, please."

"Sure, Linc. I'll tell her."

With a wave to the bemused-looking Michael, I hurried from the bakery. My thoughts were chaotic, my questions endless. Once again, I realized I knew nothing of Sunny's life for the last ten years. Whom she had been with. Cared for—loved, even. I knew there was something still strong and powerful between us, but it wasn't out of the realm of possibility that at some point she had loved someone else. That, possibly, after Molly died, Michael had begun to look at their friendship in a new light. Perhaps they were in the early stages of discovering something. Maybe my sudden appearance had come at a bad time.

Except, as I slid behind the wheel and drove the short distance to the house, one thought permeated my brain.

I wasn't giving Sunny up without a fight.

And this time, I wasn't above fighting dirty.

9

LINC

I pulled up my car beside the bright-pink SUV in the driveway of my father's house. He would have been horrified at the sight of it —and the woman who slipped from behind the wheel, her high-top sneakers hitting the pavement with a loud thump.

Abby approached my car, her blond hair, complete with a wide pink stripe to match her sneakers, piled on top of her head in a messy cluster of curls. The color caught the sun, glowing bright and gold. It wasn't the same burnished glow of Sunny's but rather like a beacon of sunshine. Abby wore a tight-fitting dress in pink and white, the material stretched over her breasts, highlighting "the girls," as she called them. Most of her face was covered by the huge sunglasses she wore, but her smile was wide, although I noticed the tension in her shoulders.

"Hey, boss man. Nice place." She snorted. "You meant it when you said ostentatious."

I bent and brushed a kiss to her cheek, taking the bag she grabbed from her back seat and throwing it onto the passenger seat of my car. Then I ran a hand through my hair.

"I hate this place."

She laid a hand on my arm. "I know."

Taking the opportunity, I hooked my finger over the top of the sunglasses and tugged them down her nose. She immediately slapped my hand away.

"Hey, stop that."

I didn't try again. I saw what I needed to see. I wasn't the only one having a bad day. The dark circles under her eyes told me all I needed to know. I had to find out what had happened, but I had to wait for the right moment. Otherwise, she would shut me down faster than the speed of light.

I slid an arm around her shoulders. "Come on in. Ned will be here soon. You can keep me company, and we can go through my schedule."

"I am dying to find out why you're staying on in Mission Cove," she admitted, grabbing her huge purse from the back seat. I swore she kept half the contents of her apartment in it. "You said you'd rather spend eternity in hell than come back here."

I glanced at her over my shoulder as I slid the key into the front door lock. "I think we both have stories to tell." I arched my eyebrow. "You know the code, Abigail. Tit for tat."

She huffed out a breath but didn't argue. From the moment I met her, that had been our code. If I shared, so did she—and vice versa. We had no secrets between us. Our unseen scars were real and open —often bleeding, and the cause of them spoken out loud in the hopes that they would cease to hurt us.

Sometimes, it worked. Other times, the scars ran too deep and would forever fester and wear at us. But still, we pushed on, baring our souls and accepting each other for the people we were—the people we had to become to break free from our pasts.

She nodded, the smile gone from her face. Inside, she followed me to the kitchen and accepted the bottle of water I handed her. To provide her a chance to collect her thoughts, I gave her a tour of the house, then we headed to my father's den.

She looked around the room. "Has the place changed much since you lived here?"

"Nope. Nothing—except a few things I removed to keep, but nothing anyone would notice. They were already packed in boxes or shoved in drawers."

She shivered. "It's cold. What an austere place to live."

I swallowed a long drink of water. "It was nicer when my mom was alive. When she died, my father removed any trace of her. It became a shrine to himself. To his power. This—" I tapped the desk "—was his throne. He commanded his world from it." I snorted. "Mine as well."

"He was a real bastard."

"I know."

"But he's gone. And you're slowly erasing him and his deeds. Spending his fortune on everything he hated. That must feel good."

"It does."

"So why the frown? What's wrong?"

I rubbed my eyes. "Sunny," I said simply. "She's here."

Her eyes widened. "*What?* Here in Mission Cove?"

"Yes, she's been here for a while."

She sat down in the chair across from the desk. "Tell me."

I told her everything. How it felt returning to Mission Cove. Walking into Sunny's bakery and the shock of seeing her. Our altercation here in the den. When I got to the part about Sunny slapping me and my response, Abby gasped quietly.

"Oh, Linc. How awful."

I shook my head. "No, it was what we needed to break the ice. She had been holding in her anger all this time, so it's hardly a surprise."

"You've been angry too." She pointed out. "Hurt as well."

"Thanks to my father, we both have." I huffed out a long breath. "I hope we can move past it."

"You still love her." It was a statement not a question.

I met her light-brown eyes. They had always reminded me of the color of caramels. Rich and, despite what she had suffered in her life, warm and open.

"I will always love her."

She relaxed against the back of the chair. "That explains a lot."

I tilted my head. "Oh?"

"It's been her all this time. I've watched you for years, Linc. The beautiful women who came and went—who threw themselves at you. Nothing. You always looked through them—not at them. There was never a spark. Certainly not the passion I see in your eyes when you talk about Sunny."

"It's always been her."

"Can this happen?" she asked. "Can you get past everything you've been through? That's a lot of water under the bridge, Linc. You're two different people now."

I shrugged. "Am I? Somewhere inside me is still the boy who loved Sunny. Who *still* loves Sunny. As soon as I saw her, something inside me settled. I felt complete again. I felt like Linc. Not the businessman, not the son bent on retribution. Just Linc."

"Is that enough?"

I thought about her question before I replied. Abby was always a straight shooter and never held back with me. "It's a start. All I know is when I kissed her, I felt whole again. I spent the day watching her, needing to be nearby. I can't explain it—it simply feels as if I belonged close to her."

She crossed one leg over the other, swinging her foot, the glitter on her shoelaces catching the light as it pumped. "I won't even address the kissing or you hanging out in her shop all day. But be careful, Linc. Sometimes the past clouds our judgment. Stirs up emotions that were dormant, making them powerful and alive. Don't confuse old emotions that suddenly have come to life with what may shape your future." She paused, her voice becoming soft. "I don't want to see you get hurt. And I'm worried the Sunny of today could hurt you even more than the memories you carry of Sunny inside your head."

"I didn't expect this," I admitted. "But I can't tell you how right it feels, Abby. I'm not blind—I know we have years to talk about, lots of distance and things to discuss and work through, but I want to try."

"I assumed so from the bag you had me bring you. You're staying here?"

"At the hotel." I looked around. "Not in this house. I will never stay in this house again."

"Too many ghosts," she agreed. "They're all around you."

"Yes." I studied her, not hiding the fact that I was doing so. When she had removed her sunglasses earlier, I had seen the fatigue on her face. Recognized the lines of pain around her eyes. That was always her tell. Regardless of the expression on her face, the neutral tone of her voice, her inner torment was always evident in her eyes. The caramel became muddy and dull. The small V between her eyes was more pronounced. Tiny lines became etched into her skin. Anyone who really knew Abby recognized it.

I was one of the few people who knew her.

I was about to ask her what was going on when the sound of a car approaching stopped me. It would have to wait until he left. "Ned is here."

She reached into her bag and pulled out her tablet. "Okay, boss, let's get some work done."

I stood, brushing off my pants. "This conversation isn't over, Abby."

She smiled sadly. "I'm aware."

I signed the last of the documents Ned gave me. "So, everything is arranged now?"

"Mostly. We've finally locked down most of the permits. I'm waiting for the last one from the city, and we should be good to go." He sat back, regarding me. "I know you don't want to hear it, but I'm going to say it anyway, Linc. I'm bringing in appraisers to go through the house. You might not care about the value, but as your lawyer, I insist on having valuations. Your accountant can write off the things you give away as donations. It makes the most sense."

I scrubbed my hand over my face. "How much longer does it delay things?"

"A week. I'll have them here to do the work, we can donate some things, then you can throw open the doors and give away the rest. The house is scheduled to be razed in about a month."

"Why so long?"

He smirked. "You don't just walk into a place and implode it. It has to be planned and wired. They'll be here tomorrow to make their assessment. I prebooked the date, and as long as things go all right, they'll stick to it. If adjustments have to be made, so will the date." He eyed me knowingly. "Step back, Linc. Think about it rationally—with your head, not your heart."

I stared out the window. Part of me wanted to watch this house implode on itself. The roof and walls collapsing like the house of cards my father had built around his life. I wanted to walk among the rubble, nothing left but dust and bricks that would be hauled away, until all that remained was empty ground. Another part of me didn't want to wait—instead, empty out the house tomorrow and let bulldozers pull it down.

But Ned was right, and I had to handle this properly. Make sure it was done correctly—all of it. The contents and the building itself.

I nodded in agreement. "Make it happen."

Abby spoke up. "I can be here while the appraisers are in the house."

"That would be great."

"Since you're staying, we can set up a temporary office. I can help you and take care of this at the same time," she offered.

"Great idea. Book yourself a room in the same place I'm staying. Come up on Monday, and we'll figure out a schedule."

"We can work from here?" she asked.

I glanced around, wondering how it would feel to work here. To conduct my business in this house where my father handled his affairs. I cleared my throat. "Maybe in the dining room." I could handle that much. Once my mother had passed, we never used it. I ate alone most of the time, and the few occasions my father and I had eaten a meal together, we'd sat in the kitchen.

She nodded in understanding. "I'll set it up."

Ned went through some more particulars, Abby busy making notes on her tablet. Then he stood. "I'll be back next week once the appraisals are finished. We'll review all the items and go from there." He shook my hand. "Be patient, Linc. I know you want this place gone, and it will be. I hope it brings you the closure you seek."

I frowned as he walked away. Of course it would bring me closure. Knowing this place no longer existed would help ease the hold my past still had on me. Destroying all the landmarks and decisions of Franklin Thomas from this town would help everyone. I wanted his memory, his entire history, erased.

"Did your father design this house?" Abby asked.

I shook my head. "No. It was being built, and the owner went bankrupt. My father swooped in and bought it for a song, completed construction, and laughed privately at the fact that every day the man who was building it had to look up and see it, knowing he would never have it. Knowing the house he planned on living in with his family was being enjoyed by someone 'more deserving,' as my father claimed."

"Wow," Abby breathed out. "That's fucking harsh."

I barked out a laugh. "The truth of it is that my father was already playing games in this town. He drove the man to bankruptcy. Then he had the audacity to act innocent while rubbing it in his face."

"What a two-faced bastard."

"That he was. Offered him a job at one of his businesses. Clapped him on his shoulder and assured him things would improve. All the while making sure his life never got better. I went to school with his son. They moved the next year. I remember my mother saying they were looking for a fresh start."

"Your mother had no idea about your father? The horrible things he did?"

I shook my head. "She knew he wasn't the man she thought she'd married, I think. But she had no idea of his twisted ego. He hid it well, but once she died, he let it out full strength. He liked me knowing what he did. What he was capable of. She did what he told her to do, aside from loving me. That was the rule she broke of his that he never forgave. Me before him. Then she had the gall to die and stick him with my care." I sighed. "I think, to be honest, she was better off dead."

"What about you, though? Were you better off without her?"

"No," I snapped. "You know that." I leaned forward. "I know what you're trying to do, Abby, and it isn't going to work. We're not talking about me anymore. Tell me what's going on."

Now it was her turn to look uncomfortable. She was silent for a moment, twisting the end of her pink streak over and again, tugging on her hair just hard enough to feel pain, so she could concentrate on something other than the horrific moment she was living through. She had done that for all the years I'd known her. She told me once at times it was the only way she could keep herself from screaming when she was younger. I let her gather her thoughts, knowing she would tell me the truth. She always did.

"My mother came to see me," she finally admitted, not meeting my eyes.

I was out of my chair, gripping the sides of the desk. "Who the hell let her in the building? She isn't allowed in there. She isn't allowed to be *near* you."

She shook her head, her eyes wide. "She didn't come into the building, Linc. She—" Abby swallowed heavily "—she was waiting for me in the underground parking lot of my building when I got home."

The implications of her words hit me. Her mother knew where she lived.

"You're moving. This week."

She didn't acknowledge my words, but a tremor went through her. "It was such a shock, seeing her. It's been so long, for a moment, I didn't recognize her."

I moved around the desk and sat beside her, taking her hand. "What did she want?"

"Money. She saw an article about you and saw me in the background of the picture they used."

I frowned. "You are never in the pictures." I approved every photo, making sure she was never around when cameras were being used.

"I think this was taken without us knowing. It's an office shot. I'm not even looking at the camera, barely even in the shot, but my mother recognized me."

"Abby, I'm sorry." I had promised to always protect her, and I had failed.

She squeezed my hand. "Not your fault, Linc. Anyway, she saw the picture and tracked me down. She followed me and, somehow, a couple of days later got into the garage and waited for me. She informed me that if I lived in such a swanky place and had a job working for someone as wealthy as you, I could spare her some money." Her voice began to tremble. "After all, I owed her."

"The fuck you do," I snarled out. "You owe her nothing, and she's getting nothing." When Abby didn't meet my eyes, I groaned. "Tell me you didn't give her any, Abby. She'll keep coming back."

She pulled her hand away and stood. She paced back and forth across the room, her hair an endless loop between her fingers. Then she stopped and stared at me. "When I told her to go to hell and stay there, she smiled. Just smiled. It was the fucking scariest smile I've ever seen." Tears glimmered in her eyes, shocking me. Despite what she had been through, it was rare I ever saw Abby cry. She was too strong, so I knew the next thing out of her mouth was going to be bad.

"She said no problem. Then she paused and said perhaps I wanted to reconsider. When I told her I didn't think so, she said fine."

"And?" I demanded.

Tears ran down Abby's cheeks. "She told me Carl got out of prison early for good behavior. She told me she would tell him I said hi and perhaps he'd drop over for a visit."

Curse words I rarely used flew from my mouth. I stood, enraged, disgusted, and frightened. What kind of human being did something like that to their own flesh and blood?

Abby pressed her hand to her mouth. "He's out, Linc. She's going to tell him where I am. I-I'm so scared—"

She didn't finish her sentence before the sobs began. I was across the room, yanking her snug into my arms and holding her. Violent tremors racked her body, and I pulled her tighter.

"He's never getting near you. Ever. I promise you that, Abby. I'm here for you." I dropped a kiss to her head. "I'm not leaving you alone, sweetheart. I promise."

A noise made me look up, and I saw Sunny, standing frozen in the doorway. She stared at me—at the woman I was holding, her mouth agape, hurt written across her face. I knew what it looked like. That she had heard the words I'd just uttered. I stared back at her, torn. I couldn't abandon Abby, but I couldn't allow Sunny to think that, once again, I had lied to her. I shook my head, frantically trying to convey with my eyes the words I couldn't yell out.

But I didn't have the chance. Before I could do anything, Sunny was gone. The door shut, and her rapid footsteps faded away. I heard the crunch of the gravel indicating she was running down the driveway and away from me.

And there was nothing I could do to stop her.

10

SUNNY

I came out of the kitchen to find the shop deserted. I frowned, a sudden frisson of fear running through my chest.

Where was Linc?

Shannon came from the stockroom, a large bag of flour in her arms. "Oh hey, boss. Got that supplier sorted out?"

"Yes," I replied, distracted, heading to the window, my fear growing when I saw Linc's car was gone.

"Michael said to tell you those towels will be back tomorrow. Oh, and that Linc guy had to meet someone up the hill. He wanted to tell you, but I said not to interrupt. He asked you to call him when you could."

My chest loosened at her words, and internally, I shook my head at my foolishness. I checked my watch and flipped the sign to closed. It was a little early, but the day was done, and luckily, I called the shots.

I had one more task to do and then I would call Linc.

Time passed quickly, and by the time I finished my task it had been over an hour and a half. Rather than call Linc, I decided to go up to the house and surprise him. It was obvious being in that house made him tense, and he might like the distraction.

As well as the surprise I made him.

My stomach dipped as I walked up the hill toward the house Linc grew up in. I had always hated the ostentatious look of it when I lived here as a teenager—and when I had moved back. It towered over our small town like a beacon of wealth and privilege no one else could hope to attain. I had only been inside it once when Linc and I were young. His father was away on a business trip, and Linc asked me to go to his house. He had taken me on a tour, showing me the massive structure room by room. So many of them were empty. Others felt staged. The family room with the big TV no one watched. The formal dining room with its gleaming table and silver that sparkled under the lights that was never sat in.

Linc looked sad as he showed me his mother's old sitting room— empty and barren.

"He threw away everything of hers," he said, the pain evident in his voice.

"You didn't get anything?"

"A few little items I grabbed. I heard him making arrangements to have it all taken away, and once I heard him go out, I packed up some things and hid them in the basement in a room I knew he never went into. Things I knew he wouldn't notice or care about, but I knew she loved." He sighed. "I couldn't take her chair or the little sofa she had. She always let me lie on it while she read to me. I had to leave the pictures she loved because if he figured out that I had taken even one, he would have hunted down everything and destroyed all of it."

I grasped his hand. "Linc, I'm sorry."

He stared at the room, the wallpaper faded, the shadows of long-lost pictures removed and destroyed leaving their imprints. I wondered if he was remembering the sound of her voice, a time when life wasn't so difficult for him because he had her. His voice was thick when he spoke. "It was better to have a few things than none at all, you know? A few of her books, some of the needlepoint pieces she had finished but not hung up. Her letters from her parents. Personal things." He shivered. *"I think my father would have killed me if he'd found me going through her drawers and cupboards taking private stuff."*

I recalled his sadness, then his intense panic when he realized his father had returned home early. We both knew what he would do if he found out I was in the house. Linc had rushed me down to the kitchen, and I'd slipped out the back door, hurrying down the path that skirted the house and making my way home in the dark. Linc had been upset for days that he'd made me walk home alone. I had stumbled in the dark, scraping my hand badly. He checked it every day, kissing the torn skin and worrying about infection, fretting over me needlessly.

I'd never ventured into his father's house again with Linc.

Until yesterday.

It had been a shock to see the boy I had loved for so long standing in front of me—no longer a boy, but a man. Gone were the developing muscles and youthful, handsome face. The shy smile and the guarded expression he often had to adopt when seeing me was absent, replaced by a confident air and demeanor.

The man in front of me wasn't shy. He was tall, his shoulders broad, his waist trim. His hair was darker than I remembered, and he wore it longer than he had when we were younger. His sharp jaw was covered in scruff, and he wore an expensive suit tailored to perfection. Something deep within me strummed with recognition at the stranger in my shop, staring at me, his body tight with tension. When he pulled off his sunglasses, revealing the eyes that still haunted my dreams, I was shocked.

Then I became angry.

Angry enough to march up to his father's house and confront him. To hurl the furious words I had kept inside for so many years. Slapping him had been one of the most violent things I had done in my life.

What transpired afterward was unexpected, wondrous, and frightening.

To hear what he went through, what that bastard of a father had done to him. Listen as Linc told me of the years spent at what amounted to a prison for him had been like. Accept the letters he had written to me that his father waylaid. All of it difficult, heartbreaking, and almost surreal.

After we separated for the evening, I sat and read some of the letters, once again transforming into the girl he had written them to. I felt his pain, his anger, the terror of not knowing or understanding what had happened, or how he could get away. His pleas to wait for him, to know how much he loved me, how much he would always love me. His loneliness, isolation, and fear jumped from the pages. His longing for me grew with each letter, the pain he was feeling soaked into the ink on the pages.

His honest, handwritten words mended some of the pieces of my heart that had shredded the day he disappeared from my life. Knowing I hadn't been abandoned. That he hadn't fucked and run. The fact that his love had been real—all of it healed a part of my broken spirit I hadn't realized I'd been holding in until now.

I stopped in confusion outside the house, staring at the bright-pink SUV. Linc had told me his lawyer was coming back today, but I doubted he drove such a feminine vehicle. The flowers and sparkle decals on the sides were not something I would associate with a lawyer. But perhaps, I told myself, it belonged to his wife or daughter and he had to borrow it.

The front door was ajar, and I followed the sound of voices to the den. I frowned at the obviously feminine-sounding tone, stopping in shock in the doorway.

Linc was holding a woman, kissing her head. Murmuring to her in a low, gentle voice. His entire stance was protective. She was wrapped in his embrace, his hand spread wide across her back. I heard his endearment as he spoke, assuring her he was wasn't leaving her and he would protect her.

Their familiarity was palpable, the intimacy of the moment clear. This was someone very important to Linc.

How important, I didn't know, but suddenly, the ten years we'd been apart seemed longer. A chasm of unknown questions, memories, moments neither of us knew about.

Who was this woman to Linc? What did it mean for us?

Had his response, his closeness the past hours, simply been a reaction to the memories of us and not actually real feelings? Did he already belong to someone else and was now realizing his actions had been just that?

When he looked up and met my eyes, his grew wide with anxiety, and he shook his head, telling me what I needed to know.

I had to leave. I wasn't any more welcome here now than I had been years ago.

He didn't have to say anything. I turned and left much the same way I had the other time.

Alone, upset, and confused.

<hr />

I paced my small apartment over the bakery on an endless loop. All the things I had loved about the space now seemed wrong. The coziness was claustrophobic, the furniture uncomfortable, the sight of the town, and the large house that loomed over it, daunting. I snapped shut the blinds, but I couldn't get the images in my mind to stop.

Linc holding another woman. Soothing her. The way his long-fingered hands drifted up and down her back in comforting, familiar touches. His voice crooning to her.

There was history. A lot of it. She meant something to him.

A voice in my head told me that was why he said he wanted me to call. He didn't ask me to come to the house. But once I finished with my supplier, and closed the shop, I wanted to see him. I looked at the bag I had dropped by my door when I'd arrived home, breathless, upset, and tearful.

Biscuits. I had made him an extra batch of fresh biscuits, and I planned on giving them to him with tubs of jam and butter. I wanted him to eat them in his father's den. Let the crumbs fall on the expensive rug and not clean them up. Do something silly and make him laugh in a room that had only every brought him fear.

My gaze fell to the pile of letters. Ones that had hurt me to read yet brought me a glimmer of hope that perhaps my future might look different from what it had the day before. That maybe Linc might once again be part of my life.

Now, I couldn't stand to look at them.

I couldn't take the apartment anymore. I needed to get out before I let my emotions swamp me. Despite what I knew the place now meant, there was only one spot I could think to go and clear my head.

I grabbed my coat, shutting the door and leaving the letters, the biscuits, and my hopes behind.

The wind kicked off the waves, lifting my hair off my neck. I stared out at the cove, the constant motion of the water soothing. It always had been. Whenever I was upset, worried, or my sisters were driving me to distraction, I would escape to this place. Eventually, I shared it with Linc and it became our place, but once he was gone, I still went there. It had been my spot first. I refused to let him take that away from me too.

Despite all the development around the town, this little spot had never changed—the land around it the same as it had been for years. The land adjacent to it, the deserted area Linc and I would meet up in was now a park loved by the community and, as Linc confirmed, named after me. But this place remained the same. Idly, I wondered if Linc had anything to do with it, then dismissed the thought. I'd come here to escape him. To let the sound of the waves and wind clear my head. I built a fire, having learned how to do it myself over the years once I started coming here alone again. I kept a small pile of wood and some waterproof matches tucked under the edge of the rock. I knew one day I would come here and find it gone. Discovered by teenagers or sold and used as part of a development, but for now, it was still my spot.

I sat beside the small fire, poking the flames, watching them dance in the dark, chasing away the chill as night descended and the stars came out. I huddled close, my knees drawn to my chest, and with a sigh, I laid my head on top of them, feeling the emotion of the day catch up with me. Tears drifted down my cheeks, and I allowed them to fall, knowing I needed to clear them from my system. Tomorrow, I would face the day and be strong, but for now I had to let it out.

Linc, the past, the letters, today, the woman he was holding...it all was too much. My head ached with too many thoughts, and my heart yearned for something I didn't think I could have. Tears dripped down my face, soaking into the fabric of my pants. I didn't bother trying to stop them.

The back of my neck prickled, and the sound of the rocks moving under heavy footsteps startled me. In all the years I had been coming here, no one else had ever shown up, except one person. I didn't have to look to know who it was. My body always knew when Linc was close. That hadn't changed.

"Please go," I pleaded. "I can't, Linc. Not tonight. Tell me your excuses another time. Just leave me alone."

He sat beside me, his warmth beckoning, his scent drifting around me. He still smelled like home, even after all these years. Ocean, cedar, and something pure Linc.

"I can't," he stated simply.

I refused to look at him, not wanting him to see the tears, or see the vulnerability he had somehow brought back out in me. I had worked for years never to show weakness to anyone again—to be a tough business owner, a capable daughter and sister, a trustworthy friend. But I refuse to care too much about anyone outside the people I considered my trusted circle. If I was being honest with myself, I even held back parts of me from them. The part that had been torn away from me the day Linc disappeared—the same part that seemed to have reemerged when he walked into my bakery.

"Please," I repeated.

"Not until you hear what I have to say. If you still want me to go, I will."

His voice was low—determined. I turned my head, meeting his gaze. His eyes were dim, worried, and grief-stricken. He gasped when he saw my face, reaching out his shaking hand.

"No, Sunny. I know what you're thinking, but you're wrong."

"You know that woman—you've known her a long time."

"Yes."

"You're close."

He ran a hand over his face. "Not the way you think."

"You love her," I stated.

He didn't deny it. "Yes. I love her. She's been my best friend for more than nine years, Sunny. If it weren't for her, I'm not sure I'd be sitting here with you right now."

A tear dripped off my nose. Linc bent close, wiping the wetness away from my skin with his fingers, making soft sounds. "Please, Sunny-girl. Let me explain. I know you don't owe me anything and I know how it looked when you came in, but please, god *please*, listen to me." He moved his fingers faster as the tears came harder. "Tell me I haven't lost you all over again."

It was the break in his voice, the catch, that hit me. He sounded as if he was in the same agony I was sinking into.

"I want the truth."

"I swear I'll give it to you. I'll tell you everything about Abigail Price." He smiled sadly. "It's only fair. She knows everything about you."

I sat up, roughly rubbing my hands over my face. I missed the gentle swipe of his fingers, but I needed the distance.

"How?" I asked. "How does she know about me?"

He regarded me in silence. "We were both sent to that place by our families. She was one of the few females there. We became close *friends*." He emphasized that word. "Just friends. When I finally left

99

and got my hands on my money, I got her out. She's been my right-hand ever since."

I frowned. *She was his business associate?*

"I have Abby's permission to tell you about her past, Sunny. As long as you promise to listen, I'll tell you."

I shivered, shifting closer to the dying fire. Linc cursed and pulled off his jacket, draping it around my shoulders. Then, as if he had only done it yesterday and not ten years ago, he reached behind him and grabbed more wood, adding it to the fire. He poked at the burning wood until he was satisfied with the flames.

"Will you listen?" he asked, sitting back beside me.

I thought of the endless hours of conversations that had happened in this spot. The plans we made, the dreams we shared. The years I spent sitting here, alone, always wondering, always wishing for another night of him here beside me. Then the broken hitch to his voice echoed in my head, and I knew I had to try.

"Yes, Linc. I'll listen."

11

LINC

When I couldn't find Sunny at her apartment, I sat in my car, swearing under my breath. I cursed Abby's mother. I wished death—a long, slow one—on Carl. On both of them. I called the lawyer I kept on retainer for anything to do with Abby and filled him in on the situation.

"Get his parole revoked, Milo. Put a tail on him. Keep him the hell away from Abby. Her mother too."

"On it." He hung up.

Then I calmed myself, centering my thoughts the way I had learned, and concentrated on finding Sunny.

The cliff—the place Sunny and I used to hide—came to mind. I had purposely never developed the land around that area, even though I owned all of it. I had never planned on going there again, but I wanted to know that somehow, some small part of us still existed.

Would she go there?

There was only one way to find out.

I started the car and headed toward that end of town.

I was relieved to have found her, grateful she agreed to listen to me, and cursed myself for not thinking of bringing an extra jacket or a blanket. Her tears gutted me, and I wanted to hold her, but I knew she didn't want that. I had to wait until she heard my story.

I stared out over the dark water, feeling the heat of the flames at my feet. My shirt didn't offer me much protection from the cold, but with Sunny beside me, I was fine. I was happier knowing she was warm and protected. I gathered my thoughts, then spoke.

"Abby arrived one day about six months after I had been sent to Toblacove."

"That was the town?"

"No, the name of the"—I held up my fingers in quotations— "'establishment' where I was held. It was really a prison—a place rich people sent their kids they gave up on and washed their hands of. They spoke of rehabilitation, but it was a holding cell, to be honest. We were fed, sheltered, and 'taught,' for lack of a better word. If you call grueling workouts, constant lectures on what ungrateful people we were, military-type discipline 'teaching.'"

"Oh, Linc," she whispered.

I kept talking. "The institution, because that is what it really was, was outside a small village." I frowned as memories hit me. "No one spoke a word of English outside the compound, and very few of the, ah, *students*, as we were referred to, were allowed to go to the village. Some who had been there for a long time, or had proven their trustworthiness, were allowed a day every month or so. Never announced, so no plans could be made. I was never allowed, as per my father's instructions. No matter what age you went in at—you didn't leave until you were nineteen, unless your parents got you." I paused. "That rarely happened. We were sent there and forgotten about."

"Oh." Sunny made a low noise in the back of her throat. "Were there a lot of girls?"

"No. Very few and they mostly kept to themselves. Everyone did.

Friendships were not encouraged. The rest of us kept our interactions to a minimum so not to draw notice. We did as we were told. Studies, gym, chores, meals. There was very little free time."

"I see. But you became friends with Abby."

"I learned how to get around some of the rules. Where to go to get away from the cameras. Whom to trust. You had to in order to survive. In order not to completely fall apart." Turning my head, I met her gaze. "To make sure they didn't drum everything remotely real and human out of you. I refused to become one of their robotic zombies. I simply let them think I was."

Her eyes shut, and when they blinked open, I saw the glimmer of fresh tears in them. I didn't think as I leaned toward her and brushed them away this time. She let me touch her, which was enough—for now. I cleared my throat and continued.

"She arrived the way I did. Unconscious and drugged out of her mind. I saw her wandering the halls, confused, disoriented, and scared. Something about her reminded me of you. Maybe the light hair or the vulnerability I saw in her eyes. She was two years younger than me, and she didn't deserve to be there any more than I did. I tried to show her the ropes. Where to eat, where things were, who to avoid, all those things."

"Was everyone drugged?"

"No, some kids came willingly. I think given the choice of what they had at home compared to what this place offered, they took it. I always assumed their life before the institution was hell. They were the ones with a little more freedom."

"I see. So, you became Abby's protector."

I lifted my shoulder, shifting on the cold ground. "I suppose. Keith, the one guy I trusted, had done the same for me. I was passing it on." I drew up my knees, wrapping my hands around them. "Her chamber was right across from mine. She had nightmares at first, and she screamed. A lot." I shut my eyes, remembering the screams.

Sunny's hand folded over mine. "Oh, Linc."

"Abby was a wild child. Her mother was a head case, and she got involved with a long list of men. Rich men. Sometimes they married her, sometimes not. Abby was ignored for the most part, sent away to boarding school, and only brought home on occasion." I cleared my throat. "She, ah, started looking for affection in the wrong places. She got pregnant and had an abortion at fifteen."

"She was desperate to be loved," Sunny stated. I squeezed her hand, hearing the sympathy in her voice.

"The abortion was botched, and Abby got really ill. Septic. She ended up having emergency surgery and a full hysterectomy."

"Oh god. That poor girl."

"She was sent home—a fact that her mother wasn't happy about. She had remarried for the fourth or fifth time, and she felt Abby was interfering with her life."

"But it was her daughter," Sunny protested.

"Like I said, her mother was a head case. Narcissistic. Self-absorbed." I exhaled hard. "Abby's latest stepfather was much the same. He was a real bastard, and he decided that Abby was part of the whole marriage deal. He tried to rape her."

"No, no, no," Sunny breathed out.

"She fought him off and told her mother. Her stepfather said she came on to him. She had scratched him when fighting him off, and he told her mother she attacked him when he said no. It got ugly. Abby said she was going to the police. Two days later, Abby woke up at the compound."

I turned and faced Sunny. "She was still recovering from every-thing else that had happened to her when she arrived at Toblacove. She was lost, Sunny. Alone. She had no idea what it was like for someone to care about her. At least I'd had you. Your mom and your sisters. My mom when I was little. I knew what it was like to *feel* love. She only knew rejection and being invisible. We became friends. Eventually, she told me her story, after I had told her mine. She knew all about my life. My father. You." I risked a glance at her. "I talked about you a lot. She knew our whole story and the fact that I was still in love with you. She listened. I understood her pain as well. Having

a parent hate you. Blame you for everything. Deny you their love."
My voice became thick. "Dump you and forget about you. Pretend
you didn't exist."

"Linc..." she murmured.

"I protected her the way I did you. She became my shadow.
Everything I learned, I taught her. Things she understood that I
couldn't, she became *my* teacher. I taught her self-defense. Made sure
she followed the rules. Kept her under the radar." I poked at the fire
with a long stick. "As my plans grew, I shared with her. All about the
business I planned on concentrating on when I got out. My strategy
to destroy my father. All the things I wanted to accomplish."

"You trusted her."

"Completely."

Her voice dropped. "You love her like a sister?"

I grabbed her hands. "Yes. Like I loved Emily and Hayley. And
she loves me like a brother. Nothing more, I swear to you." I met her
eyes, mine blazing in truth. "Not the way I loved you."

"How did she get out?"

"The day I left, I was called to the office and told to get my stuff. I
had ten minutes and I had to be gone. I refused to leave without
telling her. I had already done that to you, and I wasn't doing it again.
I left my stuff behind, and I found her instead. I swore I would get
her out. I made her promise to be strong. Keep her nose down and act
like it didn't matter." I rubbed a hand over my eyes, remembering the
panic in her eyes and the fear she tried not to show. "The first thing I
did when I got my money was to get her out. She had fooled them so
well, she got to go to the village on occasion. I had someone waiting,
and the first time she left the compound, I had her brought here. It
took two months of me waiting, anxious and worried, but I kept my
promise. The second thing I did was get that place closed down. I
gave all the information I had gathered to my lawyer, and he got it to
the right people. It took years, but it no longer exists."

"Good." Sunny inched closer. "What about her stepfather?"

"He went too far with a housekeeper. She pressed charges.

Someone else came forward with her story. He went to jail. Her mother refused to testify against him, thanks to a huge payoff from him. I assume, given her visit to Abby, the money has run out and now she's looking for more." I snorted. "Too bad she isn't gonna get it."

I shivered a little, and Sunny gasped. "Linc, oh my god, you must be frozen! We need to go."

I shook my head. "I'm not finished."

She stood, kicking at the dying fire. "I've heard enough that we can go somewhere warm and finish this conversation."

I peered up at her in the darkness. "Do you believe me?"

She held out her hand. "Yes."

In the car, I cranked up the heat and hit the button for the seat warmers. Once I had that done, I turned to Sunny. She was looking at me, worried. I needed to finish my story now.

"Abby's stepfather got out, and now she's terrified he'll come after her. Her mother basically threatened to tell him where she is unless Abby gives her money."

Sunny gasped.

"That's what you saw, Sunny. Me comforting her, promising her I would help. I will never let that lowlife near her. I can't." I wrapped my hands around the steering wheel, holding tight. "I want you in my life, Sunny. I want to explore this with you. To see if we can get past what happened and have a future with each other. But my world contains Abby, and I won't walk away from her. Or desert her. Everyone else in her life has done that."

"I wouldn't expect you to."

I relaxed at her words.

"Where is Abby now?"

"Locked in my hotel room. Probably asleep. She was exhausted." When her eyebrows rose in surprise, I explained. "I'll sleep on the sofa. Every room in the hotel was booked other than mine for the next few nights."

"It is the long weekend."

"Yeah, I forgot. I'll figure it out tomorrow. Meanwhile, she's safe, and I have someone stationed outside the door, just to make sure of it."

"You're a good man, Linc."

I turned, fully facing her. "Will that force me from your life, Sunny? The presence of another woman equally important to me, yet in a totally different way?"

"No, Linc. As long as I understand what she is to you. It hit me hard this afternoon."

I ran my knuckles over her cheek, felt the dampness of her tears and the cold of the wind lingering on her skin. "We both have a lot to learn about the other person. So many years to hear about."

She caught my hand in hers. "I missed you, Linc. I felt as if a part of me was gone." She swallowed. "But I had my family. I wasn't locked away somewhere alone. I'm glad-I'm glad you had Abby."

"She's family to me, Sunny. Part of my past and my present. I want you to be that and my future."

"I want that too."

"I think you'll like each other. I really do. You're actually a lot alike."

"I look forward to meeting her."

"Good. We'll make that happen tomorrow." I paused. "Michael—this afternoon. I sensed how close you two were."

She shook her head. "We're friends as well, Linc. I miss Molly. I promised her I would look after all of them. That's all you saw—friendship. I'm godmother to both of their kids."

A sigh of relief left my lips. "Okay. Thank you for telling me."

I glanced at the clock on the dashboard. "It's late. I know you're up early, so I should take you home."

"Are you heading back to Toronto soon?"

"No, I'm staying close to you. I'll be at the hotel for the next while. I'll work at the house with Abby and watch over her and be able to see you. If that's okay."

"It is."

I smiled and dared to lean over and brush a kiss to her cheek. "Good. I'll drive you home."

"Will you come up, get something to eat and have coffee?"

My smile grew wider. "I thought you'd never ask."

I followed Sunny up the stairs and into her cozy apartment. Inside, I inhaled with appreciation. It smelled like her—warm, sweet, and lovely. She ducked into the kitchen to make coffee, and I looked around, picking up the pictures she had scattered around. Smiling as I recognized Emily and Hayley—now all grown-up and at university. I felt sad as I looked at pictures of her mom, progressing from the woman I remembered to a frailer, older version. Sunny was in a few of them, and I could see her change from the girl I loved to the woman I met again yesterday. Growing up, her full cheeks slimming out, her body changing from angles to womanly curves, her smile sadder than I remembered, her eyes more haunted.

My gaze was drawn to one photo. High on a shelf and tucked away. My hand shook as I plucked it from the corner. Me, lying in the sun, my chest bare, sunglasses on, my head tilted back as I enjoyed the warmth of the rays on my skin.

"That was at the camp," she offered as she came into the room, carrying a tray.

"I had no idea you had taken this."

"I used the phone you bought me. You were alone by the water, relaxing. I saw you and had to take the picture." She smiled sadly and took it from my hand. "It's how I always remembered you from that summer. Smiling and happy. In the sun—loving the summer." She didn't meet my eyes. "And me." She slipped it back on the shelf and faced me. "The summer of us."

I stepped close and slid my arms around her, drawing her close.

"There is more for us, Sunny. If you want it." I pressed my mouth to her hair, feeling the silkiness of the strands on my lips. "I know I do."

She fit so well against me, even after all these years. She still nestled under my chin as if she belonged there. Her softness melded with my harder angles exactly the way I remembered. I never wanted to let her go.

She tilted her head back. Her dark brown eyes were filled with emotion. Her hair fell in waves down her back and over my hands. The urge to wrap my fists around the strands made my fingers flex. The desire to kiss her was strong. Her pupils dilated and her breathing picked up, her gaze focused on my mouth. I bent and brushed my lips over hers, a small whimper escaping her mouth.

"I want to, Sunny," I whispered against her lips. "I want to kiss you. Taste you. Everywhere—for hours. Reacquaint myself with every inch of you. But I don't want any unanswered questions between us. I want us both to go into this trusting and believing in the other person." I touched my mouth to hers one more time. "Because this time, come hell or high water, I won't be able to let you go. I will fight anything and anyone that comes between us. Do you understand me? Once I make you mine again, I will never let you go. Ever."

Her response was perfect. She pulled my head down to hers, and *she* kissed *me*. She swept her tongue into my mouth and stroked it along mine possessively. She tugged on my hair, keeping me close. She licked at me endlessly, then dragged her mouth along my jaw and over to my ear. "Me either, Linc. Me either."

Then with a final press of her lips to mine, she stepped back and grinned at me.

"Biscuit?"

12

LINC

I ate the biscuits Sunny had made for me, sitting at her little kitchen table, surrounded by mementos of her life. Pictures she had chosen, furniture she had refinished, pieces of bric-a-brac she had acquired or kept from her childhood. I picked up a saltshaker in the shape of a duck, squatting low, its mate beside it on the table, his neck stretched out. Both had ridiculous faces on them that made me smile. I traced the glaze, dull from years of being touched.

"I remember these on your mom's table."

Sunny nodded, cupping her mug. "They were my grandma's. Silly, I know, but they meant something to her. We took all that stuff with us when we went, then brought it back."

"It must have been hard to start over."

She pursed her lips. "It was. But I had my mom and sisters. Uncle Pete was great—older than my mom. He hardly knew us, but he made us welcome and gave us a home. He was a retired cop. Hayley and Emily adored him. We all did. I miss him," she added simply.

"How did he die?" I asked.

"Heart attack. He was in his boat, fishing..." Her voice trailed off, then she cleared her throat. "He died exactly the way he wanted. Doing something he loved. After he died was when Mom got sick and wanted to come back here. She missed the water and the sun." Sunny's lips turned up into a sad smile. "Where we lived had a lot of fog and rain."

"You never liked the fog."

She rested her elbow on the table, meeting my gaze. "For a long time, the fog suited me, Linc. I was sad and withdrawn, even though I tried not to show it. Eventually my heart healed enough I was able to find my feet again."

I hunched closer. "But it was never the same, right? There was always a part of you that was missing. Missing me." I kept my eyes on hers. "Because that's how it was for me. I missed you every goddamn day."

"Yes," she whispered.

My phone beeped, breaking the moment. I glanced at it, then shot off a fast reply to Abby.

"Is everything all right?" Sunny asked.

"Abby wanted me to know she is fine and going to bed."

"How long do you plan on staying here?"

I shrugged. "A while. Abby brought a bag with her—she had no intention of going back to Toronto if I wasn't there. She knew she'd be safer with me close. So, we're both staying."

Sunny's fingers drummed on the table, and she tilted her head. That had always been one of her nervous tells. She wanted to ask me something and wasn't sure how to phrase it. It made me smile to know I could still recognize her habits.

"Ask me," I murmured. "Ask me anything, Sunny."

"It's you, isn't it? The mysterious benefactor. You didn't help fix up the town or fix what your father broke. You're the person still buying up properties and basically gifting them back to the town. Making sure people who could never afford to own anything get the chance to do exactly that. My payments go to you."

I didn't deny it. "You can own the building now if you want it,

Sunny. One call and it's yours." I told her. "If I had known it was you, it would have been yours free and clear from day one."

I still couldn't believe she had been here in Mission Cove and I didn't know it. Her business was listed simply as Hilbert Inc. The name of the owner was Suzanne Hilbert. Neither had struck a chord with me when I scanned through her papers. She had been Sunny my entire life, and her new last name hadn't been the least bit familiar. I preferred Sunny to Suzanne. She suited the name more.

"I don't want it free and clear. I want to earn it."

"You have earned it. Everyone in this town has earned it. What my father did to the people here was atrocious. The way he played with people's lives. Took away their pride." Now it was my turn to tap my finger on the table. "I'm paying it back. All of it. With interest."

"A modern-day Robin Hood, Linc?"

I shook my head. "No, someone trying to make restitution."

"For what? You didn't do anything. It was your father."

I pushed away from the table and circled Sunny's apartment. She watched me pace, not speaking. I stopped by the window and lifted the edge of the curtain, peering down into the town. The streets were quiet, the house on the hill dark. I let the curtain fall back into place and turned.

"You may not like my answer, Sunny."

"Tell me anyway."

"I'm doing this because he would hate it. Because every time I spend more of his money giving back to the people he hurt, I know he must howl in rage as he burns in hell. I feel as if I finally have my hand on the knife, and I'm twisting it in him every single time I sign a check or write off another building. This is payback. Pure and simple."

"At some point, I assume it will end."

"No. I studied hard while I was locked away. Turned out I had a knack for investing. Numbers. I took my inheritance and tripled it in a year. I used the money and broke *him*, then took his dwindling funds once he died, added an equal amount of my own, and did the same again. That money will never run out, no matter how much I give away."

"So, you're a millionaire."

She had no idea of my net worth. "Hundreds of millions, Sunny. Closing in on bill—"

She held up her hand, stopping my words. She grimaced, her voice shaky. "So, we're even more unevenly matched than before."

I tilted my chin in agreement. "You're right. We are. You're far more valuable than I am."

"Yep. My biscuits make me wealthier than you can imagine," she snarked.

"I'm not talking monetary value. Your soul does, Sunny. We're unevenly matched because you're a far better person than I am. Your goodness is priceless. My wealth has come with a cost I can never repay."

She frowned. "What do you mean?"

"I lost something I don't think I will ever get back. I always disliked the way my father treated people, the games he played. Yet, I find that I enjoy this particular game of destroying any mark he has ever made on this earth. Erasing him. The hatred I have for him burns inside me. It has been the central focus of my life since the day he took me from you."

She paled, her already ivory complexion becoming almost white. "I don't like to see the hate you carry inside, Linc. It frightens me."

I hurried across the room, dropping to my knees in front of her. "Don't you see, Sunny? The hate is why I have to do this. He hated and made others suffer. I'm using my hate for *him* to help people."

"What happens when there is no one left here for you to help, Linc? What will you do with that hate then?"

Her question hung in the air, the words heavy.

"I keep hoping it drains away," I admitted.

"It won't unless you allow it to."

"Then I'll help more people. I already do, but on a lesser scale. I also run a very successful financial business. My company supports a lot of charities." I edged closer, taking her hand. "I hate *him*, Sunny. He is the only black spot in my heart. I won't become him." Our gazes locked, and I reached up with my free hand to cup her cheek, stroking the skin in gentle circles. "If I have you, I could never be him. You bring too much warmth into my life."

"That's a lot of responsibility, Linc."

"I think you're up for the challenge." I softened my voice. "I hope you are. I need you in my life."

She leaned into my touch. Then in a typical Sunny move, changed the subject. "Hotels aren't very comfortable for long-term stays."

"Better than my car," I smirked and stood. I knew she needed me to step away and break the dark mood that had descended.

"There's an empty apartment across the hall."

I frowned. "There is?"

She rolled her eyes. "Don't you know the layouts of your buildings, Linc?" she teased.

"Too many of them." I shot back with a wink.

She stood. "Come and see."

Across the hall was a duplicate apartment to Sunny's. It was furnished simply, but it was light and airy and meticulously clean.

"I was planning on trying to rent it in the summer," she explained. "I've been slowly getting it ready." She cleared her throat. "You could stay here. There are two bedrooms. Abby would be safe over the shop, and it's more comfortable than a hotel room. It has a kitchen and everything..." Her voice trailed off as I stared at her. "What?"

"You'd be okay with me sharing a place with Abby?"

She shrugged. "Better than the sofa. Plus, you said she was like a sister."

"She is."

"Then I have to trust you. And her. If she is as important to you as you say, then I need to get to know her. The back door leading up here is steel and has a good lock on it. The only other way up to this floor is through the kitchen, so she can use that entrance and always be safe. If you're busy, I'm right here. She won't be alone." She traced a pattern on the counter, not meeting my eyes. "And you'd be close."

I move nearer to her. "I'd like that."

The air between us warmed. I traced her cheek, trailing my fingertips over her soft skin. "Be my light, Sunny. I need that. I need you."

"What if it's not enough?" She swallowed, her voice quivering. "What if I'm not enough?"

"You are."

She wrapped her hand around my wrist. "Try to let go of the hate, Linc."

"If I have you, I will try. I promise."

She sighed, her eyes fluttering shut. "Stay here. Close to me."

"Are biscuits included in the rent?"

Her eyes crinkled in amusement. "Yes."

I dropped my voice, my mouth hovering above hers. "Are kisses?"

"Maybe," she whispered, her eyes locked on my mouth.

"I'll take it."

Then I kissed her.

The next morning, Abby stumbled out of the bedroom, looking half asleep. She fisted the mess of curls on her head, mumbling one word.

"Coffee."

With a smirk, I handed her a cup—strong and black—the way she liked. She took it with a grateful look and sat on the sofa, sipping. I let her wake up a little more. She had never been a morning person. At the institution, she was always the last to show up for breakfast, and often missed it.

Not that it had been much to miss. To this day, I hated oatmeal and hard-boiled eggs.

"How bad was the sofa?" she mumbled.

I shrugged, pouring myself another coffee. "Fine. It was one night."

"What time did you come in?" she asked, regarding me curiously.

"About midnight. I checked, and you were sound asleep." I squeezed her shoulder as I went past and sat on the chair across from the sofa. "You were exhausted, Abby."

"I hadn't slept much for a few days," she admitted. "But I felt safe here."

"You are."

She glanced behind me. "No breakfast?"

"We're going out for breakfast."

She snorted into her coffee. "I bet I can guess where."

I ignored her amusement.

"Sunny has offered us a small apartment over her bakery while we're here. There're two bedrooms, it's furnished, and it has a kitchen. The access is a thick steel door at the back and through her shop, so it's safe."

"So, you'll send Nick away?"

I knew she hated having someone watch over her, and since I planned on staying close and eliminating the threat to her very fast, I agreed.

"I've been on the phone with Milo. He's finding out the terms of Carl's parole." It was my turn to snort into my coffee. "I'm fairly certain he will be breaking one or more of them very quickly."

"You'll make sure of it," Abby mumbled.

"Yes. And your mother is going to get a visit. It will ensure you no longer have to worry about another surprise."

"Thank you."

"No thanks are needed."

"Are you sure it's a good idea, Linc?"

"The apartment? Or Sunny?"

"Both."

"The apartment is more practical."

"And conveniently close to Sunny," she pointed out.

"Yes." I sighed and scrubbed my face. "I know you're worried, Abby. Sunny is as well."

"Not about me, right? She knows we're only friends, doesn't she?"

I waved my hand. "Yes. She isn't worried about that. I think the two of you will get along well. She wants to meet you and get to know you. The apartment was her idea, actually."

"Oh."

"I know you don't want me to get hurt again. I'll be honest—neither do I. But I have to try." I exhaled hard. "Sunny...she thinks I have too much hate in me. She isn't sure she knows how to handle that part of me."

"Your hate is reserved for your father. You're a good man, Linc."

"She worries I won't ever be able to let it go. To be able to live my life without the hate being the driving force. I have to admit, I wonder if she's right."

"If you love her the way you say you still do, then you will. She was the one thing you grieved for the most. If you're together again, you can stop your grieving and begin to live for something else."

I stared at her, her words sinking in.

"When did you suddenly become the grown-up?"

She stood. "Always have been. I'm going to get showered so we can go meet this girl of yours. I'm hungry."

She walked away, stopping to refill her cup and disappearing into the bathroom. I thought about her words. Simple, direct, and honest. Once again, she reminded me of Sunny. I wanted to believe her. To think that I could lay the ghost of my father to rest and move on to a different life with Sunny. My hatred of him had been at the forefront of everything I'd done from the moment I woke up in that hellhole he threw me in.

Could I shift my focus and step away from the anger? Could I let go of the hatred and embrace life?

I never thought it possible. But my thoughts had never included Sunny. Now she was in my life again, and I already felt...different.

My phone beeped, the simple text message sending my heart soaring.

Biscuits hot and waiting for you. So am I.
Sunny xxx

Given my reaction to the thought of seeing Sunny?
Perhaps I had my answer.

13

LINC

Over the years, I had learned to read situations, hide any anxiety I was feeling, keep my face neutral, my hands dry, and nerves hidden. I could meet with the toughest crowd, the angriest individual, and remain cool.

Watching the two women I loved the most in the world meet was the most uncomfortable situation I'd ever gone through. I introduced them, shocked at the way my heart raced, the anxiety I heard in my voice—the way my hands grew damp with perspiration.

They sized each other up, their eyes wary, their handshake brief. Both stood, cool and unbending, waiting. It took me a moment to catch up and realize they were waiting for me to do something.

Except I had no clue what to do next.

Step back and let them at each other? I knew they both had something to say. Warnings from Abby to Sunny about hurting me. How well she knew me. What her expectations of Sunny were. Sunny would be filled with righteous indignation and inform Abby she had known me longer. That she and she alone held the key to my heart. She would admonish Abby and remind her my feelings for her were platonic and she needed to remember that.

I could sit down and watch them as the words were volleyed back and forth. Maybe snag a biscuit or two while they got it out of their systems. I really felt as if they could be friends if we could make it past the initial awkwardness.

Or should I play peace-keeper and insist they talk? Stay and point out their good points and how much each of them meant to me? Remind them of the one thing they did have in common?

Me.

My hands grew damper. What I really wanted was to walk out the door, hide for the day, and come back later and see who was still standing.

In the end, I went with what I knew best. Distraction and my stomach. I sat down at a table and slipped my hand into Sunny's.

"I'm hungry, Sunny."

She sighed. "Of course you are," she said at the same moment Abby did. Then they chuckled. Sunny shocked me as she reached out and gave Abby a hug.

"Sit down and I'll bring breakfast."

Abby smiled—a real smile, not her fake one. "Let me help. I love to bake—I've never had a friend who owned a shop before. Maybe I could help one afternoon?"

Sunny grinned. "Free help is always welcome."

I looked between them. A third option—the two most important women in my life acting as if they wanted to get to know each other and making the effort to do so. Hugs and all.

I liked that one.

"Still hungry," I mumbled.

Sunny nudged Abby to the table. "Sit. I'll be right back. You can help later."

She disappeared through the door, and Abby glanced my way. "I like her."

"I knew you would. You like to bake?"

She shrugged. "I dabble."

"Huh."

Sunny came back with a laden tray. I rose and took it from her, my mouth watering at the scent. Warm biscuits, flaky croissants, brioches, butter, jam, and coffee.

Manna from heaven.

It was a good thing I had food to occupy my mouth since from the moment Sunny sat beside Abby, I ceased to exist—for either of them.

The chatter was nonstop.

"I love your hair," Sunny enthused, flipping her ponytail over her shoulder. "I can't do anything cool with this horrid color. Pink or purple would clash."

"I love the color of your hair," I mumbled around a mouthful of biscuit. "It's like the sunset."

"Linc, stop talking with your mouth full," Abby scolded me.

"Pink is my favorite color," she told Sunny. "I love it."

"I noticed. Your little truck is so cute. Love the sparkles."

"It's an SUV," I offered to the air since no one seemed to hear my words.

"It's great. I like sitting up high."

"Short girl problems," they said in unison, then chuckled and launched into a discussion about pant leg lengths.

I picked up my phone, deciding I might as well be productive.

Being invisible had one advantage. They were so busy talking about hair, baking, and other subjects I had zero opinions on, the food was fair game. I wolfed down most of the tray while I returned emails and checked messages. When I became aware of silence at the table, I lifted my gaze from the phone to find Abby and Sunny staring at me.

"What?"

"Really, Linc, you have to be on your cell phone while having breakfast?" Sunny asked, sounding displeased.

"He's attached to that thing. Every meal, no matter what."

"Hey," I objected. "You two were busy. I was giving you some time to get to know each other."

"Uh-huh," Sunny stated, crossing her arms. I tried not to notice how that pushed her breasts together. Then I tried not to think about how much I used to love to touch them. How soft and full they were in my hands. The way her nipple—

"Linc!"

I blinked. "Sorry?"

Abby chuckled and stood. "Could I put my bag upstairs? Then I think Mr. Hornball and I had best get to work."

"Hey," I protested again. They were ganging up on me already.

I loved it.

Sunny rose. "Of course."

I grabbed the bags from the car and followed them upstairs. Abby looked around, taking the larger of the two bedrooms. When I glared at her, she rolled her eyes, hitting my shoulder as she went past me. "As if you'll be sleeping in this apartment much," she muttered. "We both know you'll be next door."

I had no objections to that idea, but I would let Sunny make that decision. Catching Sunny's eye, I winked, loving how her cheeks flushed, as if she was having the same thoughts as Abby.

That made my day.

My phone rang and I answered, watching as Abby and Sunny walked around the apartment. "Ned. What's up?"

"My blood pressure. I got news one of the permits was rejected."

I frowned. "Which one?"

"The permit from the town to destroy the house."

"What? Why the hell would they reject it? They still get their taxes, and something will replace the building. If I don't tear it down, it will fall into disrepair, because I'm not maintaining that monstrosity. Did you tell them that?"

"I can't get anyone on the phone. I'll head down and deal with it."

I scrubbed my eyes. "No, I'll go to the town hall and talk to the mayor. I'm sure it's simply an error."

"All right. Get back to me."

"I will."

I hung up. "I have to go. Abby, stay here and settle in. There are some emails I need you to address, and once I get this sorted, I'll come back. Maybe we'll work from here today."

She nodded. "On it."

I walked down the steps with Sunny, stopping her before she entered the bakery. I laid my hand on her arm. "Thank you."

"I like her. She keeps you in line."

"You know what?"

She grinned, one side of her mouth higher than the other, giving her an impish look. "What, Linc?"

"I like *you*." I bent low and brushed my mouth across hers. Then I went back for more, taking her top lip between mine and kissing it, then doing the same to her bottom lip before covering her mouth and kissing her harder. Our tongues stroked together, long, lazy swirls, curling, tasting, and discovering. When I eased back, Sunny's cheeks were pink, her lips swollen from mine, and her eyes wide.

"I have been wanting to kiss you since I walked into the bakery," I murmured and bent again for one last kiss.

"Hope it was worth the wait."

I dropped a kiss to the end of her nose. "It was." I enfolded her in my arms. "It always will be."

———

The empty corridors of the small town hall echoed with my footsteps. I frowned as I glanced around. The place was almost deserted. I had encountered one person on the way to the mayor's office. Chuckling, I reminded myself this was Mission Cove, not Toronto. They didn't even open the building until ten, and it was only a few moments past. Nothing big was happening in the town, and it would seem most employees were not yet at their desks. I hadn't been in the building for a long time, and it hadn't changed much, the layout the same as I recalled from past visits.

Not long after my mother died, my father would send me on

errands, delivering thick manila envelopes to people. Often it was to the mayor. I would ride my bike down the hill, careful to deliver the package to the right person. I was so desperate for my father's love and approval that I never made a mistake. I was fast and never gave the envelope to anyone but the person who was supposed to get it. I would rush back to the house to tell my father I had completed my task, always hoping for a glimmer of approval. It never came. He remained impassive and uncaring. Still, I tried.

Until the day after a rainstorm, when he gave me an envelope and I sped down the hill too fast. I lost control of my bike, and my backpack and I flew off, landing in a huge puddle. The papers were ruined, my knees and pants torn, and the front tire of my bike damaged. But that was nothing compared to the pain of the punishment my father inflicted on me. He was furious, screaming at me about my carelessness, wasting his time, and being irresponsible. It was the first time he had used his fists as well as his words, but certainly not the last. It was the day I realized he would never love me, no matter how hard I tried. The day I learned to fear his office as well as the man.

I gave my head a shake, pushing aside the memories. He was dead and could no longer hurt me. I located the mayor's office and pushed open the door. It looked much the same as I remembered. Neutral colors, uncomfortable-looking chairs, the walls covered in pictures of the town during festivals and tourist season. There was a desk beside a closed door, the last stronghold, as it were, that prevented you from getting to the mayor. I remembered his assistant —the mayor's wife. Mrs. Tremont was well-groomed, rigid—and to a young boy, scary as hell. She always glared at me, her dark eyes filled with disapproval over my insistence at handing the envelope directly to the mayor. She would make me wait, sitting in the corner on one of those uncomfortable chairs, sometimes for over an hour. But I waited, not wanting to risk my father's wrath.

I glanced around, not surprised to see how little had changed.

The town outside these walls was prospering, but inside, it looked as if time stood still.

The door by the desk opened, and a woman strode out. She stopped short, seeing me, our gazes locking, and for the second time that morning, I was a kid again. Cold, dark eyes met mine, a frown appearing on a face that was older but still familiar. Mrs. Tremont crossed her arms, a frosty glare etched on her expression. She recognized me, and it was plain she wasn't happy to see me. When she spoke, her voice was cold and formal.

"May I help you?"

I straightened my shoulders. "I'm here to see the mayor."

"Do you have an appointment?"

She knew damn well I didn't.

"No."

"Then, young man, might I suggest you make one?"

I refused to let her intimidate me. "I don't have time. Tell the mayor Lincoln Webber is here to see him."

Her eyebrows shot up. "*Webber?*"

I smirked. "Yes. Lincoln Webber." I crossed my arms, mimicking her stance. "He *will* see me."

She sniffed. "Too good to keep your father's name?"

My indignation rose. "That, Mrs. Tremont, is none of your business. Tell your husband I'm here to see him about an urgent matter."

She didn't back down. "He is not here. As deputy mayor, you can discuss your matter with me."

Deputy mayor? Her?

Good god, the people here needed help more than I realized.

"Fine. A permit I require was refused. I assume it was done in error, and I need that rectified. *Immediately.*"

She didn't pretend not to know what I was talking about. "The one to level your father's house."

"It's my house now. I'm having it demolished."

She didn't meet my eyes as she deposited some files onto the top of her desk. Her tone became almost gleeful as she responded, "No, I don't believe you are. The permit was denied."

"On what grounds?"

She lifted her gaze, pure hatred blazing from them. I stepped back at the blatant hostility. "On the grounds that your father did a lot for this town and his house was a symbol of his commitment to Mission Cove. It and his memory deserve to be respected."

I wanted to laugh. *Commitment? His memory?*

Was she insane?

"We decided, in the best interest of all parties, not to allow the demolition."

"I disagree. It's my property and your decision is certainly not in my best interest. I want an audience with the council. As soon as possible."

She clucked her tongue. "That won't be possible for a while. We don't meet for another month."

Anger, red and hot, filled my chest. I stepped nearer to her desk, my tight fist resting on the wood as I leaned close. "Then I insist you call an emergency council meeting."

Our eyes locked, furious blue meeting cold brown. "Step away from my desk, or I'll call security. I don't appreciate your intimidation tactics."

Seething, I stepped back. "Call for an emergency council meeting," I repeated, my voice cold, but calm.

"I'll take that up with the mayor and get back to you." She glanced around her desk. "I'm sure your number is here somewhere. A staff member will be in touch."

"Why are you doing this?"

"I'm doing what is in the best interest of the town, Mr. Webber."

"And an empty, ramshackle building on top of the hill is in the best interest of the town? I'm not maintaining it."

"Then it will be maintained and the bills sent to you."

We were locked in a war of wills. One of the things I had learned was when to stay and fight and when to walk away. I had no idea what her motivation was behind this, but I wasn't done. Not by a long shot.

I turned and headed to the door. "My lawyer will be in touch."

Her triumphant cackle followed me down the hall.

14

LINC

I parked at the country club a couple of miles outside Mission Cove. After I'd stormed out of the mayor's office, I had paced the hallways trying to get my anger under control. At one point I stopped, leaning against a wall. I concentrated, counting between long inhales of air until I felt calmer. My ears perked up when I heard a conversation occurring in the office next to me.

"Another bill from Sandy Hooks," a voice muttered. "I swear the mayor spends more time on the putting green than in his office."

"Probably getting away from the dragon of a wife he's got," another voice replied.

I glanced out the window. It was sunny and warm—the perfect day for a game of golf. He and my father used to play a lot of golf, and obviously, things hadn't changed. I headed to my car, making a call after I slid inside.

"Sandy Hooks Golf Club," a voice answered.

"Yes, I'm calling from Mayor Tremont's office. Has he already started his round?" I asked. "He left his cell in the office, and I wanted to bring it to him."

"Oh yes, about twenty minutes ago. Would you like me to get a message to him?"

"No, thank you. I'll handle it myself." I hung up.

I had a message, all right.

I approached the small group, waiting patiently as they all teed off, then crossed the tee box to the mayor.

"Mayor Tremont."

He turned, his face confused as he took me in. "Yes. How can I help you, son?"

I turned on the charm, recalling the mayor's like of alcohol—any kind. I shook his hand. "Lincoln Webber." From the blank look on his face, I knew he had had no idea who I was, or to whom I was related. "I'm sorry to bother you on a well-earned day on the course, sir, but I am in urgent need to speak to you. May I buy you a drink at the bar?" I indicated the outdoor roll cart, one of the many set up along the course.

He regarded me, then waved to his group. "Play on. I'll take par on the holes I miss."

The group all looked amused. "You never make par here."

He glared. "Well, today, I did. One of my constituents needs to talk to me."

They moved away. "Leave the cart," he barked. "My knee is acting up."

Lazy bastard. But I kept my smile in place. I needed to play this right. We strolled to the makeshift bar and placed our order, then sat on the bench located close. He took a long drink of his beer—probably not his first one of the day.

"Now, how can I help?"

I chose my words carefully. I didn't know if the mayor had any idea of how my father had double-crossed him for all those years. My father played the game so well that he made sure the mayor shared some of the wealth, but the lion's share went to my father. Always.

"My lawyer sent in the paperwork for approval on a house demolition. Somehow, the paperwork was lost," I fibbed, deciding to play this a different way than accusing his wife of treachery. "I have all the other necessary permits but lack this one. I came to see you directly." I had to pause before I uttered my next lie. "My father always told me to go directly to the source of power." I clenched my fist so tight, my nails dug into my palm. "His praise for your take-charge handling of things was limitless."

More like scathing contempt for what a spineless bastard you were, but potato-potahtoh, I added silently.

He frowned. "Webber isn't a name I'm familiar with. Who was your father?"

I swallowed, barely able to push out the words. "Franklin Thomas."

His eyebrows shot up. "You're Frank's son?"

"Yes."

"Why the name change?"

I was prepared for his answer. "Out of respect, sir."

Not for him, I thought silently.

"Ah, not riding on his coattails."

I nodded, taking a sip of my water in order not to speak.

He stroked his chin. "I don't recall seeing any paperwork come across my desk."

I knew it. There had been no discussion. That cow of a wife of his must have hidden it. But why?

"It somehow has been lost in transit, I think." I waved my hand. "It happens."

"What are you planning on pulling down?"

"My father's house."

"Why?"

I waited for a moment to answer him, as if I was having trouble finding the words.

"I cannot bear to look at that house without him in it, sir."

Because I wish he were alive so I could blow him up with it.

"What are your plans?"

"I'm working with my team to decide," I lied smoothly. "Something benefiting the town."

"Your team?"

"Webber Holdings Inc."

His eyes widened. He had heard of my company. He knew the power I had. What I could do for him if I chose to do so. I could feel his mind racing—wondering how to leverage this for himself.

"I plan on spending more time and money here," I murmured. "As long as things go according to plan. Otherwise, the house will sit, empty and abandoned." I tsked. "An eyesore."

"Why don't you sell it?"

"No," I snapped, then backpedaled as his eyes widened. "Too many memories."

"Ah. I always wondered why you never joined your father's company. He said you had other aspirations."

He was digging. I held my temper in place and chose my words carefully.

"I couldn't compete with his image," I explained.

He grunted. "The master."

I barely withheld my snort of derision. "Something like that."

"Let me call my office."

I ran a hand through my hair, trying to look abashed. "I was there, sir. I'm afraid your wife misunderstood me and thought I was threatening her. I was simply upset. Dealing with all this is very personal, as I'm sure you understand."

He clapped his hand on my shoulder. "Of course. Your father was your idol. Let me make a call or two. That's what we do, right? I scratch your back, you scratch mine."

"Of course," I lied again. The only thing I planned on scratching was an item off my list.

Three hours later, I had my permit. I refused to leave until I knew it was complete. We moved inside to the clubhouse, and I spent three hours listening to the man drone on about my father. All the great things he'd done for the town. Then he went on about the way the town was prospering. "Business is up, rent is down, and the occupancy level is high everywhere," he boasted. "Even better than when your father was around. We're very solvent."

He neglected to tell me it was due to the mysterious benefactor, instead making it sound as if it were his doing. I let him ramble, the alcohol he was imbibing loosening his tongue. There was no doubt who ran the show here—and it wasn't him.

He tapped his head. "I'm constantly projecting expansion. I have more great things planned."

I crossed my legs. "I would be interested in hearing them."

He floundered, then waved his hand. "My group is coming. We'll have to put that off for another day."

"Uh-huh."

The mayor's golfing party reappeared, not seemingly put out he hadn't rejoined them. I made sure to keep him plied with an endless supply of rye and water, followed by lunch. His wife had not been happy on the phone. I had heard her loud argument from where I sat on the bench, sipping a bottle of water. Not the actual words, but the tone of her voice was enough to let me know she was furious. Still, somehow, the paperwork was miraculously found and approved. When I received a message from Abby telling me she had the paperwork in hand, I was grateful I could leave. I'd had quite enough of the mayor, his wife, and his stories to last me a lifetime.

I stood and shook his hand. His eyes were clouded with all the alcohol, his words slurred. "Remember, you owe me," he said, pointing his finger at me. "I'll be in touch."

"You do that."

I walked away, trying not to laugh. He'd probably not remember any of this, or if he did, the details would be sketchy. All I had done the entire time was make a lot of noises and nod my head. Like all politicians, no matter how small-time, he liked to hear himself talk. I stopped at the clubhouse entrance and spoke to the manager. "The mayor is a little under the weather. Make sure he gets home safely. Don't let him drive."

He looked past my shoulder with a resigned stare. I had a feeling it wasn't the first time the mayor had been under the weather at the course. But I refused to allow him to drive in case he had an accident. I didn't want that on my conscience.

There was enough there already.

Back at Sunny's, I found Abby at a table in the bakery. She looked up as I walked in.

"Hey, boss."

I sat down heavily, feeling exhausted. "Hi. Why are you working down here?"

She grinned. "You're right. The biscuits are addictive. I could smell them all morning, and I was hungry. I came down to have something to eat and decided I liked it down here."

I inhaled the sweet smell of cinnamon, sugar, and butter. "It does smell good."

Abby's eyes danced. "Sunny let me help in the kitchen for a bit." She held out a plate. "I made these."

I took a cookie from the plate, taking a bite. "Good job," I mumbled around my mouthful. "If you get tired of being my sidekick, maybe Sunny will hire you."

"She has a job here anytime she wants. I get the feeling you're a bit of a tyrant." Sunny's arms draped around my neck, her voice a low hum in my ear.

I wrapped my hands around her wrists, pulling her tighter. I looked up, meeting her amused gaze. "I think I'm an awesome boss."

She dropped a quick kiss to my lips. It took everything in me not to pull her back and kiss her harder. Longer.

"Uh-huh," she responded, releasing her embrace and sitting beside me. She studied me. "You look exhausted."

I ran a hand over my face. "I am. Between the mayor and his wife, it's been a day."

Sunny made a sympathetic noise in her throat. "She's a handful."

"When did she become deputy mayor?"

"Not long after your father died, I think."

I shrugged. "She hated me as a kid, and it appears she still does. She didn't try to hide the fact this morning." I snorted. "Pretty sure after today, the hatred has grown to loathing. She'll make any request that has to go through town hall difficult."

"Why does she hate you so much?" Abby asked. "I mean, who hates a kid?"

I shrugged. "No idea, but she always has."

Sunny pursed her lips, looking over my shoulder. There was something in her expression that made me lean forward. "What?"

"It's probably nothing."

"Tell me anyway."

"I went to meet my mom at work at the hotel one day after school. I always used the employee entrance. It was a nice day, so I waited outside, sitting on a picnic table the staff used for breaks. It was sort of off to the side where no one would see it." She paused, looking nervous.

My curiosity was piqued. "Keep going."

"I saw Mrs. Tremont come out the back door and head to her car. She looked around as if she was making sure no one saw her. I remember wondering why she came out the back and not the front. She always *liked* to be seen." Sunny swallowed. "As soon as she drove away, a man came out the same door. He did the same sort of sweep of the area, then he left."

"So, she was having an affair," I surmised.

"I think so."

"Did you know the man?"

Sunny nodded, her voice quiet. "It was your father, Linc."

15

LINC

Hours later, I was still reeling from what Sunny had told me. Mrs. Tremont and my father had an affair. I had no idea how long it lasted, but obviously, she must have had strong feelings about him, given her actions and the words she had flung at me this morning.

So many things made sense now. How my father always seemed to be one step ahead of the mayor in so many things. His wife must have been feeding my father information. I wondered how often they met and how they kept it a secret for so long.

I wondered if perhaps that was why she hated me. Had she thought she would be a beneficiary in my father's will? Had he made her promises while I was younger about them being together once I was gone?

He must have been an even better actor than I gave him credit for.

The man I knew had no emotions. At least no positive ones. Once my mother died, any sort of decency in him had gone to the grave with her. He used people, then discarded them when they no longer had a use. I was sure he knew exactly how to manipulate the mayor's wife—string her along with false promises, use my presence as an excuse for whatever was needed at the time. I could imagine vague assurances, untrue murmurs of the future, declarations of feelings that were false, since he was incapable of any.

The mayor had always been easily led. My father made fun of him behind his back, often stating he was the one pulling the strings. He had them both duped—in fact, he still did. She felt wronged, not by the affair they had, but the promises he had never fulfilled, and she was blaming me—the way he had all those years. The mayor still thought my father was a great man, proving he was the idiot my father always said he was. I would give him that much.

I was so lost in my musings that a hand on my shoulder caused me to jump. Sunny smiled in apology and sat across from me, sliding a plate in my direction.

"You've been in here for hours, Linc. You must be hungry."

I looked at the plate, my appetite strangely absent. I pushed it away. "Maybe in a while."

I rested my elbows on the table. "You never said anything to me—years ago—about this."

Sunny frowned. "I never had any proof, and I only saw them the one time, so I couldn't be certain. I thought at the time it was possible for it simply to be a coincidence."

"But you don't think that now."

She shook her head. "My mom and I talked once, years later. I told her what I saw. She said your father had a permanent room at the resort. One on the main floor, at the back. He also had keycards to get in any door. It wasn't common knowledge, although there were rumors." Sunny sighed. "She saw the mayor's wife leave his room more than once."

"Nobody talked about it? No gossip?"

"I'm sure there was behind the scenes. But your father owned the resort, Linc. No one was going to speak up and risk their jobs."

"Too scared of repercussions."

"Exactly."

"It makes a lot of sense, when I think about it. He was using her, and I'm sure, in some fashion she was using him, but I think, somehow, it changed for her. She was certainly passionate about his 'memory' this morning. I'm sure in order to dissuade her, he used me and my presence as an excuse for years. No wonder she hates me."

"Does it matter?" Sunny questioned. "Her feelings, I mean?"

"Not really. It explains a lot, though." I pulled the plate toward me, the tempting pile of biscuits too much to ignore anymore. "I am grateful all the business dealings I have in this town are hidden in numbered companies. If she knew I had anything to do with them, I'd have roadblocks going up left, right, and center."

"I think you're right."

I bit into a biscuit, the texture light and airy. I chewed in appreciation and swallowed. "Where is Abby?"

She chuckled. "Downstairs with Shannon. Preparing the dough for some of the cookies for tomorrow. We often make it the night before and then bake as needed. We'll be busy this weekend."

"Tourist season starts."

"Yes."

"I had no idea she liked to bake. She certainly never shared anything at the office."

"I think maybe she keeps a few things to herself, Linc. Some private parts of her life that are only for her."

I finished the biscuit, wiping my fingers on a napkin. "But she shared with you."

Sunny looked past my shoulder. "You see Abby as strong, capable, and a force to be reckoned with. Your right-hand. I think she associates baking with a—" she paused as if searching for the right word "—softer side of herself. Something she doesn't show many people—including you. She hates to be vulnerable."

"You are amazing," I murmured. "You see all that in such a short time. You barely know her."

"I see myself in her, Linc. I've had to hide the softer side of myself away so I can be the business owner, the boss, I need to be. I had to find the tougher side to survive everything."

"Everything, including my leaving you."

She met my gaze. "Yes."

"You know now I didn't want to leave you, Sunny."

"Yes. I know. I just need..."

"A little time. I understand."

"You do?"

I lifted her hand, sliding it into mine, staring down at the way my palm encased hers. Covering her small hand entirely. Holding it safely, the way her heart held mine.

"I knew the truth for ten years, Sunny. You had no idea of the depths of treachery my father had sunk to. You really thought I had abandoned you."

"I did." She paused, looking at our joined hands. "Especially after I confronted him."

"What?" I gasped. "You went and saw him?"

"Yes."

I held her hand to my chest. "Did he hurt you? Tell me he didn't touch you. I swear to god, I will find him in hell and drag him back up here and kill him all over again if he touched you," I raged.

Her eyes widened in response to my rant. "No," she assured me. "He didn't have to. He used his words to hurt."

"Tell me everything," I demanded.

"I wanted to confront him. After I got back from camp, I went to the house. He came to the door, looking amused. He told me to go away—as if I were a fly he was shooing off his arm. He said he had no interest in talking to one of Linc's castoffs."

My grip on her hand tightened. "There were no *castoffs*. There was only ever you."

"I know."

She frowned, losing herself in the story.

"He told me to get off his property and not to come back. 'Forget you ever knew my son,' he instructed. 'I guarantee you he's already forgotten about you.'"

I shook my head. "I would never forget about you."

She smiled sadly. "I refused, demanding that he give me your contact information. He had me follow him to his den. He picked up his phone and sent you a text. Then he showed me your reply."

"He never sent me anything. I had no cell phone."

"I know that now, but I didn't at the time."

"What did it say?"

"*Linc*," she quoted. "*Sunny is here and wants to talk to you.* Your reply was—*No, not interested. Tell her to move on. That part of my life is over. I'm not coming back.*"

She swallowed. "I was sure it was a trick. I grabbed the phone and texted you myself. I begged you to call me, talk to me. Your reply said it all. *Leave me alone, Sunny. You were a great pastime, but my life is heading in another direction. One you are not a part of. One you will never be a part of again.*"

She wiped away a tear that ran down her cheek. "I dropped the phone, and your father picked it up. He looked at the screen with a smirk and told me that 'should do it.' Then he told me to get out, leave him alone, or he would cause so much trouble for my family, life wouldn't be worth living. He was careful to state he was sure I didn't want to jeopardize my mother's job or the welfare of my sisters."

"He threatened you."

She nodded. "I ran to the door, and he followed me, laughing at my pain. He grabbed my arm before I could leave and told me that girls like me were a dime a dozen. He knew it and you knew it. He made some other scathing remarks about me and my family and pushed me out the door. I fell on the porch, sobbing, and he kept laughing. It was the cruelest sound I ever heard. Then he slammed the door shut. I wept all the way home. I couldn't reconcile the boy I loved with the words I read on the screen."

"Sunny," I begged. "Baby, it wasn't me."

"I know that now. If I'd been thinking clearly, I would have

known he'd never let me touch the cell phone if it was really you."
She shrugged. "But I wasn't, and he knew that."

I stood and paced the room. "But can you get past that? All the
mistrust and pain?" I spun on my heel, facing her. "You are the opposite of everything he said. Priceless. I thought of you every damn day.
Sometimes it was the only way I could make it through the days.
Jesus, Sunny, seeing you again is like a miracle." I dropped to my
knees in front of her. "I never stopped believing in us—loving you.
But it was different for you. You thought I betrayed you. You thought
I used you. Can you get past that? Can you reconcile the truth you
know now with the truth you believed all those years?"

Her eyes searched mine, her dark gaze soft. "Yes, Linc. I know
the truth now. I'm coming to terms with it." She cupped my face.
"You have to as well."

"I hate him more than ever. I hate him for the years he stole from
us. The pain he caused you. All the what-ifs he stole."

"What-ifs?"

I leaned into her touch. "I imagined us married, maybe a baby or
two by now, Sunny," I said quietly. "Building a life together as a
family. He stole all that from us."

"You wanted to have babies with me?"

"Yeah," I breathed out. "I still do."

"Oh."

"I used to dream of a little girl who looked like you whom I could
spoil. A little boy I could carry on my shoulder and teach about baseball and fishing. A house we'd share. The love we'd give our kids.
Each other."

She tilted her head to the side, studying me.

"Sometimes, our dreams change," she whispered. "Or sometimes,
they're put on hold."

I pushed closer to her. "Are you saying you'd still have my babies,
Sunny?"

Pink tinged her cheeks. "It's not impossible, Linc. We're still
young, and we can rebuild our dreams."

"Sunny." I captured her mouth with mine, running my hands up her neck and bunching them into her hair. I kissed her with everything in me. The years of pain, the emotion of the moment, the joy of realizing my future—the one I had thought I had lost all those years ago—might still be possible. Of knowing that regardless of what had transpired, she was back in my life. I kissed her until we were breathless. Until she knew, without a doubt, the boy who loved her then, was the man who loved her now. That I was here and not leaving her.

I kissed her until my knees ached, and I knew if I didn't stop now, then I wouldn't stop. Not until she was under me, naked and pleading, and I was inside her. And I didn't want that to happen with my assistant not far away and no privacy. I needed to take Sunny somewhere we could be alone. I wanted to rediscover her all over again.

And I had an idea of where we could go. I would have to arrange for Sunny to have some time off, but I would wait until this weekend was over before I told her about my plans. For now, I was all hers—whatever she needed me to do, I would help.

But then, she was mine.

16

LINC

I sipped coffee and watched Sunny race around the bakery, her owner hat firmly in place. She directed, moved, adjusted, instructed, and never once lost her patience or the smile on her face. She was in her element, and I felt a glow of pride observing her.

I had put aside my own work for the next few days. The long weekend would bring in a flurry of tourists, many of whom would want to buy cookies, biscuits, or other tempting treats. Sit for a few moments and eat a sandwich or sip a coffee. Sunny had extra staff, lots of her delicious baked goods, and tons of supplies for sandwiches and coffee on hand. She also had one area set up with samples. Her idea was simple. Let them taste before they buy. Because, she assured me with a wink, once they taste, they *always* buy.

That was my job this weekend. Official sampler overseer. I had a T-shirt and hat, both branded with Sunny's logo. Abby was helping in the kitchen. She was excited and relaxed, which was great to see. Much to my delight, she and Sunny had become friends, and the two of them worked well together. We were both eager about helping out Sunny.

The door opened, and Michael came in, his arms filled with

towels and linens. Sunny liked white cloths on the tables, and she went through a lot every day. Michael kept them clean, as well as all the towels, aprons, and other items she wanted pristine. Her entire shop had an old-fashioned feel to it. The soft color on the walls, the woodwork, linen cloths, and the mismatched pieces of china all gave it a homey vibe. It suited Sunny.

Sunny hurried forward with a smile. "I'll take those, Michael."

He gave them to her, then came over and shook my hand. "Linc."

Sunny came back through the kitchen door. "Sit, and I'll bring you a coffee."

He smiled as he sat, pulling off his baseball cap. "A cinnamon bun would go well with that," he called out. "I've been smelling them baking all morning," he informed me. "A man can only take so much."

I chuckled. You could smell the bakery for blocks. The rich scent of cinnamon, sugar, and butter drew you in.

Abby came out of the kitchen, carrying a tray of the cinnamon buns. Her wild curls were held back with a hairband, her bright-pink stripe vivid against the blond. She was wearing her pink high-top sneakers and swaddled in an apron. After talking to Sunny, she slid two buns onto a plate and carried it over to the table, along with a coffee. As she approached, I turned to say something to Michael, except he wasn't looking at me. He was staring at Abby, his eyes focused entirely on her.

"Holy mother of god," he mumbled.

I tried not to laugh, especially when I looked at Abby and saw her returning his stare with one of her own.

She slid the plate and mug in front of Michael, their gazes never wavering. "I think I'm made for you," she announced.

He gaped at her, and I snickered. Abby blushed and stammered.

"I mean, I made these. The buns. I brought them to you. Yeah." She shot me a look. "Sunny asked me to bring them to you. So, I did. Here they are." Then she turned and bolted back into the kitchen.

Michael stared after her, then turned to me. "Who was that?"

I crossed my arms. "My assistant."

He ran a hand over his face. "Shit." He looked down at the cinnamon buns. "She made these?"

"She's been in the kitchen with Sunny all morning, so I assume so."

"Does she have a name?"

"No. I whistle, and she shows up."

His head snapped up, his eyes glaring at me, and I smirked. "Of course she has a name. It's Abby."

"Abby," he repeated. He lifted a bun and bit into it, chewing slowly. He closed his eyes with a low groan. "This is so good."

I stood and went to get a refill. Sunny smiled at me as I bent over the counter.

"Did you catch that?" I asked quietly.

"I think someone is smitten. Two someones, actually. Abby keeps peeking out the door."

I glanced behind me. Michael was eating, his gaze fixed on the kitchen door as if he were willing it to open and Abby to reappear.

"Is he ready for that?"

Sunny sighed. "It's been almost two years, Linc. That's a long time to be alone."

"He has kids. I'm not sure how Abby would feel about that. And she is younger than him."

She stepped closer. "Why don't you butt out, Linc, and let them figure it out. Abby's a grown-up girl." She brushed a kiss to my mouth. "I love how protective you are, but honestly, leave it alone."

She was right, although I couldn't resist pushing Michael a little when I returned to the table.

He had eaten both buns and drained his coffee. "I should get some of these to take home to the kids," he said. "They'd love them."

"Good idea. Want me to ask Abby to box up some?"

"Ah, no. I'll do it."

"Are you sure? It's not a problem."

"I said I'd ask," he growled. I chuckled, and he relaxed in his seat. "You're being an ass, Linc."

I sipped my coffee. "Yep."

"What's her story? Is she single?"

"Single? Yes. Complicated? Yes. The closest thing I'll ever have to a sister? Yes."

He studied me. "Gotcha."

I held up my hands. "Just saying. She's important to me."

"Okay."

Abby came out of the kitchen, her bravado back in place. She approached the table with a smile.

"How were the buns?"

"They're my new favorite thing," Michael said. "I could eat you, um, I mean *them,* every day."

I choked on my coffee.

Jesus, these two were going to kill me.

Color stained Abby's cheeks, and my eyebrows flew up. Abby never blushed.

"Oh...good. That's good," she mumbled, her eyes never leaving his face.

Silence hung as they stared at each other. With a groan, I stood. "Abby this is Michael. Michael, Abby." I pushed Abby down into my chair. "Why don't you two *talk?* I'll go help Sunny."

I paused at the door and looked behind me. They were still staring at each other, both of them looking as if they were the only two people in the room.

I shook my head as I entered the kitchen. Abby getting involved with a local hadn't been in my plans. Then I laughed. Me working in a bakery on the long weekend while in Mission Cove after finding Sunny again hadn't been in my plans either.

Yet, here I was. And I wouldn't trade it for the world.

"**A**re you ready?" Sunny asked.

"It's going to be fine." I squeezed her shoulder. "I'm right here with you."

"Okay." Sunny's fingers flew over the keyboard, and a few moments later, the screen filled with her sisters' faces.

"Hey, girls." She greeted them.

Hayley and Emily both started to talk, and I sat to the side, listening as they chatted, filling Sunny in on their news about school, their part-time jobs, boys they were dating and/or interested in—their lives in general.

I could see their faces from where I sat. They were both grown up—no longer the little girls who loved hugs and treats. As I listened to their voices and heard their laughter, they were still in the echoes of my memories that lingered. I hoped once they heard Sunny's news, they recalled some good memories of me.

There was a lull in the conversation, after they asked if Sunny was ready for the busy weekend coming up.

"Yes," she replied. "I, ah, have some extra help." Her gaze drifted my way. "And some news."

Hayley came closer to the screen. "Sunny, are you seeing someone?"

Sunny reached for my hand, and I gripped it hard for encouragement. "Yes, I am."

"Tell us!" Emily demanded.

Sunny's cheeks turned a soft pink. "He's special. Very special."

"Oh my God, it's serious," Hayley said.

"Yes, it is. He's here, in fact, and wants to say hello." Sunny paused. "You met him before."

"Really? Who is it?"

"Linc."

Silence filled the room. Then Emily spoke. "Linc? As in Linc Franklin? The boy who broke your heart?"

Sunny swallowed. "It's Linc Webber now. There are things about that time you don't know."

I loved hearing her say my name and the way she defended me. It made me want to kiss her.

"Sunny," Emily hissed. "Are you sure about this? He almost destroyed you."

I stepped in behind Sunny. "It almost destroyed me too."

They looked shocked, both of them silent.

I pulled my chair beside Sunny and sat down, wrapping my arm around her shoulder. "It's a long story. I didn't leave her. I was taken away from your sister—from my life here. I searched for her when I came back—all of you—but you were gone. Then, by accident, I found her again." I tightened my hand on her shoulder. "I'm not leaving her again—ever."

Emily leaned forward. "Sunny—"

Sunny cut her off. "I know what I'm doing, Emily." Then she smiled, her voice softening. "I'm happy. Really happy."

Hayley tilted her head. "You look happy."

"We both are," I stated. "I will do whatever it takes to keep your sister. To earn your trust again. I've been half alive without her."

Emily sniffled. "We missed you."

I smiled. "I missed you too, kiddo. We have a lot to catch up on, but I think you girls need to talk. So, I'll leave you to it. Sunny can give you my cell number, and I'll answer any questions you have."

"Don't hurt her," Hayley demanded. "Don't do that again, Linc."

"I won't," I swore. I stood and kissed the top of Sunny's head. "You know where I am."

I walked into the bedroom, the girls' voices following me.

"Is he staying with you?"

"Tell us everything, Sunny!"

"God, he got handsome. Is he that good-looking in person?"

I shut the door to give them privacy, but I did hear Sunny's reply to the last question.

"Even better. And he's so amazing, girls. You have no idea."

I hoped they would accept my presence in Sunny's life. I knew I had to work and earn their trust, but I would do it. I would take care of them as well as Sunny.

I knew their forgiveness would take time, but I would be patient.

I would do anything for Sunny.

An hour later, Sunny appeared, her eyes red-rimmed but peaceful. I held out my arms, and she lay beside me, her head on my chest. I had heard parts of the conversation through the door, at times serious, at times more lighthearted with sisterly teasing and jibes. She had assured them she was fine and explained in brief detail what had happened. The girls had a lot of questions she answered, then they moved on to how we found each other and what the future looked like for us.

"You defended me." I kissed the top of her head.

"Of course."

"Did they come around at all?"

"Yes. You can expect a lot of texts and calls, though."

"No problem." I paused. "I can fly them here to see us anytime you want."

"Maybe later in the summer. They usually come for a visit. Emily likes working in the bakery. She and Abby would get on well."

"All right. Whatever you think is best. I can fly us there as well for a weekend. Just say the word."

She traced her fingers on my shirt. "Maybe." She snuggled closer. "Right now, I kinda don't want to share. I like having you to myself."

I tucked her tighter into my side. I felt much the same way.

"I'm good with that."

That weekend, Sunny sidled up next to me at the counter. "You know," she murmured with a teasing grin, "if this whole millionaire thing doesn't work out for you, you could become a barista."

I chuckled as I slid another cappuccino toward her. I had been replaced as sample passer because I was eating as many as I was giving away, and that was frowned on. No one had outlined the rules, so I didn't feel it was fair, but my protests fell on deaf ears. Now, some kid had the best job in the whole place, and I was moved. I found out quickly I sucked in the kitchen, dropped too many things to be of any help serving people, and my cash register skills were lacking, but I caught onto the whole coffee thing well. Luckily, Sunny's shop only offered coffee, simple lattes, and cappuccinos. Or a shot of espresso. Not fancy drinks. Otherwise I would be lost.

I was shocked at how much I was enjoying the weekend. Sunny's bakery had been busy since Friday afternoon as the tourists began to trickle in, drawn by the nice weather and the chance to escape the big city. By Saturday afternoon, the place was packed, and on Sunday morning, there was a line waiting outside when Sunny unlocked the door.

She was amazing to watch, always calm—warm and pleasant to her customers, helpful and efficient with her staff, never sitting or not busy—she worked as hard as anyone, if not harder.

I had forgotten how much I liked simply being around her. Listening to her voice and laughter, being able to touch her hand or steal the occasional kiss. Observe her with other people and the way they reacted to her genuine warmth. This was her element, and I loved seeing her in it.

"I know, Sunny-girl," I deadpanned. "I'm an awesome coffee guy. I was thinking of applying for a part-time gig here." I winked, leaning over the counter. "I'm dating this woman, and I want to be able to wine and dine her in the finest establishments. Impress her, you know? I bet with my tips alone, I can win her over."

She met me halfway, her dark eyes dancing in the bright sunlight that filled the bakery. "Save your pennies, big spender. You already have."

Unable to resist, I wrapped my hand around her neck and pulled her in for a fast, hard, and surprisingly satisfying kiss. Her cheeks were flushed as she pulled back amidst the claps and whoops my action caused.

"Enough of your lip." She smirked, the sexy pull of her full mouth making me smile. "Wash your hands and get back to work."

I grinned, doing as she instructed, then returning to the small line that was waiting patiently. I worked steadily for a few moments, pausing to wipe my hands between orders.

"What can I get you?" I asked, looking up and freezing at the cold gaze that met mine.

"Quite the show," Mrs. Tremont uttered. "Not exactly family friendly."

I rolled my eyes. "Affection between loving partners is hardly something to be ashamed of, *Martha*." I stressed her name, knowing it would piss her off.

"Not the place for it." She sniffed.

I couldn't resist the dig. "You prefer dark hotel rooms, I suppose?"

Her eyes narrowed, her glare becoming frostier. I swore I felt the temperature around us drop. Her voice became icier. "Not hygienic either."

"Don't worry," I assured her. "I won't lick your cup."

"I've changed my mind. I don't want anything."

I bit back my retort. This was Sunny's business, and I was out of line. Instead, I offered her a smile, using my most conciliatory tone.

"I'm sorry. I didn't mean to offend. I was simply caught up in the moment. Allow me to make you a coffee—on the house." I wasn't surprised when she accepted it. Snobs like her could never resist something free.

"A latte. With sweetener. Two."

"Coming right up."

A moment later, I handed her the cup with another fake smile. "Enjoy."

She swept out of the bakery without another word. I bowed my head, pretending to be absorbed in wiping off the nozzle, when, in fact, I was trying not to laugh. I hoped she enjoyed the weak, tepid brew I made. And the real sugar—I'd even added extra. Maybe it would help her disposition—at least it would startle her taste buds.

Sunny stepped up beside me. "You okay?"

"Fine. Definitely not my biggest fan."

"I saw what you did. Making it with used grounds, and the sugar. She hates sugar. Calls it the white death."

"Oh, ah..."

She nudged me in the ribs. "I could fire you for that. Messing with a customer. Shame on you."

I faced her fully. "But you won't. In fact, you're going to reward me."

"Is that a fact?"

I leaned over, dropping my voice. I gripped her waist, pulling her a little closer. "Meet me in the storeroom in five minutes, and I'll remind you."

She giggled, slapping away my hands. "Stop teasing. It's too busy for that."

I looked around the shop. It was packed. People coming and going. Tables full. Staff filling the trays as fast as possible. The sample kid was run off his feet, but Sunny was correct. Once they tasted her cookies, they joined the line to purchase them.

"We'll be lucky if we last the day without running out of everything," she whispered triumphantly. "I have to go and start baking for tomorrow. Sales are even better than I hoped." She met my proud gaze. "I might be here all night, baking."

I planned on being there to help her. I knew Abby did as well. I also knew Sunny would be exhausted on Monday.

I took advantage of not having a line. "I want you to come with me on Tuesday."

"Where?"

"Toronto. I have a meeting in the morning, then I want to spend the rest of the day with you. We'll come back on Wednesday."

I let her take that in.

"We'd stay overnight?"

I nodded, my hand tightening on her waist. "At my place. Just us."

Her pupils dilated, making her dark eyes almost black. Her voice was breathless when she replied, "Us?"

"Us," I confirmed. "Alone."

"The shop—"

I shook my head, interrupting her. "I spoke with your staff. You can leave them their orders, and they'll take care of it. Abby is going to stay and help."

"But Abby—"

Again, I was ready for her. "I spoke to Michael. He's going to keep an eye on the shop." I chuckled. "He's brought his kids in here three times. He finally lucked out and Abby was out front. I watched him introduce them to her."

"How did that go?"

I grinned. "He acted all casual and Abby was flustered, but I think it was fine. When I told him about having to be in Toronto and why I was worried, he offered, so that's covered. Now, next objection?"

"You really want that? Me at your place?"

I met her gaze, mine never wavering. "Yes. And there is no pressure, Sunny. I want some time alone with you. More than an hour at night or a few moments when I see you here. Time to be us. To talk." I slid my hand down to hers and gripped it. "I'll wait. I told you I would. But we need time alone. That's all I am asking."

"Okay."

My smile couldn't be contained. "Really?"

"Yes."

"Can we grab one minute in the storeroom?" I murmured. "I really need to kiss you."

A throat clearing in front of me gave me my answer. Another customer.

Sunny surprised me, leaning up on her tiptoes and kissing my cheek. "I'll owe you."

She hurried away, disappearing into the kitchen. I faced the older man, who was waiting patiently.

"I wish my boss looked like that." He grinned. "And kissed me for a job well done."

I laughed. "Perks of the job."

"Is she taking applications?"

I shook my head, still amused. "Nope. Position is filled —permanently."

"Lucky bastard."

He was right.

17

SUNNY

I rested my head back against the luxurious leather interior of Linc's car and watched the scenery go by. Mission Cove faded from view, the landscape becoming more urban, the highway active with traffic. Ahead was Toronto—one of the busiest cities in the country. I hadn't been there in years, and if it weren't for Linc, I wouldn't have been heading toward its towering skyscrapers and overcrowded boundaries.

I rolled my head, peeking over at Linc. He was driving with one hand on the wheel, the other wrapped around mine, resting on the console that separated us. His car smelled of rich leather, cedar, and ocean. Of Linc. It was a scent I would always associate with him.

I could scarcely believe I was here, with him. The day he walked back into my life was one I would never forget. Seeing him standing in front of me was a shock. The boy I had loved had grown into a man who was a stranger—yet the moment he breathed my name, he became Linc again. He had lost his gangly, awkward gait and the boyish shape to his face. His stride and movements were confident and sure, his face all sharp angles, his jaw covered with scruff, no matter how closely he shaved in the morning. But it was his eyes. His eyes still looked at me the same way, with fierce devotion and fire. As in the past, I could sense when he was close. And when he pulled me into his arms and kissed me, it was as if I had finally come home.

All the years we were apart, a piece of me was missing. I learned to smile and pretend, to hide my pain away so nobody saw it. To act as if what we had shared had been a teenage love, when in fact, it was so much more. I knew I would carry it with me for the rest of my life. Carry him in my heart. I had tried to get over him, date other men—but it never worked. The closer they wanted to get, the more I pulled away. It was as if my heart refused to let him go.

And now he was here.

"Hey." His voice broke through my musings.

I startled. "Hi?"

He smiled, lifting our entwined fingers to run his knuckles over my cheek. "You okay, Sunny-girl? You're awfully quiet."

"Just thinking."

"Are you worried about the bakery?"

"No, I know Shannon, Mack, and Lori will take good care of it. I'm only a call away, if needed. Now that the rush of the weekend is over, they can handle it." I smiled as I thought about the busy weekend and how Linc and Abby had pitched in to help. "You were awesome. So was Abby. That girl has some serious baking skills."

He checked over his shoulder, then changed lanes. "I know. She kept that hidden all these years. I'm not sure why."

"I told you—it was something personal. She told me she would bake and take whatever she made to a shelter or her neighbors," I explained. "It was something she did just for herself. She wanted to be a strong woman in your eyes," I reiterated.

"She is. She always will be—I know what she went through. I think she is incredible." Linc smirked. "And it seems I am not the only one who does."

I squeezed his hand. "Michael is a good guy. He'd treat her well. Isn't that what you want?"

"Of course. It's just that he lives in Mission Cove, and she lives in

Toronto. Long-distance relationships are hard. And her lifestyle is very different."

"It's the same for us, Linc," I reminded him, my heart in my throat.

"No. We're different."

I had to say it. "Linc, I have no desire to live in Toronto." I indicated the huge city we were engulfed in, the traffic flow heavy around us, and the crowds of people. "I don't like big cities."

"We'll work it out, Sunny. All of it. My business is transportable. And despite my wealth, I don't think we're that different. I'm still Linc under my fancy suit."

"A suit you look hot in," I teased, making him grin. Then I became serious again.

"I love Mission Cove. Despite our past, despite everything, it's still home to me. I don't think you feel the same way."

He glanced my way with a frown. "Where *you* are *is* home, Sunny. You always have been, and you are that again. I was lost for years without you."

"I felt the same way."

"You're my compass, Sunny. My true north. I swear, we'll figure it out."

His words warmed my heart. He was so serious and confident. Certain we would work things out. I wanted to believe him, to trust that he wanted this as much as I did. I smiled at him, letting the subject drop for now. I covered my mouth as a yawn escaped.

"We're almost there." He chuckled. "I'm going to take you to my house. You can have a nap while I'm at my meeting, then we have the rest of the day together. I've made dinner reservations for tonight, and I have tickets to a show."

"That sounds wonderful. I hope the dress I brought is okay."

"You'll be beautiful."

I felt my cheeks warm at his sincerity. "I think you're biased," I mumbled as we pulled into a quieter neighborhood. The houses were all tall, with garages on the main floor and a long flight of steps leading to the front door. Huge windows and spotless brick exteriors glinted in the morning sun. The street he turned onto was wide and circular with a fountain in the middle, an unexpected sight. Linc hit a button, and the garage door on a house with charcoal-gray brick, trimmed in glossy black, slid open. He parked the car, the door shutting behind us. He stepped from the vehicle and came around to open my door. I loved the fact that he still did that for me. He held out his hand, pulling me from the passenger seat. Bending down, he brushed a kiss to my mouth. "Welcome to my house, Sunny."

I looked around in awe. Linc's house was stunning. We climbed the steps inside from the garage. I spied a workout room on the lower level and some other areas, but when we reached the main floor, my jaw dropped. Glossy marble floors, dark hardwoods, and light were all around me. A spacious living room, an elegant dining room, and a massive kitchen took up the entire level. The furniture was masculine and large. The walls a warm white, offset with colorful artwork. The kitchen was sleek and modern, and I may have squealed at the Keurig built into the fancy refrigerator. The floors were warm under my feet, and I gazed longingly at the massive gas stove.

"Do you cook?" I asked, running my fingers over the glossy surface.

"No," he replied, sounding amused. "I have a housekeeper. I can do the basics, but she handles the rest."

"Oh."

He held out his hand. "I'll show you upstairs."

I followed him, studying the framed images on the walls, marveling at the thick carpet on the stairs. He waved toward the left. "My home office and a guest room." He opened a set of double doors.

"My room."

My eyes widened as I took in the expansive room. A king-sized bed faced the large windows that overlooked the fountain on the street. The walls were a rich blue, the molding a crisp white, giving the room a cozy, warm feel. I peeked into a massive walk-in closet, then followed Linc as he entered the bathroom. I stared at the large shower with multiheaded jets, then in longing at the gigantic tub.

Linc stepped behind me, wrapping me in his arms. "Maybe you can have a bath. You used to love soaking in the tub."

"I still do," I replied quietly, feeling overwhelmed as I looked around.

He spun me in his arms. "Hey, what is it?"

I shook my head, but he refused to let me go, tipping up my chin to make me look him in the eye. "What?" he demanded. "Tell me."

"I'm embarrassed," I admitted. "Having you stay at that little apartment. You seeing my place—compared to this, it's a hovel," I admitted.

"Stop it," he growled. "I love the little apartment, and your place is not a hovel. It's yours—it's you. The fact that you're in it makes it special." He indicated the room. "They're just walls, Sunny. It's a place I sleep, eat, and work. It's always just been a house." He bent down and kissed me. "With you standing in it, it feels like a home now."

He always said the right thing. His words were like a soothing balm over my heart. I stared up at him, his blue eyes sincere and warm, darkening with intensity as he met my gaze. His hands, resting on my hips, tightened, and the air around us bubbled with heat. My breathing picked up, and before I could stop myself, I flung my arms around his neck and kissed him.

If I shocked him, he recovered fast, yanking me close and taking control of the kiss. His mouth dominated mine, his tongue pressing in, stroking over mine with long, sensuous passes. I gasped as he wrapped his large hands around my thighs, lifting me to the counter, stepping between my legs as he continued to work my mouth. I whimpered as he tugged me close, and I felt his erection trapped between us. He slid his hands under my shirt, gliding them up my back, spreading his fingers wide, his touch warm and sure. He dragged his lips down my neck, across my cheek to my ear, his voice raspy.

"Fuck, Sunny. I want you."

I wrapped my legs around his waist.

He hissed and cursed. "Baby, I have a meeting."

"Okay." But I offered him my mouth again, and he took it.

He devoured me, trailing his fingers up and down my back, sliding them under the fabric of my camisole, feathering them over the sides of my breasts. My nipples hardened, and I felt the pulse of desire grow in my core. "Linc," I whimpered.

"Jesus," he panted. "I want to spend hours with you, Sunny. Kissing you. Holding you. Making love to you," he added with a low growl. "Not fuck you in the bathroom and leave you alone right away." He rested his head on my shoulder, then raised his chin and met my eyes. His were dark with desire. "You are too beautiful. I can't resist you."

I cupped his face in my hands and kissed his mouth. Then his cheeks, nose, and finally his forehead, peppering light kisses on his skin. "Then go and do what you have to do. I'll be here when you get back."

He stared at me, a wondrous look on his face. "How did you do that?"

"Do what?"

"Make me feel...adored," he breathed out, his voice incredulous.

"You are."

Our eyes locked, a moment of clarity and silent conversation happening between us. He nodded as if answering a question, then scooped me into his arms and carried me into his bedroom. He set me on the bed gently as if I was the most delicate of sculptures. He kissed my forehead. "Sleep while I'm gone. It's Mrs. Ellis's day off, so you won't be disturbed."

"I'm not sure I can sleep. I'm not used to morning naps."

He grinned so widely his eyes crinkled. "Then have a bath.

Snoop around, Sunny-girl. Open my drawers and find a shirt you like and wear it. Dig through my closet. Bake some biscuits. Whatever you want. Just relax."

I understood what he was telling me. His life was an open book, and I was to make myself comfortable in it.

I snuggled into the cradling mattress with a contented sigh. Turning my head, I inhaled the scent of Linc on his pillow. Suddenly, I felt exhausted.

"Maybe just a few moments," I murmured, shutting my eyes.

Linc pressed his lips to my forehead again, and I felt a soft blanket being drawn over me. I burrowed back under the warmth, the pull of sleep hitting me.

"I'll be back soon," Linc promised.

"M'kay," I mumbled.

I heard the sound of his camera phone, then his footsteps as he walked away. He paused at the door, his breathing the only sound in the room.

"What a beautiful sight," he muttered.

I was asleep before he reached the main floor.

LINC

Sunny was on my mind all morning. I kept glancing at the photo I took of her in my bed. Curled under the ivory blanket, her hair spilling across my pillow—a bright ribbon of color against the pale hue of the sheets. For the first time in years, my concentration was muddled. It wasn't on the business in front of me. I wanted to be back at the house with Sunny. Lying beside her, feeling her soft skin on mine. I wanted to feel her under me, hear her calling my name as we rediscovered each other.

Not sitting in an office listening as a bunch of power-hungry men tried to outdo one another.

I cleared my throat. "Gentlemen, as much as I appreciate that you all have an opinion on this matter, the bottom line is, it is my decision. I thank you for your input, and I'll send my determinations to you soon." I glanced at my watch. "I have another meeting to attend, so excuse me. My assistant is off today, so you can show yourself out."

I strode from the boardroom straight into my office, shutting the door. At my desk, I watched as they filed from the office, all muttering and angry. I didn't care. They wanted my financial backing; they could play by my rules.

I picked up the phone and called Milo. He had sent a couple of messages while I was in the meeting, and unlike the men I dismissed, I was eager to hear what he had to say. He wasn't the same sort of lawyer as Ned. He leaned more toward the darker side of the law and had a lot of contacts that came in handy on the rare occasion such as this. We had met at Toblacove and had stayed in touch once we both got out.

"Linc," he drawled by way of greeting me.

"Milo. Tell me you have good news."

He chuckled, the sound low and dark. "It worked. I had him tailed to a bar, so he was already breaking parole. He was all over a young-looking girl in about five seconds. How the police got tipped to him violating his parole restrictions, I have no idea. Add in the drugs in his pocket? He's back in jail, and he ain't getting out for a long time."

"How did you get an underage girl into a bar?"

"I never said she was underage. I said she was young-looking—the way he likes. She was twenty-one. And one hell of an actress. Everyone in the bar heard her telling him off and knew he was getting handsy without permission. She almost screamed the place down."

"So they have enough to hold him?"

"His parole restrictions were no bars, no alcohol or drugs, and he was to keep a fifty-foot radius from women under the age of twenty-five. He broke all the rules in one fell swoop."

I tried not to laugh and failed. A gift of a bottle of rye delivered to Carl in the afternoon had ensured his bad decision-making. He liked the hard stuff, and being in jail would have made him thirsty for the taste. I had hoped it would set him back on the path to destruction, and I was pleased it had happened so quickly.

"Her mother?"

"I can't locate her. I think she heard about Carl and went back into hiding. Hopefully, she left town, but I'll keep checking. If she has nothing to hold over Abby, she knows there's no point in bothering her. Keep Abby in Mission Cove for a while. I have someone watching her building in case her mother shows up."

"Good job. Pay everyone involved and send me the bill."

"Already done."

I hung up and rubbed my eyes. Abby was safe again. I wasn't sure about her mother, but I knew Milo would keep a careful watch. She was easier to deal with than Carl. He was a nasty piece of work, and I didn't want to chance him going after Abby. He shouldn't have gotten parole, and while there was no doubt in my mind he would wind up back in prison sooner rather than later, I'd decided to help him along. I wasn't sure how Abby would feel about my actions, or Sunny. I wondered about not telling them, simply informing Abby that I found out Carl was back in jail. I had a feeling, however, she wouldn't buy it.

I sat lost in my thoughts for a moment, then shook my head. I had better things to do right now than weighing the pros and cons of my actions.

Abby was safe again, and to me, the ends justified the means.

And besides, Sunny was waiting.

I pulled into the garage, wondering if Sunny was still asleep in my bed. Part of me hoped she was. She worked too hard, and I wanted to spoil her today.

But entering the house, I had my answer. All I could smell was biscuits. I found Sunny, not in my bed, but in the kitchen, wearing one of my dress shirts, the tails hanging down to her knees, and a pair of my heavy socks. Her hair was pulled into a ponytail, her face free from makeup, and she looked adorable.

She looked up as I came around the corner, her welcoming smile bright. I headed straight for her, catching her in my arms and lifting her off the ground. I crashed my mouth to hers and kissed her long, hard, and passionately. She plunged her hand into the hair at the nape of my neck, kissing me back with equal fervor. I eased back, dropping my face to her neck with a groan.

"You have no idea what seeing you in my kitchen is doing to me right now."

She wrapped her legs around my waist, laughing low in her throat. "I think I can, um, *feel* your reaction." She rubbed against me. "I think you're happy to see me. Or your cell phone is in your pocket," she deadpanned.

"Baby, my cell phone doesn't take up that sort of real estate."

She giggled, the sound lilting and strange in my house. I liked it. I was about to kiss her again when the timer on the oven went off and she pushed away.

"Cockblocked by biscuits," I muttered and set her on her feet.

She pulled the tray from the oven, the scent wafting over. She brushed butter and honey over the tops, the glistening sweetness making me salivate. She carried a plate to the table and slid it in front of me, then sat down.

"You have no jam in the house, but there was honey, so you'll have to settle for that."

"Okay. I think Mrs. Ellis got it in case I liked it in tea. I didn't have the heart to tell her I never drink tea."

She leaned over and kissed me, her lips lingering on mine. "You're a good man, Linc."

What happened earlier flitted thought my brain, and I frowned.

"What?" she asked.

I inhaled, then blew out a long breath and told her everything. Milo, what I asked him to do—what he had made sure happened.

She was silent for a moment, crossing her legs, pumping one foot slowly.

"You manipulated the situation."

"It was going to happen," I insisted. "Sooner or later."

"But you made it happen now."

"Yes. Abby needed to be safe. I won't apologize for that."

"I understand that, Linc, and I get where you're coming from. But you need to be careful—this is a slippery slope you're on."

"What are you talking about?" I asked, reaching for a biscuit and taking a bite of the warm, dense dough.

"Your father did the same sort of thing."

I froze, narrowing my eyes at her, the biscuit now dust in my mouth. I swallowed and cleared my throat. "You think I'm like my father? I didn't do it to hurt anyone or for any sort of gain. I wanted Abby safe." I tapped the top of the wooden table, driving my point home. "He deserved what he got. I could have done far worse."

She bit her lip, sadness washing over her face. "That's what frightens me, Linc." She stood, walking toward the sink. Her shoulders were slumped, her posture defeated. I dropped the biscuit on my plate and followed her.

I had done that. Upset her. Worried her. Her words from the other day came back to me. *"I don't like to see the hate you carry inside, Linc. It frightens me."*

I wrapped my arms around her, holding her tight. She didn't pull away, leaning back into me.

"I didn't mean that, Sunny. I wouldn't do anything else. I did what I thought I had to do to make sure he went back to jail and stayed away from Abby."

"And her mother?"

"If she is a threat, I will keep her away from Abby."

"Would you-would you hurt her?"

"No," I insisted. "She'd be given a stern warning, and we'd give her money to go away. Take her to the bus station and make sure she moved on."

"If she refused?"

"Then we'd get a restraining order. I don't hurt people like that, Sunny." I tried not to feel insulted she had to ask, but I did feel a pang of hurt.

"You don't feel that you're manipulating people?"

"I suppose, in this case, I am," I admitted. "I'm sorry if that makes you uncomfortable."

She sighed. "I get the feeling you're not really that sorry."

"I'm not the boy I was, Sunny. Too many things happened, too many years have gone by. But I am still the man who loves you. Who is trying. Can that be enough?"

She turned in my arms and gazed up at me. I could see her struggle. I hated the wariness of her gaze. She wanted the boy who was only ever good. The one she remembered. But I had changed, and part of me was hard and did what I felt was best for the people I cared about. But I didn't do things to hurt people the way my father did. I protected them.

I *wasn't* my father. She had to see that. I had to make her see that.

I tucked a loose curl behind her ear, trailing my finger over the tender lobe. I felt her shiver. "Sunny," I whispered. "I'm still me. A little tougher toward the world, but not you. Never you."

"I want to believe that."

"Trust me. Give me that chance."

Her eyes grew round as I moved closer, lifting her to the counter. She squeaked as her thighs hit the cold granite, making me grin. I leaned in, ghosting my mouth up her neck, stopping to sweep my tongue along her skin. She gripped the fabric of my shirt, bunching it in her hands.

"Promise me you'll tread carefully."

"I will," I vowed against her shoulder, nosing the loose collar out of the way and teasing her skin with my lips, nipping at her softness.

I licked and bit my way back up her neck, threading my hand into her curls and pulling her mouth to mine in a soul-shattering kiss. The world ceased to exist around us—all that existed was her. Me. This moment. I stroked her tongue with mine, tasting the honey, tasting her. Losing myself in the sweetness of her. I always loved kissing Sunny, and time hadn't changed that fact. The feel of her close, the way her mouth moved with mine, the low, sexy sounds she made—all of it amped me up. My cock ached, wanting to be inside her. My body longed to feel all of her against me—her soft skin gliding along my rougher body. The way I remembered feeling, wrapped in her embrace. The warmth of being joined with her. The intense intimacy we had shared that one night. I wanted to repeat it. Over and again.

I dragged my mouth from hers, desperately trying to find my control. "We have to stop."

"Why?" she whimpered, trying to close the distance between us, pulling my head down toward her again.

"I promised you dinner and a show. If we don't stop, neither is happening, because once I get you upstairs and in my bed, you aren't leaving it until we go back to Mission Cove tomorrow, Sunny."

Our eyes locked, and the sweetest smile curled her lips.

"I love pizza in bed."

I gripped her hips.

"And I really don't like theatre."

"Are you sure?" I asked, my heart pounding in my chest.

"I'm on the pill."

"I haven't been with anyone for a long time. A very long time. I'm clean."

"Take me upstairs, Linc."

I scooped her into my arms and took the steps two at a time.

I laid her on my bed and stepped back. She was a vision to behold. Dressed in my shirt, the white of it bright on the creamy sheets, her hair a mass of sunset curls around her face, and her dark eyes wide with desire as she looked at me—she took my breath away.

I yanked my shirt over my head, too eager to bother with the buttons. I cupped my erection through my pants, groaning.

"See what you do to me, Sunny?"

She lifted her arms over her head, her slender legs moving restlessly on the sheet as her breathing picked up and a warm flush tinged her cheeks, spreading down her chest as I disrobed in front of her. She licked her lips as I made fast work of the belt and zipper, pushing my pants off my legs, taking my shoes and socks with them, and standing in front of her in nothing but black boxers, my cock so hard, it strained against the waistband.

I crawled up the mattress toward her like a lion stalking its prey. I straddled her hips, leaning on my fists, looming over her. Teasingly, I tugged on the collar of the shirt she wore.

"One of us has entirely too many clothes on."

Her words were low, sexy. "Take them off, then."

She gasped as I gripped the tails of my dress shirt and ripped it open, the buttons flying like small UFOs in the air and landing scattered on the carpet. I let the torn material fall to the sides and feasted my eyes on her. Smooth, ivory skin, dotted with faint freckles and flushed pink along her collarbone, greeted me. Her breasts, her beautiful breasts that always fascinated me, were fuller than I remembered, her nipples a deep, dusty-rose color. They lifted and fell in rapid succession with her shallow gasps of air. I slid my hands along her arms, trailing my fingers over her warm skin, and entwining our hands over her head. I bent down close to her mouth, touching my lips to hers.

"Sunny, you are the most beautiful woman in the world." I kissed her softly. "More gorgeous than my memories." Another kiss, this time harder, longer. "Lovelier than my imagination."

She shivered as I ran my lips down her neck, over her sexy collarbone, and between her breasts. Goose bumps broke out on her skin as she arched her back with a silent plea, and I closed my mouth around her nipple, sucking gently. She gripped my fingers with hers, a low moan in her throat as I moved between her breasts, kissing, sucking, licking. I released her hands to cup them, stroking my thumbs over her hard nipples.

"I've always loved your breasts," I confessed. "Your *tits* starred in my nightly dreams." I shook my head in amusement. "The things I wanted to do to them."

"Tell me."

I lowered my head, demonstrating as I spoke. "Lick them. Suck them. Squeeze them. Play with them." I rose over her, close to her ear. "Fuck them." I flicked my tongue on her earlobe. "I still do."

She whimpered.

I smiled against her skin. She was so responsive, exactly the way I remembered. I sat back, lifting her, pulling the shirt away from her body. I wrapped her in my arms, holding her tight, needing to simply feel her against me. I knew how big this moment was going to be for us, and I didn't want to rush it.

She gripped me hard, her fingers digging into my skin. I felt a tremor go down her spine, and I pulled back, tilting up her chin to look into her dark eyes. "Sunny, baby, what is it? Too fast?"

"No," she whispered. "It's overwhelming at times. I never thought I'd be here, like this, with you again."

"I know." I brushed a kiss to her lips. "I feel the same."

"Linc..." Her voice trailed off, uncertainty filling that one word.

"Talk to me," I begged. "If this is too much, we can stop, Sunny. I swear."

"No, it's just—" she swallowed "—I might not be what you expect."

I cupped her face. "What I expect? I expect *you*. Nothing more."

"I, ah, don't have a lot of experience." She huffed a sigh and looked up. "In fact, other than you, none."

Her words hit me, and I stared at her, stunned.

"Sunny, you've never been with anyone but me? All these years?"

"No."

For a moment, I said nothing. We hadn't talked about the years we were apart. The people in our lives. Our experiences. I had assumed...well, apparently, I had assumed wrong.

I stroked her face with my thumb, trying to phrase my words properly. "Can I ask why?"

She shrugged. "Sex was never just about sex for me. What we shared that night meant something. I dated a few guys, but none of them ever touched my heart. I didn't want them to touch my body if that was the case." Her gaze looked everywhere except at me. "I just... didn't."

I pressed my forehead to hers. "Sunny, baby, you overwhelm me." I exhaled hard, the air moving the curls around her forehead. "My experience was, ah, different," I confessed, feeling shame at my words.

She wrapped her hands around my wrists. "It's fine, Linc."

"No, listen, please. I dated a few women. I had relationships with two. But they never touched my heart because you still owned it. They were both smart enough to recognize that, and we took the relationship for what it really was. We enjoyed each other's company, and the sex was an outlet—nothing more."

"So you only had sex with two other women?"

I nodded. "The last one was two years ago. Like I said, it's been a long time."

She met my eyes. "And you've been alone ever since?"

"Sunny, I've been alone since the day I lost you."

"I'm here, Linc."

I leaned my forehead back to hers, shutting my eyes. "I'm not worthy of you."

"I think you are."

I gazed down at her, her eyes damp with unshed tears, her lips trembling with emotion. Her confession shook me to the core. This woman, this beautiful woman, had been mine all these years. As alone as I was—and somehow waiting for me.

"I want to tell you everything. All the words, all the thoughts I never got to share the first time around. I want to build a lifetime of new memories with you, Sunny."

"I want that too."

"I'm going to make you mine again," I murmured, tracing her lips with my finger. "Only this time, I'm not letting you go."

She kissed my finger, a single tear sliding down her cheek.

"I never stopped being yours, Linc."

With a groan, I crashed my mouth to hers.

The girl in my memory was simply that. A memory. A body on the cusp of changing. A mind beginning to explore and absorb the world around it. A girl on the brink of becoming a woman.

That woman was with me now. Beautiful, vibrant, and here in the present—not a shimmering mirage of a ghost from long ago. Real. Warm. Waiting.

Our mouths molded together, reacquainting themselves with everything familiar, discovering all the new richness of the moment. Sunny's taste filled my senses—sweet, hot, and addictive. She kissed me back, her passion matching mine. I dragged my mouth over her cheek, nibbling on her ear, kissing the sensitive skin behind it, smiling as she shivered. She always liked that.

I explored her with my hands and my mouth. Tasted and teased the juncture where her shoulder met her neck. Licked her sexy collarbone. Keeping our gazes locked, I lifted her arm, trailing my mouth along the inside of her wrist, up her elbow to her shoulder, then doing the same with the other arm. Her breasts beckoned, and she gasped as I licked and sucked at her nipples, teasing them into hard points under my tongue. I kissed my way down her stomach, listening to her whimpers as I worshiped her curves, trailing my fingers over the swell of her hip, gliding them along the indent of her waist and sliding them back to her breasts, playing with the hard nubs as I went lower.

Sunny gripped the sheets as I slid farther down the mattress, lifting one leg, kissing my way up from her ankle, swirling my tongue under her knee, making her moan as my mouth drifted higher. I stopped before I reached her apex, then started on the other leg. She strained under my touch, her voice pleading and begging.

"Linc, oh god, Linc—"

I grinned against her soft skin, taking my time. When I finished my torturous route, I paused, then slowly drew my finger against her core. One light, fluttering touch.

Jesus, she was soaked.

She gasped and arched, her legs opening farther, silently begging.

I gave her what she asked for.

I closed my mouth around her clit, lapping, flicking the hard nub. Sunny moaned, lifting her hips to get closer. I slid one finger inside her, feeling the way she gripped me. She was hot, wet, and tight around my finger.

"My cock wants inside you, Sunny. He wants to feel you choking him." Turning my head, I kissed her thigh, biting down and leaving a small mark.

My mark.

"You are going to feel amazing wrapped around my cock."

I added another finger, pumping harder. I wanted her to climax for me. I wanted to watch as she lost herself in pleasure before I buried my cock completely inside her. She gripped one hand in her hair, grasping at my shoulder with the other. She made a keening sound, her voice high and wanting.

"Linc, oh god...*Linc*—"

I couldn't tear my eyes off her. I pressed my thumb to her clit, stroking and teasing. Her back bowed off the bed, her cries getting louder.

"*Fuck!*" she cursed, the sound breathless and sexy.

"Give it to me, Sunny. I want to hear you come."

With a long shudder, she did. Crying out my name, pleading with me for more, begging me not to stop.

So, I didn't.

I rose on my knees and yanked her up my thighs. With one thrust, I was inside her, her heat searing me. Marking me forever. She cried out as I began to move. Thrusting hard into her warmth, the slick welcome of her desire. She pulled at the sheets, gripping them with her fists, then reached blindly for me as I rode her. I bent low, pulling her to my chest and sitting back up, surrounding her with my embrace. I spread my hands wide across her back, holding her to me. She wrapped her legs around me, taking more of me, and I growled at the intensity of the sensation. She tugged at my shoulders, dug her nails into my back, pulled my head down to kiss me, yanked on my hair, all while making the most erotic noises. Sweat glistened on our skin, the bed creaked, the sheets in disarray around us. My body was on fire, the flames licking at my skin. I was certain I would be a pile of charred ashes left at her feet when we were done.

I didn't care.

We moved together, the years disappearing, the pain and worry gone.

There was only *now*. Only her. Only us.

And blinding, soul-shattering ecstasy.

Her head fell back, a low, frantic scream falling from her lips. I buried my face in her neck as she tightened around me, milking my cock as I came. My hips jerked, my balls tightened, my cock sank deeper inside her, and my world imploded.

Pleasure had never been so intense. Every part of my body felt it. Thousands of tendrils exploded under my skin. My nerves snapped and twisted as I rode it out. I bellowed her name. Gripped her to me so hard, I knew I would leave bruises on her delicate skin. I saw colors I had never seen behind my tightly closed eyes.

And through it all, she held me. Until I was spent. Until I began to tremble with her in the aftermath. I ran my hands up and down her back, my heavy breathing drifting over her cooling skin.

"Sunny," I whispered.

Her arms tightened, her face still buried in my chest. I felt the wet of her tears on my skin, and as carefully as I could, I laid her down, running my hands over her.

"Baby, I hurt you? Tell me where?" I demanded, cupping her face, forcing her to look at me. "I lost myself in the moment, I didn't mean—"

She lifted a finger to my mouth, silencing me. I met her eyes and relaxed. There was no pain in her expression. There was love. Satisfaction. Happiness.

I pulled her hand to my mouth and kissed her palm. "Overwhelmed?" I asked tenderly.

"Yes," she whispered. "I never thought... I never knew, Linc. We were so young before..."

"I know."

"Was it, ah, okay for you?"

"Sunny," I whispered. "That was the most profound experience of my life. It was a dream come true and better than any fantasy I had in my head all these years."

"Oh. Well, good then."

"And it'll get better, Sunny-girl."

She giggled, the sound making me smile. "If it gets any better, I might not survive."

I bent low and kissed her. Sweetly. Softly. "I'll catch you, baby. I promise."

She pulled me to her chest, and I rested my head against her warmth.

"Okay, then. I look forward to it."

And for the first time in years, I fell asleep with my Sunny beside me.

I never wanted to be without her again.

LINC

I woke with Sunny curled around me. She was awake, tracing abstract designs on my chest with her finger in long, lazy motions. I snickered. "Is this a game, Sunny-girl? Am I supposed to guess what you're writing?"

She tilted back her head, smiling at me. Her dark eyes were soft and warm, her smile wide. Her hair was a total mess from my fingers, and I spied a small bite mark or two on her neck. I had a feeling I was going to hear about those marks later. But for now, we were good.

"No, I was enjoying touching you."

I grinned. "Touch me all you want, Sunny." To demonstrate, I spread my arms wide. "Everything you see is yours."

She pushed up on her elbows, a mischievous look in her eyes. Her fingers danced down my chest, drifting lower. "Everything?"

I groaned as her fingers ghosted over my cock. He was ready to be owned by her, growing steadily and tenting the sheets. She bit her lip, sitting up and straddling my thighs, gazing down at my dick, her eyes wide.

"You look as if you have a problem there."

I reached for her face, cupping her cheek and stroking it with my thumb. "If I remember right, you were a *great* problem solver, Sunny."

"Hmm," she hummed, tracing along my shaft with her finger. Up, down, over, circling the crown, then repeating the circuit. She added her thumb, swirling it along the head, making me groan low in my throat when she wrapped her hand around me. "I am good at zeroing in—" she pumped me "—on the issue."

"Oh god, yes. Zero in, Sunny. For the love of god, zero in."

Bending over my torso, she hovered over me, her mouth almost touching mine. Her breasts brushed against my chest, her nipples teasing the hairs scattered along my skin. She licked my jaw, trailing her tongue along my neck and shocking me when she bit down at the juncture, sucking in the skin with a sharp nip.

She winked. "Payback."

Before I could even react, she sank down on my aching cock. I shouted, gripping her hips at the sudden rush of heat, the warmth enveloping me. The intense pang of pleasure that shot through my body.

"*Fuck*, Sunny."

"Yes," she deadpanned. "That is exactly what I had in mind."

Then she began to move. Long, slow rolls of her hips. Pressing down, lifting up, stroking my cock with her inner walls as I groaned and hissed at the sensations. She grabbed my hands, lifting them to her breasts. I fondled and stroked her nipples, held her full curves in my hands as she moved over me. She bent backward, her hair brushing my legs as she took me deeper than I had ever been before. Her walls clamped down on me, rippling and clenching around my shaft. The effect of her altered position blew my mind.

Destroyed any control I thought I held.

Cursing, I grappled for purchase on her hips again, straining to get closer. Thrust up into her warmth. Shouted her name. Came without warning. My cock pulsated, emptying within her. Sunny gripped my thighs, a low, pensive cry escaping her lips as she arched and shuddered.

"Linc," she moaned. "Linc...Linc...Linc."

Then she collapsed on my torso, breathing heavily. I wrapped my arms around her, cuddling her to my chest, lost in the moment of warm intimacy with her. I dropped kisses to her head, whispering words of adoration and love to her. "Sunny, baby..." My voice trailed off.

She lifted her head, sleepy and sated. "Hi."

"Hi."

She tapped my chin, a goofy smile on her lips. "Hi."

I chuckled. "Did I fuck the words right out of you?"

She giggled. "I think I was the one fucking *you*, Linc."

"I love it when you talk dirty."

She wiggled a little. "I am dirty." She wrinkled her nose. "Messy."

I chuckled. "How about a shower?"

"Sounds good."

"Then pizza?"

She hesitated.

"Would you like something else?'

"I love Chinese. I mean, *love* it. Where we lived in Nova Scotia, we knew an Asian family that had a restaurant. It was amazing and I was spoiled. Their noodles and ginger chicken were so awesome. I crave them. Mission Cove has one place, and it's pretty bad. There must be some good places here?"

"There are and, in fact, there's a great one close. I'll order us all your favorites."

She pushed off my chest. "Race you to the shower."

I watched her hurry away, enjoying the way her hips swayed and admiring the curve of her ass. She always had a great ass—even in our teens. It was the only thing that made watching her leave enjoyable. Still, I jumped from bed and followed. I wasn't ready to let her out of my sight yet.

S unny gazed around the table, her eyes wide. "How much food did you order?"

I slid a plate in front of her. "A lot. I wasn't sure what you liked aside from noodles and ginger chicken, so I got what I thought you would enjoy, plus my favorites. We can pack up the leftovers and take them back to Mission Cove."

She sat down, reaching for the noodles. I grinned at her eagerness. One thing I had always loved about Sunny was there was never any pretense. She never hid the fact that she was hungry or enjoyed eating. I had always kept extra treats in my car for her when we were younger. So many girls at school picked at their food, refusing to let anything pass their lips that wasn't in the form of salad or vegetables. I had observed the same thing in many of the women I had encountered in my adult life. It was a mystery to me, and I was glad Sunny had never adopted that mind-set. I liked seeing her enjoy the food in front of her. It made me less self-conscious about my own appetite, which to this day, was massive.

We loaded up our plates, the kitchen filled with the low moans and exclamations from Sunny. I watched her chew a dumpling, slurp noodles, pick up some spicy beef in her fingers when her chopstick skills failed her, all while making noises that were oddly erotic. My dick hardened as she licked her lips, closing her eyes in satisfaction as her tongue lapped at the spicy sauce from the ginger chicken.

"That, right there," she groaned. "Oh my god, it's better than sex."

I slapped my hand on the table. "You wanna bet on that, Sunny-girl?" I growled. "My cock is willing to take on that challenge—right on top of the counter behind me. You wanna throw down?"

Her eyes flew open, her tongue frozen mid-lick. "Um, what?"

I pointed my chopsticks at her. "The noises, the mutterings. You have no idea what you're doing to me. You either need to tone it down, or we're taking a break from dinner."

She blinked. Had the audacity to lean over and peek under the table. My casual pants were tented obscenely. She sat up. "Wow."

I narrowed my eyes at her. She grinned, winked, then twirled a long strand of noodles on her chopsticks and, never breaking our gaze, slurped them loudly, licked her lips and hummed. "So...good," she moaned. "So-so-good."

My chair fell back as I stood, towering over her. "I warned you."

She was out of her seat fast, grabbing a dumpling as she did. "You're going to have to catch me."

I grinned maniacally. "Oh, baby, you're on."

Sunny lifted her leg, bubbles drifting down her wet skin, sinking into the steaming water around us. I nestled her tighter to my chest, pressing a kiss to her damp curls. Our chase had ended fast, and I'd had her up on the counter promptly. I was inside her not long after, both of us climaxing quickly, in long, breathless shouts. Then, sticky from sex, she sat on my lap and we fed each other mouthfuls of food, the spicy morsels often dripping on our chins. I licked it off her smooth skin, but we were a mess. A bath was definitely in order, and I carried her upstairs, filled the tub, and we sank under the mounds of foam.

Turned out body wash made great bubbles, and I had been over-generous with my squirts.

"You okay, baby?" I asked.

"Hmm," she responded. "I'm great."

I held her tighter. "You are."

She tilted up her head, and I dropped a kiss to her full mouth. I would never tire of being able to kiss her again. I was addicted to her mouth.

She sighed in contentment. "I love this tub."

"It's yours. Use it whenever you want."

There was a beat of silence.

"It's a little far away from Mission Cove," she reminded me, her voice gentle.

"Whenever you're here," I assured her, the reality of our situation breaking in. She lived there; I lived here. Fewer than a hundred miles away, but when we were apart, it would feel like an entire continent.

She was quiet, but I felt the tension creeping back into her shoulders. I bent over her ear. "We'll figure it out, Sunny. Just live in this moment with me, right now."

"It's more than I thought I would ever have again," she admitted.

"It's the start," I insisted. "We'll find a solution."

She pulled away and turned in the water to look at me. Her curls were damp, tendrils falling down her neck and over her forehead. Her skin glistened pink and wet from the heat and water. She was beautiful but looked troubled, a V forming between her eyes. I rubbed my thumb over the crease. "Stop, Sunny. Stop questioning this."

"How will this work, Linc? You pop down on the weekends, and I come visit once a month? We have enough sex to tide us over until the next time? Talk and text during the week?" She looked away. "Eventually, you'll get tired of that."

I was honest. "Yes, I would. Very quickly, in fact." Her eyes flew to mine, wide and worried. "Which is why that isn't going to happen, Sunny. I lost too much of my life with you already. It's not happening."

"My bakery—"

I held up a finger to her lips. "I know your bakery is important, Sunny. And for now, yes, I will be there with you as much as I can. We will talk and text every day. I won't even address the 'have enough sex to tide us over,' because there will never be enough with you. But as the future becomes now, we'll figure it out."

"You don't ever want to live in Mission Cove again." It was a statement, not a question.

"It was never in my plans, no," I admitted, running my knuckles down her cheek. "But I didn't know you were there."

"And now?"

"Now that I found you again, I'm not letting you go. Ever. So, whatever we have to do, we'll decide it—together. Here. There. Somewhere in between. But it will be us, Sunny. Not a summer of us, but a lifetime of us. Understand?"

She regarded me in silence, then turned back in my arms and sank down in the water again. "Fine," she huffed. "Bossy man."

She pushed away a mound of foam.

"Possessive bastard," she added, muttering under her breath.

I hauled her up my chest and bit her neck. "Damn right, I'm possessive. Don't forget it."

I heard her muffled giggle. I tightened my hold. "We'll work it out, Sunny. Trust me."

"I do."

I liked those two words. I planned on her saying them again—in a totally different setting and with witnesses.

And soon.

I liked waking up with Sunny beside me. Even more, I liked being able to make love to her in the early dawn, listening to her low moans and feeling her clench around me as I took her from behind, holding her leg over my hip and slowly thrusting into her until she cried out my name. I followed not long after, with my face buried in her neck, her light scent filling my senses.

We showered, ate the biscuits she'd made the day before, then left for Mission Cove. On a whim, I took a detour, and we stopped at the old summer camp. The camp had closed and the land sold, but Gerry and Cindy retained a small piece of the property and still lived there.

I followed the road that led up to the old dining hall. Gerry and Cindy had converted it, and it now looked like a comfortable home.

I stepped out of the car as Gerry opened the front door, stepping out on the porch. He was older, his hair gray, but he still walked tall, his shoulders straight. He approached the edge of the porch.

"Can I help you?"

Sunny opened her door and she slid out. "Hi, Gerry."

He beamed at her. "Hey, Sunny." He indicated me. "Who's your friend?"

I pulled off my sunglasses. "Hey, Gerry."

His eyes widened. "Well, son of a bitch." He hurried down the steps, shouting over his shoulder for his wife, then grabbing me in a bear hug. "Linc."

Cindy came out the door. She hadn't changed, although her hair was white and her face had a few more wrinkles. But her warm smile was the same, and her hug was firm.

They insisted we come in. Cindy bustled around getting coffee, Sunny offering to help her. Gerry showed me around, explaining how they'd remodeled the large building. "Cindy had knee surgery a while back, so we needed one floor. This is perfect for us."

"It's great, Gerry."

We sat on the porch they had added, facing the lake.

"I often wondered about you, kid," he mused. "Your father—he made you disappear?"

"Yeah," was all I could get out. Memories of that summer, that perfect summer Sunny and I spent here, were overwhelming me.

"I should have done something."

I shook my head, facing him. "There was nothing anyone could do, Gerry. My father was too powerful and determined to keep me away from Sunny or anything that made me happy." I slouched back in my chair, staring at the water. "But he's dead now, and his control is gone."

Sunny and Cindy joined us, a tray of coffee and cookies sitting on the table. I grinned around a mouthful of the oatmeal raisin cookie. It was another memory come to life. "So good," I murmured, reaching for another.

"We use Cindy's recipe at the bakery," Sunny informed me. "They are one of our biggest sellers."

I grabbed a third, not at all embarrassed.

Cindy chuckled. "I see your appetite hasn't changed."

"Nope. I was denied all the things I loved for so long. Now, I have them anytime I want." I met Sunny's gaze with a subtle wink, causing pink to spread across her cheeks.

Gerry caught me and chuckled. "Nice to see the two of you together."

I lifted Sunny's hand and pressed a kiss to her knuckles. "It feels nice. Really nice."

We all laughed, and Gerry and Cindy caught me up on their life.

"About four years after you disappeared, we decided to close the camp," Gerry mused. "We were getting on, kids didn't want to be counselors anymore, and our numbers were dwindling."

I nodded, already knowing what he was about to say.

"We put the land up for sale, with the stipulation we keep a small piece for our retirement." He sighed. "It was a hard decision, but we knew it was our nest egg."

He rested his arm on the chair. "Imagine my shock when we got an offer—a really good offer on the land—that allowed us to keep, in what was my opinion, the most valuable piece of the property. I was given a free lease that expires when both Cindy and I are gone."

I took a sip of my coffee, not meeting his eyes.

"A further shock has been that the land has never been developed. A crew shows up twice a year, cuts back trees, makes sure it's clean, even does the same work on my property, then leaves. No surveyors, no real estate people, no developers have ever been here."

"Hmm," I muttered. "Odd, I agree."

No one would ever develop the land around them—I'd made sure of that. They had been good to me. Treated me well. It had been one of the first things I had bought when I put my plan into place. I was determined to look after them.

"It's amazing," Gerry mused. "Same thing seems to be happening in Mission Cove. Unexpected gifts of property. Houses being rebuilt and sold at a fraction of their value. Almost gifted, some say."

Sunny looked between us, putting the pieces together.

Gerry rested his elbows on his knees. "What are you doing these days, Linc?"

I waved my hand. "This and that. Finance mostly."

"Uh-huh. Any property investments?"

"I have my fingers in a lot of pies, Gerry," I said smoothly.

"I bet you do," he said with a smirk. "I bet you do."

I let his remark pass.

Cindy and Sunny got up and took the tray inside. They were talking about recipes and a new cookie for the bakery for Sunny to try.

"She's become a lovely woman," he stated.

"Yes."

"She part of your future, Linc? Or only for now?"

"My future," I stated firmly.

"Good. She suffered greatly when you left."

I snorted. "I didn't do so well myself, Gerry." I shut my eyes. "I was locked up, no way to contact anyone, and scared most of the time."

"But you survived."

"I survived," I agreed.

He was quiet for a moment. "Are you living in your father's house?"

I shuddered at the thought. "No. I'm having it destroyed."

"Going to rebuild?"

"I haven't decided," I said honestly. "Maybe nothing."

"That would be a waste."

"As long as the monument to his stranglehold on Mission Cove is gone, I'm happy."

He didn't say anything for a moment, rubbing his bottom lip. "Maybe you need to think again, Linc."

"What do you mean?"

"You are obviously rebuilding this town, Linc. Don't think I haven't noticed that all the improvements that have happened are in some way connected to your past."

I didn't say anything. I wasn't looking for thanks or glory.

"I get you want to destroy the legacy of your father."

I snorted. "Legacy isn't the word I would use. Reign of destruction, more like it."

"Fine. Then think, Linc. Destroying your father's house—fine. But leaving the land empty? You're missing an opportunity."

I faced him fully. "An opportunity?"

He nodded. "Your father was all about keeping everyone down. Being king. He never reached out his hand to help people—he liked to keep them beneath him. You want to purge his memory? Then do something positive with the land." He grinned evilly. "Something your father would hate."

"Do you have an idea?"

He leaned forward. "I do."

We shook hands goodbye. "Don't be a stranger," Gerry said and waved his hand toward his house. "And I know, kid. I know this was you."

"I don't know what you're talking about."

He clapped me on the shoulder. "Okay. Keep your secret. But I am forever in your debt. It broke my heart, thinking I would have to leave this place."

"That will never happen," I vowed, then snapped my mouth shut.

He winked. "It's okay, kid. Your secret is safe. Remember what we talked about. Think hard."

"I will."

I slid into the car, and we headed for Mission Cove. I knew Sunny was already thinking of the list of items she had to take care of. My head was swimming with Gerry's idea. It was simple but perfect.

"It was you who bought his land." Sunny's voice interrupted my thoughts.

"Yes."

She reached over and squeezed my hand. "Linc, you have so much good in you—even if you refuse to see it."

"Gerry had an idea about the land that will be left when the house is gone."

"Oh?"

I turned my head and met her gaze briefly. "He thinks I should build a library and community center. A place where kids could hang out after school, have access to computers, maybe someone to talk to if they need it."

"That's a great idea."

"My father would have hated it. He never wanted to help kids. Not those less fortunate, anyway," I added. "In fact, no one else less fortunate, regardless of their age. He thought it was his place, *his right*, to keep them down, not help them up."

"That's where you're so different."

I ignored her remark.

"The library in town is pretty small. I could triple its size. The whole top floor could be the library. The main floor, a place for kids to hang out. Play games, do their homework." I thought of how often I went home to an empty house and hated it. "Have other people around."

"That would be awesome. It would benefit someone like Michael. He's always juggling to make sure his kids have a place to go to after school—even in a small town like ours."

I warmed to the idea. "We'd have a shuttle bus. I bet I could get Gerry to help plan it. He knows kids and what they need. Maybe Cindy would want to hold some baking lessons. We could add a kitchen at the back."

Sunny sealed the idea for me. "You could call it the Amanda Webber Community Center after your mother. Have her picture on the wall when you walk in. It would be hers then, not your father's."

My heart warmed at her words.

"Perfect."

LINC

I dropped Sunny off in front of the bakery, then parked the car. I used the key she gave me and carried our bags upstairs. I took them to her place—there was no point in pretending I would stay next door. Wherever Sunny was, I would be as well.

I went downstairs, wandering through the kitchen and wondering why there was no one baking or cooking. That seemed unusual. I pushed open the door to the shop, freezing when I heard Sunny's distressed voice. "I don't understand. None of this makes sense."

I hurried forward. All the staff, including Abby were gathered around a table. Sunny was standing, holding an official-looking document. Everyone turned as I walked in, and from the look on Sunny's face, I knew it was bad. I wrapped my arm around her waist, pulling her close.

"Let me see."

I scanned the document, my frown growing as I read it. "What the hell is this bullshit?" I muttered. "Health violations?" I looked around in shock. I had never seen a shop or a kitchen in a business as meticulous as Sunny's. "When the hell did this show up?"

"About two hours ago," Shannon offered. "We knew Sunny was on her way home, and we didn't want her upset."

"When were they here?"

"Shannon said they were here yesterday," Sunny said, her voice shaking. "You never know when they're going to show up."

"Did they say anything? Act strangely?"

Shannon shook her head. Mack spoke up. "I followed him around, and Abby was there. He was really thorough. But he didn't say anything and only asked the basic questions about our routine." He met Sunny's eyes. "I was certain we'd pass with flying colors. We always do. So I didn't even think to call you."

"No, it's fine," Sunny murmured. She was shaking, and I knew she was feeling anything but fine. Gently, I pushed her down into a chair and read the list of violations.

"Mack, come with me."

We went into the kitchen—I knew nothing about kitchen equipment, so I had him point out each infraction, my anger growing as the moments passed.

Frayed wires—fire hazard.

One plug had a piece of electrician's tape on it. "I put that on the plug so I knew which one it was. There isn't anything wrong with it," Mack stated.

Inadequate hand-washing stations.

"We meet code," Mack insisted. "In fact, we exceed it."

Equipment, utensils, multi-service articles, and food contact surfaces are not properly constructed or sanitized.

The kitchen was spotless. I frowned and looked at Mack. He shook his head.

"We were baking when he showed up. Of course, it was messy—but not unclean. Never in this kitchen. Sunny is very particular. So am I."

Maintain and arrange appliances to permit a clean and sanitary condition.

"Our arrangement has passed every other time. The interiors are impeccable," Mack insisted.

The list went on in the kitchen and included the temperature of the display cases and the cleanliness of the washrooms.

All of it bogus.

I growled under my breath. I already knew who was responsible for this. I pissed off Martha, and this was retribution. She saw Sunny and me kissing. She knew how my father had felt about our relationship. She was doing this to get back at me. This was my fault.

I glanced at the list. Every "violation" was ridiculous.

I returned to the shop. Someone had given Sunny a cup of coffee. She was calm, almost removed, when she met my eyes.

"It's bullshit," I insisted.

"Michael had a visit from an inspector. They told him his shop and the chemicals he keeps on hand are dangerous, and they are going to recommend the closure of his shop and relocation," Abby said. "He's beside himself with worry."

"Did Martha see you with him?" I asked, my voice icy.

She furrowed her brow in thought. "Yes, I think so. I was sitting with him and his kids when she came in."

I wanted to storm up to the town hall and have it out with that bitch. Call her every name under the sun and tell her husband exactly the kind of woman he was married to. But the bottom line was the affair I thought she'd had with my father was a rumor. The mayor might have heard it already. Maybe he didn't care. I had no idea.

Sunny stood. "Well, we need to regroup. Take pictures of the before and after. Fix one item on the list at a time. We have a week to clear the list, so the inspection certificate on the window goes back to a pass—" she swallowed heavily "—not a conditional pass."

I glanced at the window, narrowing my eyes at the sign. I wanted to rip it down, but I knew that would cause Sunny more trouble. Shannon, Mack, and Abby stood. "We've been baking all day. We'll finish it, and you can decide what to tackle first," Mack stated. "We'll get it done, Sunny."

"Thanks, Mack."

They filed into the kitchen, leaving Sunny and me alone.

"This is on me."

Sunny shook her head. "Not even Martha would go this overboard for a bad cup of coffee, Linc."

"No. She saw us. She knew the lengths my father went to in order to keep us separate. She's carrying on his work. She's furious with me over the house. Abby was sitting with Michael, so she's put the two of them together and is making Michael suffer."

Her eyes widened. "If that's true, then nothing I do will work."

"Unless she thought we broke up." I threw out wildly, hating myself the instant the words were out of my mouth.

"No!" Sunny gasped. "I will shut this bakery before I even allow you to say another word, Lincoln Webber. You take that back right now. I am not living in secrecy again. We did that, and it was awful."

I pulled her into my embrace. "I couldn't do that, Sunny. Not really. I'll figure this out."

She tilted back her head. "Leave it, Linc. Leave it alone."

"I can't."

"I'm asking you to. This is my business. I will handle it."

"Stop being stubborn."

She pushed away. "Being stubborn is how I made it this far. This is my problem, and I'll handle it."

"A problem you have because of me," I seethed. "I'll handle it."

"No, you will not. I'm telling you right now—leave it alone." She crossed her arms. "If she is doing this out of revenge, then you being involved will make it worse."

Her words stung, even if they were true. She kept talking. "And don't tell me what to do, Linc. You are not the boss. This is my business, and I'll handle it the way I see fit."

"I can solve it."

"How exactly?"

"I'll figure it out. I'll find a way to take her down or—"

"*No,*" she snapped, interrupting me. "It's a problem I need to solve legally. I don't have time to stand here and argue with you. Go deal with what you came here for, Linc. Get the revenge you need on your father. Maybe then you can find some peace." She sighed. "Maybe then the Linc I knew will be back."

"I already told you, this is me. This is Linc now. I thought you accepted it."

She ran a hand over her face, suddenly looking exhausted. She sat down, looking at me. Her expression frightened me. It was one of resignation.

"I thought I could. But I'm not so sure I was right." She ran a hand up her neck, leaning on her palm. "Right now, I don't know what to think. But I need to work. And I think you need to go."

"What? No, Sunny—"

She spoke the words before I could stop her.

"Maybe this was a mistake, Linc. Visiting the past. Thinking we could outrun it."

"Don't say that."

She stood, her shoulders slumped. "I can't do this again, Linc. Our entire relationship when we were younger was shrouded in secrecy and anxiety. We had to sneak around, hide our feelings. I lived in constant fear that you'd walk away."

She held up her hand before I could speak. "And when you disappeared, it took me years to find my life again. To stop looking for you. To be able to smile and get on with life."

"Sunny—"

"You insist you're here with me in the present, but the truth is, you're still so mired in the past, you can't see through it, Linc. Your first instinct is to react with anger. Seek revenge. Just like your father." She sighed. "I can't live in fear again. I won't."

"What are you saying?"

"I'm saying we need to step back and think. This is all too much. It's all...too much."

She turned and walked away.

I paced the den in my father's house. I went around the room over and again, too restless to sit. I had no idea why I'd come back here, to this house, but I had. Maybe the darkness suited my mood.

Abby had tried to come with me when I left the bakery, but I told Abby to stay with Sunny. I knew she would accept Abby's help. She certainly didn't want mine.

Sunny was furious with me. Her words echoed in my head.

I couldn't lose her. I had just found her again.

Why couldn't she see I only wanted to help?

There was no doubt why Martha Tremont was doing this —payback.

I flung myself into the chair, my knee hitting the drawer. I cursed, grabbing at my knee. The key inside the drawer rattled and I slid the drawer open. I had put the metal box back inside the drawer once I gave Sunny my letters. I had, in fact, forgotten about the box until now.

Since I couldn't concentrate on anything else, I decided to go through the rest of the papers. It would be interesting to see what secrets my father had hiding.

The box was fairly full. In his usual methodical way, my father had copies of all pertinent documents in the box. His will, the deed to the house, various other documents no longer required. A copy of my birth certificate. My mother's death certificate, still sealed, never even looked at by him. I set that aside to take with me.

Then it got interesting. An envelope containing some USB drives with names on them. Many of them ones I recognized. I would have to get my computer to find out the contents. Somehow it didn't come as a surprise that my father would keep files on people he wanted to destroy or threaten. I had a feeling he was an expert at blackmail.

There was one last envelope. I lifted out the manila pouch, noting the thickness of the contents and the initials in the corner.

MT

I opened the envelope, my eyes widening at the contents. Pictures of Martha Tremont. Personal pictures. Some of her. Some of *them*. Intimate. Graphic. All taken, I was certain, without her knowledge. All kept, I knew, to blackmail her.

I shut my eyes, feeling ill. I pushed away the ones of her and studied my father's expression. Even in passion, he was cold. Removed. He stared at Martha as if he'd just as soon strangle her as have sex with her. She was simply another tool in his destructive arsenal.

That woman, who, to this day, fought for my father's honor, harbored feelings for him, was as duped by him as the rest of the town.

He was, indeed, a complete bastard.

I stared down at the pictures. At the files on the desk. The USB drives. I could only imagine what they all contained. The power they once held over the people of this town—probably other places as well.

Movement caught my eye, and I looked up. Sunny was in the doorway, her face pale. I stood, rounding the desk. "Sunny?"

She rushed forward, flinging herself into my arms. I held her close. "Hey, baby, shh," I soothed. "Whatever it is, it's okay. I'm here."

"I'm sorry. I was upset," she sobbed.

"I know," I assured her. "And I know it's my fault, Sunny. I never wanted to bring hardship back into your life." I ran my thumbs under her eyes, wiping away the tears and I gazed sadly at her. "But I have. People with scores to settle with my father will take them out on anyone related to him. Me—and of course, you, since you'll be associated with me." I pressed my forehead to hers. "I hate that."

"Is that why you remain anonymous with all the improvements? Why you refuse to take credit?"

"Yes. If some people found out it was Franklin Thomas's son making the changes, roadblocks would be thrown up. People would wonder about my end game. It's better to remain nameless."

She sighed.

"How goes it at the bakery?"

"We made a list, and we're going to start early tomorrow morning. We'll check off one thing at a time. Michael is challenging the findings on the dry cleaners."

"Good. Are you still angry with me?"

Sunny wiped her face. "No, I know you wanted to help, but you have to let me handle it. I can't allow you to step into my business, Linc. I have to draw the line."

I sighed—we were never going to agree on this.

Sunny tilted her head. "What are those pictures on the desk?"

"Nothing," I said, cursing inwardly. I moved to hide them, but Sunny caught my arm. She stared at the photos.

"Where did you get these?" She gasped, horrified.

"My father had them in the box. Along with a bunch of other things he kept on various people."

"Why?"

I shrugged. "To blackmail or use against them, I presume."

She looked around. "Is there a shredder?"

"No."

She indicated the fireplace. "You need to burn them."

I took the photos from her hand. "I'll handle them."

Her voice changed, becoming fraught with worry. "Linc, what are you thinking?"

"Leave it, Sunny."

"No!" she gasped. "You can't, Linc!"

"If she knows I won't bend to her, she'll back off."

She held up a picture. "And by using these, Linc, you'll become exactly what you keep saying you don't want to be. You'll become your father."

"I'm not my father. I would do this to protect you."

"Protect me, by threatening another person."

"I would never really do anything with the pictures, Sunny. She just has to think I would. The health violations go away, Michael's business is safe, and no one gets hurt."

She shook her head. "Your *soul* gets hurt. The way I feel about you will change, Linc. Don't you see that? You use these today, then something else in a few weeks. Then you'll start hiding secrets and manipulating everyone to get what you want. Sound familiar?" She paced the room, facing me with her fists closed. "Maybe that was how your father started. There must have been some good in him at some point. Your mother loved him enough to marry him. But she couldn't save him from himself—from his quest for power—and she lost him."

"This isn't for power," I insisted.

"Really. I think you need to think long and hard about that, Linc. Be honest with yourself. Because you're not being honest with me right now."

"I can't sit by and let you suffer because of me."

Her eyes filled with tears. "If you do this, you lose me, Linc. *Forever.* Don't you get it? I would rather have you than the bakery. *My Linc.* The boy I loved. Who loved me back. But not the man bent on revenge and holding the power. That's not the Linc I know.

"That man is your father. For the first time ever, I'm seeing Lincoln Thomas in front of me. And the loss of the man I thought you were is going to wreck me for the rest of my life. You're forgetting the one common factor here—Mrs. Tremont is a person. A fellow human being. You don't know her story. You are threatening to hurt a person. Think about it. Think hard."

Her parting words hit me in the chest, rendering me mute.

She shut the door behind her, the silence screaming in ferociousness.

21

LINC

I trolled the house for hours, unable to stay still. I walked through rooms I hadn't been in for years, staring at walls, pictures, opening closets. I wondered if any of the items I saw were picked by my mother, or if my father had destroyed everything she touched and replaced them. It was an endless loop, and eventually I was able to discern a few items I could recall her touching fondly or watching her hang. I picked them up and found a box, then transferred them to the trunk of my car.

Most of the rooms on the upper floors were empty, my father long having cleared them out after he sent me away. The attic was a vast cavern of dust and emptiness. The basement produced an unexpected find of a case of rare scotch. My father never stinted when it came to his own pleasure. Business associates received a simple glass of decent scotch, while my father's cut crystal glass held the finest of spirits. God forbid Franklin Thomas sip something from a liquor store shelf.

I dusted off the bottles, staring at the label. A memory stirred from the far recesses of my mind. My mother, holding out a glass of scotch to my father, a playful look on her face, refusing to give it to him until she got a kiss. His face, which I could usually see in my mind with a permanent scowl, had softened, and he kissed her with a gentleness I never associated with him. Then he snatched the glass and walked away, laughing.

I blinked as the memory took hold. It was the one time I had ever heard my father laugh. Or seen real intimacy between my parents. I would have been two or three at the time, and every other memory I had was of my mother. The ones including my father were filled with coldness on his part, sadness on my mother's. Sunny's words came back to me.

"Maybe that was how your father started. There must have been some good in him at some point. Your mother loved him enough to marry him."

She was right. My mother must have loved him at some point. When had things changed for them?

I carried the scotch upstairs, planning on giving it to Ned. He was a scotch man, whereas I preferred whiskey. I paused as I wondered if that was because I associated the liquor with my father.

I drove the car down into town, parking it behind the darkened bakery. I knew I wouldn't sleep—the war inside my head was too loud for that to happen, so once again, I walked. I covered miles as the town slept. I went around the center of town, pausing as memories stirred. Older, forgotten memories surfaced of my parents. My life before my mother died. There were a few good ones, but mostly sad. My mother's face, pale and forlorn as she stared out the window. Picked at her dinner, looking over at the empty chair my father usually sat in. I recalled raised voices, my mother's pleadings, and so often, my father walking out of the house, the door slamming behind him.

I ended up at The Sunny Place, sitting on the swings, gazing at the spot where we used to hide out in my car. I walked down to the bluff, staring at the water, the breeze stinging my eyes. I didn't light a fire or stay too long—my restless feet wouldn't allow that. I circled everything old but familiar, all that was new and helping the town. I grunted in grim satisfaction that at least I had done that right.

I stood across from the bakery, staring at the simple sign and the large plate glass windows. The health inspection certificate stating the premises was "under inspection" made me furious, knowing why it was there and the damage it could do to Sunny's business, especially given the time of year.

I fisted my hands, my determination growing once again. I crossed the street, using the back door, and went upstairs. I slipped into the apartment, finding Abby asleep on the sofa, no doubt waiting for me to return. I had shut off my phone, wanting to be alone. She stirred as I walked in, sitting up, rubbing her eyes.

"Where have you been?"

"Walking."

She peered at the clock. "It's three in the morning."

"A lot of walking," I added.

"Have you come to your senses?"

Obviously, Sunny had told Abby what had occurred between us. I didn't want to fight with her too. I ran a hand through my hair, feeling weary.

"If you mean, am I going to do everything I can to protect Sunny, then yes, my senses are perfectly clear."

She stood, gathering the blanket around her. "Linc—"

I held up my hand. "I don't want to hear it."

"You are going to regret this."

I leaned against the counter, resting on my hands. I took in a long breath, letting it out slowly. "I will always regret losing Sunny. But once I fix this and leave, her life will be better. She's right. Our past is always going to get in the way. At least I'll live knowing she's been taken care of. I'll deed the building to her so she's set financially, and we'll carry on without each other."

"You don't mean that."

I pushed off the counter, suddenly angry. "Sadly, this is real life, Abby, not a romance novel. I can't make it better and have the girl.

Bottom line is once we got over finding each other again, we would probably discover we had grown too far apart. It's for the best."

I ignored the voice screaming in my head that I was wrong. I had to be strong right now.

Abby shook her head, but I didn't want to listen to her.

"I'm leaving today. You can stay here—it's fine. I'm going to take some time and do some rearranging of the business. Anything I need, I'll contact you. At least here, you're safe."

She crossed her arms. "So, that's it, then. You're going to blow off the best thing in your life and turn your back on me as well."

"I'm sorry you see it that way."

She tilted her head, narrowing her eyes as she studied me. "I have never been ashamed of you before, but I am now," she huffed, then turned and stormed off to her room, shutting the door firmly behind her.

I didn't react.

There were no emotions left to react to.

Except my anger. And that was burning hot and bright.

I showered, dressed in a suit, then threw the last few things in my bag that had reappeared in the apartment. No doubt, Sunny had given it to Abby. I paused before heading out the door, laying the key on the table. My fingers brushed the metal, the dull ache in my chest I had been feeling for hours becoming more toxic. With a low curse, I picked up the bag and headed down the staircase. My steps faltered as I reached the bottom, the sound of Sunny's voice reaching me. I listened as she gave instructions to her staff, her tone calm, steady, yet authoritative.

"We're taking the list one item at a time. Once it's done, we'll move on to the next. I've closed the bakery for the day so we can concentrate. Together, we'll get it right."

I paused, unable to move. I turned my head, catching a glimpse of

Sunny. She was beautiful under the lights of the kitchen. She looked as exhausted as I felt, but her smile was firmly in place. Leading her staff. Positive.

Despite everything, I was proud. She was capable, smart, and a real leader.

And better off without me.

She moved her head, spotting me in the back. For a moment, our eyes locked. All the love I felt for her was in my gaze. The words I would never get to speak. The memories we would never create together. I shouted all my pain at her in that glance.

She turned her back.

I walked out the door and left.

M y mind was blank as I drove to my father's house. I sat at the desk, motionless, then reached for my phone and placed a call.

"Martha Tremont, deputy mayor, speaking."

"Martha, it's Lincoln Webber."

"How did you get this number?"

I chuckled, the sound without humor. "You should be far more concerned about why I'm calling than the fact that I have your number."

In truth, it had been very easy to get. The town hall staff really needed to be updated on privacy policies.

"What do you want, Mr. Webber?"

"I'm at my father's house. You know it well, Martha. I'm sure you've been here many times."

There was silence.

"I'll be waiting. And Martha, like my father, I'm not a patient man."

I hung up.

I heard her car arrive, the sound of her BMW engine breaking the silence. I hadn't moved from behind the desk. My legs wouldn't let me. I felt out of control of my body, as if my limbs were no longer attached.

The front door opened, slamming shut behind her. She stalked into the den, leaving no doubt how well she knew her way around this house.

I swallowed the bile that threatened to escape.

"I am not one of your flunkies you can command," she announced, crossing her arms.

"And yet, here you are."

Silence stretched. The ball was firmly in my court. I only had to say a few words, show her the pictures, then assure her they would remain a secret as long as she stopped harassing Sunny. It was a scenario I was certain had been played out many times in this room by my father. Countless people he held under his thumb.

"Slippery slope," Sunny's voice whispered. "You are not your father."

I picked up the envelope, my fingers not cooperating as it slid from my grasp, hitting the top of the desk. Her eyes followed my movements.

"What is that?"

I opened my mouth to start, but the words didn't come out. Instead, all I heard was Sunny.

"If you do this, you lose me, Linc. Forever."

"The loss of the man I thought you were is going to wreck me for the rest of my life."

I cleared my throat.

"You're forgetting the one common factor here—Mrs. Tremont is a person as well. A fellow human being. You don't know her story. You are threatening to hurt a person. Think about it. Think hard."

The words that came from my mouth shocked me. "Why do you

hate me? Even as a kid, you did—even though I never did anything to you."

"You kept your father from me."

A humorless laugh escaped my throat. "I think, Martha, perhaps you have been misguided in your judgment. My father spent no time with me at all unless he was telling me to do something or punishing me."

She didn't say anything. I stood, rounding the desk, leaning on the edge. I copied her stance, crossing my arms over my chest. I started to talk, not stopping for over fifteen minutes. I spoke of the way my father ignored me, held me responsible, somehow, for everything—including my mother's death. She grew pale as I talked about the inflicted punishments. How he'd pound my chest or sucker-punch my gut.

"Always with the intent to hurt badly—but not leave scars others could see," I told her.

Silence fell between us as we stared at each other. Looking—perhaps really looking for the first time. Martha gave off a polished vibe. Her makeup was flawless, her hair perfect, her outfit becoming. But when I regarded her, I saw underneath the façade. The pallor the makeup hid. The anxious tremor in her hands she was trying to hide. The fear in her gaze.

I wondered briefly if that was what my father saw when he brought people to heel. If he reveled in it—the power he held in his hands to destroy a fellow human being—because he could. I bet his euphoria was high, his ego swelling at his power, his chest inflating with his own sense of supremacy. I wondered if it turned him on sexually.

All I felt was ill. And disgust.

Right then, I knew Sunny and Abby were correct. I couldn't do this.

I reached behind me and handed her the envelope. She frowned, opening the flap, staggering to the left as she saw the contents. I gripped her elbow and helped her sit.

"What? Where did you get these?"

"From my father's personal files."

"He... I... No. He *wouldn't*."

I sighed and stood, needing the distance. I sat back at the desk. "He did."

Her head bent as she shuffled through the pictures, sounds of distress escaping her lips on occasion. She sat in the chair, her shoulders slumped in resignation. When she lifted her head, her voice was defeated.

"What do you want?"

"Nothing. I'm giving you those pictures, Martha. There's only one set. Do what you want with them. I will never tell anyone about this. Ever."

"Why?"

She was right to be suspicious. "What good would it do? Destroy your marriage? Cause an unnecessary scandal? Allow my father to carry on his reign of destruction?"

She shook her head. "I thought...I thought I meant something to him. He always promised once you were out of the way, we'd be together. Then when you left, he spent all that time trying to mend fences with you..." Her voice trailed off at the look on my face.

"He hated me," I told her. "He sent me away—there was no mending fences. He was cruel and stole my life for falling in love with someone he didn't approve of. Because I didn't follow his rules, everyone I cared for suffered."

"I-I didn't know. He said...he told me so many lies," she murmured, then held up the pictures. "Why are you giving these to me if not to manipulate me?"

I sighed. "Rightfully, they belong to you. I think, Martha, your esteem for my father has been misplaced. I thought if you saw them, you would realize the memories you are clinging to perhaps weren't real." I cleared my throat. "I suggest you try to make your peace with it and move forward."

"You aren't going to say anything?"

"No."

"Ask me to do something for you?"

I barked out a laugh. "That had been my plan. But I can't. I have to step back and let Sunny deal with her business on her own, as much as it kills me. I'll be leaving Mission Cove today."

"But you'll be back?"

I shook my head. "No, the history here is too much to overcome."

She looked down at the pictures in her lap, then stuffed them into the envelope. "I want these destroyed."

"I don't have a shredder."

"A match?"

I indicated the fireplace. "Help yourself."

She placed the envelope in the grate and I obligingly opened the flue, not really wanting to choke on the fumes. I handed her the box of matches and a piece of paper I crumpled into a loose ball. She bent, lighting the match, and we both watched as the flames curled and flickered, growing as they gained strength, the envelope catching fire, the edges coiling, the photos slowly disappearing into nothing.

Deciding it was as good a time as ever, I grabbed the other files and added them to the pile, watching as my father's legacy of fear died in a pile of ash. I would destroy the USB drives. I wasn't remotely interested in their contents.

It was over. And despite what I had lost, I felt lighter.

Martha turned, heading toward the door. There was too much bad blood between us for there ever to be anything but the most tenuous of business relations, but perhaps going forward, the hate would begin to dissipate. Maybe she could forge a new relationship with her husband.

Stranger things had happened.

She paused at the door.

"I knew your mother."

I snapped up my head, prepared to fight.

"She was one of the kindest girls at school. Always willing to help someone out. She refused to let bullies win. She used to lecture them, pointing out their wrongs. Your father was one of the worst ones in school—that was how they met. He seemed to change, but I suppose he never really did."

"I guess he hid it for a while."

"Or maybe he tried, but his true nature won out. He was very selfish—even when he was younger. Your mother was the exact opposite. I think she thought she could make him a better person."

"That obviously didn't work."

She smiled. It was the first real one I had ever seen from her. "Even angels can't always perform miracles." She tilted her head. "You are very much like her."

No one had ever said that to me. No one ever spoke of my mother.

"Thank you."

She turned to leave, stopping as she gripped the door, not looking back. "She would be very proud of you."

Then she was gone, her footsteps hurrying away and fading.

I blinked at the empty doorway.

I wasn't my father.

I was like my mother.

Her son.

And that, going forward, was how I would act.

22

SUNNY

I wiped my hand across my eyes as I scrubbed the already clean wall. My shoulders burned with the strain, the pain radiating down my arms.

I ignored it, the throb in my bones nothing compared to the pain in my chest. My heart ached with loss.

Linc.

He was all I could think of. What he insisted he had to do. It was going to kill him. All of his work—everything he'd strived so hard for would be wiped out with one horrible move to try to protect me. He refused to listen to me. To Abby. He was hell-bent on destroying himself, refusing to believe there was any other way.

I would clean this bakery a hundred times over—close it, in fact— if it meant he didn't stoop to the level of his father. I had been serious when I told him he was on a slippery slope. He would justify this action. Then do it again. Over and over until it became a part of him —until the good I knew he had within him was gone, and he became the one thing he fought against.

The wall in front of me became blurry, and I had to blink my eyes to clear them. The sound of a throat clearing behind me was startling.

"Um, boss? Someone here to see you."

"Tell them to come back," I ordered. Lots of people wanted to see me today, asking why we were closed, what the notice on the door was about, demanding to be allowed to help.

"I think you'll see me."

At the sound of Martha Tremont's voice, I froze, turning my head to meet her gaze.

"A moment of your time, Ms. Hilbert."

I slid from the stool, wiping my hands, wondering what was about to happen. She looked like herself, but different. The usual frown was missing from her face, the look of distaste she always wore when she looked at me, gone. Her expression wasn't friendly, but it was no longer hostile.

"I received an incorrect report about your bakery. The notice has been removed." She handed me the green and white pass form. "You can stop cleaning now."

I shook my head, but she held up her hand. "It was a mistake. A novice inspector going overboard. I have rectified the situation."

"Linc," I mumbled.

She cleared her throat. "Ah, yes. Mr. Webber. I saw him earlier today—we had an eye-opening chat. Cleared the air, so to speak. I do hope he changes his mind and returns to Mission Cove." She crossed her arms, staring at me meaningfully. "He is *always* welcome here."

I didn't understand. What had happened?

"He is so much like his mother." She paused, and I was certain she almost smiled. "Nothing like his father. *Nothing.*" Then she turned. "I have to go to the dry-cleaning store now. More errors to follow up on. The work of the deputy mayor is never done, you know. My citizens need to be cared for." She lifted her hand and disappeared.

I stare after her, blinking.

What had transpired between her and Linc? Something big—but not what I feared, judging from her demeanor. It wasn't friendly, but the hostility was gone—or at least lessened.

Her words rang through my head. *"Nothing like his father. Nothing."*

I had to find out what happened. I needed to talk to Linc.

Except, Abby had told me he was leaving. I had heard him walk out this morning, my heart breaking as I turned my back on him before I lost my nerve and ran to him, begging once more for him to choose us over doing what he felt he had to do. Choosing the light he so often said I was to him, over the dark.

Abby came up beside me, and I handed her the form. "We can stop cleaning now."

"Did he...?" Her voice trailed off.

"I don't think so."

"What happened?"

I yanked off my apron. "I don't know, but I have to find out. I need to get to him before he leaves, Abby, or I may never see him again."

She pressed her keys into my hand. "Go."

I drove up the hill, my heart in my mouth. Linc's car wasn't in the driveway, but the front door stood open. I ran inside, heading to the den. I stopped in the doorway, horrified at the sight before me. The room was wrecked—the desk overturned, the chair smashed. Pictures were torn off the walls, flung around. The fireplace was wet, rivulets of water running onto the expensive floors and carpet, a pile of sodden ash in the grate.

What the hell had happened here?

I dialed Abby, panicked. "He's not here," I gasped. "The den is wrecked, his car is gone." A sob escaped. "He's gone."

"Wait," she instructed.

I looked around the room, noticing the metal box Linc had dug my letters from open and lying on its side. I bent and looked inside. It was empty. Another smaller box was upside down on the rug. I didn't touch it.

"Okay, we track each other's cell. He's still in the area. East of you. He's stationary."

"East? Oh god, I know where he is."

"Go to him, Sunny. He thinks he's lost you."

"I'm on my way."

Linc's car was parked on the deserted area of land by the park. I hurried toward the ridge, frowning at the rhythmic sound that grew louder as I approached.

Linc was sitting in our hideaway, a pile of USB drives in front of him. He had a large rock in his hand, a look of determination on his face as he pounded the small pieces of metal into tiny, broken fragments. Soot streaked his face, one hand showing an angry burn. He was so focused, he didn't even notice me at first. When he met my eyes, the heartbreak and pain in his gaze would forever be embedded in my mind.

"All gone. All of his dirty, horrible secrets gone," he raged, his expression wild.

"Linc," I murmured. "I was at the house—what happened?"

"I couldn't do it. I tried—*fuck*—I tried. But I can't." He held up a mangled piece of metal. "I can't be the kind of person who does these things to people. Lord their mistakes over their heads, makes them pay over and again for a moment in their life they want to forget."

"I know," I soothed. "It's okay, Linc. You made the right choice."

"We all make mistakes. *He* made mistakes, but no one ever took the great Franklin Thomas to task."

"I know," I repeated. "You don't have to do anything for me, Linc, except be Linc."

"It was never enough for him!" he roared. "My mother tried. Jesus, Sunny, I've remembered things—the fights, her pleading with him to come back to her. The way he would sneer and call her weak." He rubbed his face, ignoring the fact that he smeared the soot even more. "And all the time he was fucking around on her." His voice dropped. "And I don't think it was only with the mayor's wife."

"You aren't him," I said and, with a bravado I wasn't feeling, grabbed his hand, stilling his frantic movements. "You. Are. Not. Your. Father," I repeated slowly.

He stopped, blinking. "No. I am my mother's son."

"Yes." I dared to inch closer, pressing my knee to his. "You are. You are Lincoln Webber. You have so much good in you."

"I'll help if you let me, Sunny. I can wash walls, fix things. I'll have my lawyer there when they come back, and we'll fight it. Let me do that. Let me do something," he pleaded. "Tell me I didn't lose you." He hung his head, his shoulders slumping. "I-I can't take it if I did that."

I took advantage of his sudden stillness and crawled into his lap. I wrapped my arms around him, holding him as tightly as I could. He buried his face in my breasts, enfolding me in his embrace. "Sunny," he whispered brokenly.

I slid my hands around to his shoulders, running them up the tightly corded muscles of his neck. I cupped his face, forcing him to meet my eyes.

"I'm here, Linc. I love you, and I'm not going anywhere."

He stared up at me, blinking. "You still love me?"

"I never stopped."

He yanked me to him, holding me so tight, I could barely breathe. It was as if he couldn't get close enough. I touched my mouth to his ear.

"I love you," I promised, over and again. I had a feeling he needed to hear me say it. I wouldn't stop until he believed me.

He gripped me, his shoulder shaking with the force of his emotions. Incoherent words fell from his lips. I didn't try to make sense of them. I knew he had to get them out, not let them fester. I let him rage until he was spent. A long shudder went through him. I dropped more kisses to his head, stroked his neck, and held him.

Slowly, I felt him return, the feeling around us changing, growing—becoming heated.

His body trembled, his already tight embrace turning into a vise. "Sunny," he moaned. "I need you." I could feel his need in the tightness of his body, the desperation in his voice, and the rigidness of his cock pressed between us.

"Yes," I gasped. "I need you, Linc. *Now*."

I tore open his shirt, wanting to feel his skin. I reached between us, yanking on his belt, tearing the material as I pulled and grasped at the closure and zipper. I reached inside, his hot cock filling my hand. He groaned as I stroked him.

Linc's large hands delved under the cotton shorts I had worn to clean the bakery, and with a low growl, he tore them off my body. I hadn't bothered with underwear this morning. I gasped as the cool air met my skin. He grasped my buttocks, cupping them, stroking and squeezing. "Sunny," he mumbled over and again. "Inside you. I need inside you."

"Up," I commanded, marveling at the ease with which he lifted his body and mine off the hard ground just enough so I could pull his pants down to free his cock. Seconds later, he was inside me, one hard thrust making us both cry out. He slid his hand up my back, burying it in my hair, holding the nape of my neck. He fastened his other hand on my hip, using it to guide me. I buried my face in his neck, moaning in long gasps at the sensation of him filling me.

There was nothing tender or sweet in our actions. This wasn't making love. This was our possession of each other. Our need to feel something besides sadness and pain.

We moved together wildly. Pushed and pulled. Gave and took. My body was on fire for him, and Linc was frantic in his desire. He groaned and cursed, guided me up and down, pulled my face to his to kiss me, his tongue mimicking what his cock was doing to me. He gripped my shirt so hard I felt the seams rend, and I wondered if either of us would make it out of this with any clothes left intact. His suit was ruined, my clothes in tatters.

It didn't matter.

He pulled back, our gazes locking. Passion, want, need bled from his eyes. So did love. I could feel it soak into my skin as we stared. His expression was fierce, his need rampant, but the Linc I knew, the one I loved so desperately, was still there—with me.

The moment was powerful—life-changing for us both.

Then his body locked down, and he pulled me to him, shuddering, filling me. His orgasm kicked off mine, and I cried out, my walls clamping down, my body spasming. Through it all, Linc held me close, his voice now tender, the sweep of his hand gentle. I collapsed into his chest, and he wrapped his arms around me, holding me securely. I felt his lips pressing to my head repeatedly, soft words being crooned as we slowly returned to earth. Returned to us.

I shivered as a cool breeze drifted around us, and Linc sat up, reaching for his jacket. He pulled it around me, then gathered me up in his arms again.

For a moment, there was only the sound of his rapid heartbeat under my ear, then he chuckled.

I lifted my head. "What?"

"I have never done a walk of shame before, but I'm pretty sure this one will be epic."

I glanced down. My shorts were in shreds, my shirt so badly stretched it hung off my shoulders. Linc's shirt was torn and dirty, his pants covered in grass and mud, hundreds of small tears in them from the rocks. I couldn't help the giggle that escaped my lips. "Oops."

"You can wait here, and I'll go to the car and grab some things. We can change before we head back into town."

I snuggled back into his chest. "Not yet."

He stroked my hair, his voice low and tender. "Okay, Sunny-girl. When you're ready."

I couldn't look at him. "You're not-you're not leaving now, right?"

He tightened his arms. "No. I am never leaving you. I'm not complete without you, Sunny." He sighed. "I'll stay and help you whatever way I can. Legally."

I lifted my head. "What happened, Linc? I saw the den."

He exhaled, pulled me to him and rested his chin on my head. "I couldn't threaten Martha. I tried, but the thought made me ill. I kept hearing your voice, and I knew you were right. If I did that today, I was well on my way to becoming my father. So I gave her the pictures and let her burn them. She told me she knew my mother at school, and I was like her. I had never heard that before. I started thinking, remembering things. Fights, angry words, my mother pleading with my father to come back to her. I was too young to understand, but now the words make sense."

He paused, and I trailed my fingers over his skin. "What happened next?"

"I got angry. With him. With everything. I took it out on his office —he valued it more than me or my mother, so I destroyed it. I wanted it ruined before the house is gone. When the desk overturned, I found another hidden box with more documents, pictures. I burned them all. It got a little out of control, and I had to get a bucket or two of water to put out the fire. I was going to let it spread, but I knew the fire department would arrive before the house totally burned, so I put it out."

"Good choice." I touched his hand. "Is that how you burned yourself?"

"Yeah, one of the embers landed on me." He chuckled, the sound low and dark. "I really want to watch that place implode."

I let that go. He was entitled.

"Then I had to get out of there. I was upset, disgusted, and furious. With him. With myself. I think-I think I lost it. I came here and decided to destroy the drives and get rid of them forever." He paused. "I don't even remember driving here."

He swallowed. "All I could think of was I lost you. I loved you so much and you were gone again and, this time, I wouldn't be able to get you back. You would never trust me again."

He glanced down. "Then you came. Why did you come, Sunny?"

With a sigh, I pulled back and told him. About the bakery. Mrs.

Tremont's unexpected visit. Going to the house. Racing to get here, desperate to find him.

"She removed the notice?"

"Yes. On Michael's store as well."

He frowned. "Do you think she still felt threatened?"

"No," I replied honestly. "I think she realized the past is done and it was time to let go of grudges and move on." I regarded him. "Can you do that, Linc?"

He studied me, then ran his fingers down my cheek. "The one past I want to cling to is ours, Sunny. And I want the future that goes with it." He swallowed. "Can *you* do that? Can we?"

I smiled, feeling the weight of the past few days lift from my shoulders.

"Yes."

23

SUNNY

Linc and I stayed wrapped around each other for over thirty minutes. We didn't talk, but simply held on, needing the closeness. Finally, he broke the silence.

"Are you scared to leave, Sunny? Afraid of what will happen once we go back to the world outside this little nook?"

"Yes," I admitted. "I am."

He tilted up my chin, meeting my eyes. "Nothing bad, Sunny. I promise. We'll find our way together. I promise. You ready to be brave with me?"

"All right."

He smirked. "Good. Because my ass is numb and frozen, and it might take a while to get out of here anyway."

That made my lips twitch.

"My legs don't have any feeling either," he admitted, barely holding back his amusement.

I began to chuckle.

"This walk of shame is going to look like a drunken stumble."

Then we both laughed, the sound freeing and loud. It felt good to let go and enjoy the moment. I pushed off his chest and stood, giggling when I realized how unsteady I was. Linc followed, grimacing as he stood, grasping at the rocks around us. "Holy shit," he mumbled. "Pins and needles."

We spent a few moments shaking out our arms and legs. He yanked up his pants, buckling his belt and tucking in his shirt. He was still a mess, covered in grass, dirt, his hair windblown and wild, soot across his face. But his expression was peaceful. Content. It startled me to realize it was the first time I had ever seen him look at ease since he came back into my life. The look of wariness and worry was gone from his expression.

He regarded me, his eyes wide. "Wow—I did a number on you."

I looked down. My shorts were in shreds on my legs, my shirt barely covering my chest. He held out his jacket. "Put this back on."

I slid into the jacket, trying not to giggle as he buttoned it up. I looked down at the ground. "What do you want to do with those?" I indicated the pile of mangled metal. They were already destroyed, but I knew he didn't want to leave them here.

He ran a hand through his hair. "Not sure."

I bent and gathered them up, stuffing them back into the envelope Linc handed me. "Let me take care of it, Linc. You destroyed them. Now let it go."

He hesitated, his hand already reaching out for the envelope. I met his gaze—mine sure and steady, telling him to trust me. Give me this task and let me share the burden.

His hand fell and he nodded. "Do what you think is best."

"I will." I already knew what I would do with them. There was a loose floorboard in the hallway at the house on the hill. I would bury them under the floorboard, and when the house disappeared, so would they. He would never have to think about them again. I stuffed the envelope into the pocket of his suit jacket. "Thank you for trusting me."

His smile was warm, his lips cool as he pressed them to mine. "Always. Thank you for being here with me."

"Always," I repeated.

218

He straightened, indicating I should stay where I was, and I tried not to laugh again as he peered around the corner, disappearing, then his hand appearing. "Coast is clear, Sunny. Let's go."

I grabbed his hand, and he pulled me around the corner and we hurried toward his car. He pushed me into the back seat, then grabbed his bag from the trunk and joined me. He dug around, handing me a pair of sweats and a shirt, finding a set for himself. We changed, and he grunted as he bundled his suit into a ball.

"So much for that one." Then he glanced my way, his expression warm. "So worth it."

I giggled. "Odd we're in our favorite spot and we're putting clothes on. It used to be the opposite."

He smirked. "God, I lived for those moments you'd let me stick my hand under your shirt. Your tits fascinated me." He leered at me. "They still do."

"If it wasn't light out and this wasn't a public parking lot, I might let you cop a feel again, Linc."

He winked. "I might anyway."

A car pulled into the parking lot, and we both laughed.

"Damn," he muttered. "Cockblocked." Then for the first time, he noticed Abby's SUV. "What is that doing there?"

"It was closer and faster than the bakery van."

"I'm buying you a car."

"I don't think so."

"As your husband, it's my right to buy you anything I damn well want."

"You're not my husband, Linc."

"Not yet," he agreed. "But that is going to change."

"Oh really?"

He nodded, his voice firm when he spoke. "Soon."

With a grin, I opened the door and stepped out, heading over to Abby's vehicle. Linc stepped out of the car, watching me.

"If that's your idea of a proposal, Mr. Webber, you are sadly lacking. I will have to say no to your tempting offer at the moment."

He leaned on his door, a wide grin on his face. "If that tempted you, just wait. You won't be able to resist."

I snorted. "Such ego."

In three long strides, he was at my door, leaning into the SUV. He bent inside, his chest warm and hard against mine. "Challenge accepted, my Sunny-girl."

Then he kissed me. Until I was dizzy. Until I would have agreed to anything he asked at that moment. His mouth was tender but demanding. Firm but gentle. Possessive and dangerous. When he eased back, we were both gasping for air. He smiled and traced my lips.

"See you at the bakery."

LINC

Escaping the parking lot was easy. Making it through the bakery was a different story. Even though the only people in it were Michael and Abby.

When we walked in, Abby at first looked relieved, then her eyebrows shot up and her lips twitched, looking at the outfits Sunny and I wore. My shirt and sweats hung off Sunny, showing all the love bites I had left on her neck. Her hair was wild, her cheeks and neck pink from the scruff on my face. She looked well and truly fucked and no doubt, so did I. I certainly felt it. I was sure my ass was covered in bruises from the rocks.

Michael blinked, looked at Abby with a grin, and stood. "I, ah, should be going."

I refused to feel ashamed, although I didn't want Sunny embarrassed. But as usual, she surprised me.

"Oh, sit down, Michael. It's not as if I didn't see you making out with Abby this morning while you were supposed to be cleaning the supply room."

He gaped at her. "I was helping her reach something on the shelf."

Sunny snorted as she poured us each a cup of coffee and reached for a plate of cookies. "What was her mouth reaching for? Your tongue?"

I barked out a laugh and sat down, pulling Sunny to my lap. I wrapped my arm around her, holding her close. "Your mouth looks a bit swollen, Mike. Allergies acting up?"

Abby chuckled and pulled on Michael's hand. "We're all adults here, Michael. Relax."

He shook his head and sat.

"Everything okay with the store?"

"Yes. Martha canceled everything. Business as usual again tomorrow." He cleared his throat. "Thank you for, um, anything you did."

I shook my head. "I did nothing but talk. I think our deputy mayor realized she had made an error."

"Well, I still appreciate it."

"No thanks needed."

We sipped our coffee, and they chatted. Talked about the baking to be done for the weekend, plans for a barbecue maybe on Sunday— all normal, everyday things most people would take for granted. I loved listening to it. Being part of it.

I let the conversation drift away as I thought about what I'd said to Sunny earlier. I meant it. I was going to marry her—and soon. We had lost enough years, given up enough happiness already. I wanted my life with her to start now.

I simply had to figure out the how-to's.

The touch of her hand on my cheek startled me, and my eyes flew open. I blinked, confused.

"Where are Abby and Michael?"

She smiled, stroking my hair. "They left about ten minutes ago. You fell asleep."

"Holy shit."

"You're exhausted, Linc. Abby is going to have supper with

Michael and his kids. We're going upstairs, and we can have a shower. I'll make you something to eat and you're going to bed."

"You're coming with me." It wasn't a question.

She smiled softly. "Yes. I will come with you. I have a busy few days ahead of me."

I stood, swinging her up in my arms and heading to the kitchen and the stairway.

"I'm gonna help."

"Can you bake at all?"

"No, but I am an awesome quality control person. Nothing but perfection will leave the kitchen, Sunny. You have my word."

She laid her head on my shoulder. "I would expect nothing less from you."

I dropped a kiss to her head. "Good."

I woke late into the night, Sunny tucked beside me, her head next to mine on my pillow. I watched her slumber, lost to her dreams. She looked peaceful and content, and a part of me hoped I was there with her.

Carefully, I slipped from the bed, making sure she was covered, then headed out to the kitchen, grabbing a drink of water and snagging a handful of the cookies from the jar on the counter. I wandered to the window, staring out on the silent town. For the first time in my life, I felt no anger or bitterness. I felt nothing but the peace of the town at rest.

I glanced at the clock. It was two a.m., but given the fact that we had fallen asleep early in the evening, I knew I wouldn't be going back to sleep anytime soon. My mind was awake and active now.

An idea I had been thinking about was taking hold, and the more I thought about it, the more I liked it.

I had been serious earlier when I told Sunny I would marry her—

and quickly. I was determined to start our life together sooner rather than later.

Logistics was one of the problems we were going to have to address. I knew how she felt about her bakery. The people she cared about here. The simple life a small town allowed her.

At the moment, my world centered around Toronto. I also knew Sunny would suffer terribly there—away from the water and everything familiar, and although I had no desire to move back to Mission Cove, there were compromises we could make. My office was transportable. My business would run no matter where I was.

But I had to be where Sunny was. Of that, there was no question. I had to make that happen.

I grabbed my laptop and opened it, scrolling through my contacts, until I found my favorite architect. I composed a long, detailed email, attaching files I had saved, as well as a sketch I quickly did and took a snapshot of, knowing it would amuse him.

I sat back, rereading the email, and satisfied, I sent it off.

I reached for the last cookie, munching on it, when arms wrapped around my neck.

"Why are you out here?" Sunny's sleepy voice murmured in my ear. "I woke up and you were gone. I didn't like it."

I turned and tugged her to my lap. She was a warm, soft weight on my legs, nestled happily into my chest.

"Sorry, I couldn't sleep. I got a little work done."

"Hmm." Her lips drifted up my neck. "I could have helped you go back to sleep."

I chuckled at her drowsy attempt at seduction. "Is that a fact?"

She tugged my head down, nipping on my earlobe. "I have ways."

"I bet you do." Turning my face, I captured her lips with mine, kissing her. It took my body about three seconds to catch up with Sunny, but my erection kicked up fast and hard.

"Mmm," she whispered. "You taste like ginger."

"And you taste like mint, you little seductress. You planned this."

She peered up at me, shifting on my lap. "I think it worked. Take me back to bed, Linc. I promise you'll sleep well once I'm done with you."

That was an offer I couldn't refuse.

The following Monday, I was busy working on my laptop. Abby was at the house with Sunny and the town librarian, letting her have first choice of the books on the shelves. After my meltdown, it was decided perhaps it was better if I didn't return to the house. I was fine with the idea. I had what I wanted from the interior, and the one thing left on my list was to watch it disappear. In less than two weeks, I'd have my wish. Until then, I was happy to stay away. There was nothing else I wanted to take from it. Or at least I thought so, until Sunny burst in, her arms filled with picture frames and looking strangely excited.

I saved the item I was working on and shut the lid. If Sunny saw the car I was building for her, she would call a full stop to my endeavors, and I was having too much fun making it for her. She loved Abby's SUV so much, I decided to get her one of her own. I was looking forward to seeing her reaction to it. I hoped delight would override her independent streak. Especially the way I planned to present it to her.

I smiled at her flushed cheeks. "What's got you all excited, Sunny-girl?"

"Linc, did you know your mother used to paint watercolors?"

I scratched my head. "No."

"Mrs. Miller was telling me as we looked through the books. She said your mother always loved to paint, even back in school. She says there's one of her paintings in the library."

"Wow. I'll have to go see it." A fragment of a memory floated in my head. "I recall an easel, I think. In the back sun-room. I remember a pencil behind her ear a lot. At least, I always thought it was a pencil. Maybe...it could have been a paintbrush." I indicated the pile of items in her arms. "What are those?"

She laid the pile in front of me. "Your mother's paintings, Linc."

I gaped at her. "What?"

"They were in a box, upstairs in one of the closets."

I picked one up, studying it. Pretty, light, and feminine, it was a good painting. The use of light was wonderful, and I could see how talented she had been. And priceless to me because of who painted it. "Are we sure these are my mother's?" I asked.

"Yes. Look at the bottom. She always signed her pictures the same way. With simply a W. Mrs. Miller said she always used her initial."

I spread out the collection, looking at them. There were six in all. All similar in composition, all signed with a W.

I gripped Sunny's hand. "I remember these. In the hallway. There used to be one over the mantle in the den, but then it was gone. They all disappeared."

"That's the one in the library, Linc. Your mother gave it to them. Mrs. Miller said you could have it back if you wanted."

I gazed at the paintings. Pieces of my mother I didn't even know existed. Small treasures. I swallowed the lump in my throat. "These would have gone when the house did," I murmured. "I never would have known." Another memory hit me. "I remember a pile of canvases. They were piled by the door and then gone the next day. He must have gotten rid of them. But he must have forgotten about these."

"We could try to find them. Advertise. Check out secondhand shops in the local area. Abby is searching the entire house in case we find any more, but she wanted me to come to show you these right away."

I stared at the canvases. "No. I would like to think someone else is enjoying her work." I turned to Sunny, pulling her close. "What a gift you've given me. Even if we don't find any others, these are such amazing things to be able to have." I dropped a kiss to her head. "Thank you."

She beamed up at me. "You're welcome."

"I love you, Sunny-girl."

She wrinkled her nose with a smile. "I know."

24

LINC

The next two weeks proved two things to me.

One—the fact that I thought I couldn't love Sunny more was wrong. The more I got to know *this* Sunny—the calm, sweet, vibrant woman she had become—the harder I fell. Gone were the days of hiding and of fear. I could touch her, kiss her anytime I wanted. Show her my affection. Accept hers. I loved her independent streak, the way she handled herself with her business, and all the people that involved. I was proud to stand beside her on the weekends, making coffee, stealing cookies, gorging on biscuits. I wasn't too proud to clear tables, help take out the trash, or do anything that made her life a little easier.

And I was well rewarded for it.

Which led to my second discovery. Leaving her behind was simply not an option. We had a brief discussion about me returning to Toronto, coming back on weekends. It sounded like a good idea until we decided on our future. I kissed her in the early morning dawn and headed into Toronto, comforted by the fact that I would see her in a few days.

But by three a.m. on the third night of not being able to sleep, I knew I was fucked. Without Sunny beside me, I couldn't rest. And even with Abby in the office, I couldn't concentrate, and neither could Abby. I didn't even wait, driving back in the middle of the night. I left Abby a message, and by the morning, we were both back in Mission Cove, and neither of us planned on leaving for any great length of time.

The apartment over Sunny's was now Abby's. I'd planned to rent a hotel room for the sake of appearance, but Sunny had laughed and called me old-fashioned. She was right. No one cared, and I was happier with her. Abby felt safe in Mission Cove. Carl was back in jail and her mother had disappeared, but knowing Abby was among friends who would watch out for her when I wasn't around gave me a sense of comfort I never thought I would get from the town of Mission Cove. Abby and Michael were growing closer, and we hoped they were able to help each other heal.

Another odd thing happened. As more people discovered who I was, there was no censure, no looks of dislike or distancing. I was surprised at the number of hugs I received, the welcome from people still living here that I used to know. Even odder, not a single person offered condolences on my father's passing. Many of them spoke of my mother, and I was grateful to hear so many wonderful stories. It felt good to know her memory would live on here while my father's terrible legacy died off, a mere whisper of the past. When they discovered the house was being taken down, there was a lot of excitement and curiosity about what would replace it. I kept my mouth shut, waiting for the final drawings to take to the town council on both matters. I wasn't shocked when the mayor dropped in and told me he expected there to be no problem with my proposals. I had sat with him and his wife and laid out my plans, then left, allowing them to talk in private.

They were both smart enough to know what my ideas meant for their little town. The economic implications were staggering. I expected zero pushback. It was a good feeling though, to be able to go forward without using anything but my ideas and plans. I didn't have to drop any veiled threats or use the past. My future was in my hands, and I was in control—nobody else. It felt right.

I sat in the sun out back of the bakery. Sunny had shown me the wide cement wall that ran along the edge of the property. She had a ladder propped against it and often sat with her back against the even higher wall beside it while she did work on her computer and enjoyed the sun, she explained. I had taken advantage of it a few times, using the privacy to make calls and arrangements I didn't want her to know about. It also provided me with an unobstructed view of the house on the hill. I watched as people went in and out. Trucks pulled up, filled, and left. The final purge of my father's things. Luckily, thanks to Sunny, I now had everything of my mother's. It was she who pointed out the heavy copper pots in the back of the cupboards in the kitchen. The delicate china gathering dust in the bottom of the dining room hutch. The crystal I never remembered being used.

"*Your mother would have chosen these things, Linc. Not your father. You should have them. They were part of her.*"

They were all now safe, along with some other items Sunny unearthed. I was grateful she had a better eye than mine to spot them.

Knowing how my father would have raged seeing people traipse through *his* house, *taking* his things—for free—as if they were worthless, gave me a great deal of satisfaction. I didn't try to deny that it pleased me. And the bottom line was many of the items would benefit the community. The dining room table would have a family sit around it and make memories. Children would jump on the beds and run on the carpets. Each family or individual was given a number and a limit, and it appeared to be going well. I bit back my grin. With Abby and Ned in charge, I had no doubt it would remain so.

"Hey." Sunny's head appeared beside me.

"Hi."

She looked worried. "You okay?" She indicated the hill. "Is that upsetting you?"

I patted my legs. "Get up here."

I helped her settle, then wrapped my arms around her. "No, it's very cleansing. I know all those things will be used. Maybe loved. It actually gives me some peace."

She leaned into me, her shoulders relaxing. "Good." She played with my fingers. "What about next week?"

"Sunny, that is going to be a banner day for me."

She peeked up at me. "Are you sure you really want to...blow it up?"

I chuckled. "I wish I could blow it up. Watch it explode and scatter for miles. But sadly, that is illegal and dangerous. When they hit the switch, it will implode—almost sink into itself. I watched a lot of the videos—it's fascinating. A building is there one moment, and when the dust clears, it's a flattened pile of debris they'll truck away." I pressed a kiss to her head. "And I get to push the button."

Her voice was low. "And then what?"

"Hey."

I waited until she turned her head and met my eyes. "Then it's done, Sunny. My past will be exactly where it needs to be—in the past. My father will no longer have any part of my thoughts." I slid a hand under her chin, angling her face up to mine. "I have a whole new life to live—with you. I plan on living the hell out of it. You with me?"

Her answer was to pull my head down and kiss me. A kiss of love, promises, and the future. A kiss of yes.

That was all I needed.

I walked through the house with the foreman. The house had been gutted down to the studs. He explained in great depth about the wires and charges attached to all the exposed beams. How the charge would be relayed and the structure would crumble. I stood in the vast space, knowing it was the last time I would be inside this building. The last time anyone would be. It would be locked down tonight and be gone tomorrow. Ned was beside me, frowning. "How do you know no one sneaks in before you, ah, hit the switch?"

Ed, the foreman, chuckled. "We do a final sweep today, and we have heat signals we check before the last call. The house is guarded all night."

"Makes sense."

I tried not to laugh. Ned still felt this was over the top, but I didn't care. I clapped him on the shoulder. "Thinking of stashing a troublesome client in before the big bang, Ned?"

He eyed me with a frown. "I think your absence would not go unnoticed."

That made me chuckle. Ed did too before turning serious. "We take every precaution. The perimeter, the building, who is allowed on site. Our measurements for the explosives are precise. Our safety record is perfect."

"Good to know," Ned mumbled.

"You should be here for the show." I winked.

"I wouldn't miss it for the world."

Ed turned to answer his radio, and I faced Ned. "Really? I didn't think you supported this."

"When you first told me, no. But I've changed my mind."

"May I ask why?"

"I know better than anyone what your father did to you. What he took from you. I was worried this would feed your hate—make it stronger. But I sense, I *see*, a change in you, Linc. I see the boy I met so long ago with your mother. I think you need to do this to close this chapter. This book. Start a new one." He paused, lifting one eyebrow. "With a pretty girl who makes the best biscuits I've ever tasted. And who has given you back the one thing your father took from you that I feared you would never get back."

"What is that?" I asked quietly.

He put his hand on my shoulder. "The ability to love, Linc. I feared in your quest, you would forget your heart. You would become him. But you didn't. Instead, you found yourself."

"Sunny did that for me."

He met my gaze. He knew my plans, all of them, and he was on board with me.

"Then let's do this."

I t was a gloomy day. The skies overhead dark with rain, the air cooler than it had been. Sunny shivered beside me, and I tucked her closer. "This all feels very ominous," she mumbled.

I chuckled. I personally thought my father was writhing in hell, screaming in rage and shaking his fist at me as he saw what was about to happen.

I hoped the devil gave him a front row seat.

We were far from the house, the hill blocked off and no one allowed to be close. I knew the town was gathered below, watching in anticipation. To the younger generation, it was simply something cool happening—something they would probably never see again in Mission Cove. For others, today had a far more significant meaning.

None more than me.

Anticipation built within me, making my body shake. I hadn't slept all night, up pacing—wanting, needing, this done. I had planned it for so long, and now that the day was here, I wanted it over. I wanted to move on with my life, my plans, and Sunny.

Beside me, Ned and Abby spoke together. Sunny clung to me, her fingers digging into my waist. I knew she was concerned about my emotional reaction when it happened, but I wasn't worried.

I had waited too long for this moment.

Sunny had been in the house with Ed earlier, and I knew the drives were somewhere inside. She came out looking resolved and smiling, so I had slipped my hand around hers and squeezed, silently thanking her. She squeezed back, then I tucked her into my side, needing her close.

Ed approached, his entire crew with him. "All the checks are done, Linc. Cameras set up as you asked. Crew accounted for. No heat sources have suddenly appeared. We're ready."

"Excellent."

"Ear protectors," he yelled, and we all slipped them on our heads. "Come with me."

I held Sunny closer, needing her with me for this moment. We stood behind the huge electronic control unit, and Ed nodded. Horns blew, loudspeakers began the countdown. He flipped open the switch. He lifted one side of my ear covering. "When we hit one, you press this. Hard. Got it?"

I swallowed thickly. "Yes."

Sunny's breath stuttered, and I stepped forward but reached for her hand. "It's fine," I murmured knowing she probably couldn't hear me, but having to say it anyway. I couldn't hear the countdown due to the cans over my ears to protect against the sound of the implosion. I held my finger over the button, the digit hovering in midair, watching as Ed counted down the numbers on his fingers.

At ten, my hand began to shake. By five, I was sweating. Adrenaline pumped through my body, making my head hum. Ed nodded in encouragement, and when the count hit one, I didn't hesitate. I pressed down.

For a second or two, nothing happened. I stared dumbfounded, then it started. Explosions, one after another. The house shook, groaned, fought back, and then with a long, low scream, gave a lengthy shudder and crumbled inward.

Sunny jumped back, startled. I held her tight, watching as plumes of dust shot up as the building settled into the earth. It was exactly as I pictured. Looming one moment, gone the next.

The skies opened, torrents of rain falling, dissipating the dust. It was as if the heavens had decided they, too, wanted no reminder of the house drifting up their way.

That house that had caused me nothing but pain, held a lifetime of tears and sorrow within its walls, was gone.

"Good riddance, old man," I hissed.

I looked down at Sunny. She gazed up at me with love. "Are you okay?" she mouthed.

I bent down and kissed her. "Yeah. Yeah, I am."

"Good."

I pulled off the ear protectors. "Let's go home, Sunny. I need a biscuit."

She pulled my arm close.

"Okay."

25

SUNNY

I looked in the mirror, eyeing my reflection critically. I had bought a new sundress, hoping Linc would like it. It was a soft yellow with bursts of gold, rust, pink, and white scattered around the fabric. It hung from my shoulders with two pretty bows and had a long lace flounce around my knees. I hadn't bought a dress like this in a very long time, but tonight was a special occasion.

Linc was taking me out on a date. A real, honest-to-goodness date. He was even getting ready next door at Abby's so he could "pick me up properly." He had called me yesterday, his voice unusually serious.

"Sunny."

I grinned into the phone, peeking through the door to make sure he was still sitting in the corner of the bakery where I had left him. "Linc," I replied, biting back my amusement—he must need more biscuits. "How lovely of you to call."

"I wanted to hear your voice."

My heart melted. I loved how he talked to me. "Well, now you have."

"I have a question, though. Do you have plans for tomorrow evening?"

Other than getting naked with him as soon as possible, my schedule was pretty clear. We couldn't keep our hands off each other.

"No."

"Excellent. I would like to take you out on a date."

"A date?" I repeated.

"Yes, a date. A real date. If you're willing." I heard his swift intake of air. "I am asking you, Sunny, to go out with me—tomorrow night."

Suddenly I understood. We'd never been able to date openly. Linc was trying to make up for it, and once again, my heart constricted at his sweet gesture.

"I would love to go out with you, Linc."

"Excellent. I will pick you up at six."

"All right. I'll, ah, see you then?"

"Yes." Then he paused. "Wait, Sunny?"

"Yes?"

"I'm out of biscuits."

I burst out laughing. "I'll make sure you get some."

"Great. Love you."

He hung up.

He'd been gone all day, and I heard his steps on the stairwell about an hour ago. His toiletry bag was gone from my tiny bathroom and Abby told me his suit was at her place, so I knew he meant what he said about picking me up.

Linc was different these days. In the month since his father's house was demolished, he had changed. Gone were the shadows that constantly lurked in his eyes. The suspicious glint whenever anyone would approach him. It was as if he'd let his hate implode with the house, dispersing it into the air. He smiled more. Laughed loudly. I had forgotten how loud his laugh was. It boomed out and filled whatever room he was in. It happened frequently now. He no longer spoke of his father. It was as if he had never existed. As memories—good ones—surfaced of his mother, he talked to me about them.

People in town talked to him about her, sharing their memories and he loved it, soaking up their words like a sponge. I hung his mother's artwork in the apartment, and I often saw him staring at the pictures with a tender look. We visited the library, and he stood in front of the large framed watercolor.

"*I remember this now,*" *he said softly.* "*She hung it in the den. One day after a fight, it was gone.*"

I squeezed his arm. "*It was here and safe.*"

"*And here it stays,*" *he said firmly, tracing the small plaque under the painting.* "*I like knowing people see her talent.*"

He slept peacefully as long as he was beside me. We had tried to find a balance between Toronto and here, but the third night he was gone, he strode into my apartment in the early hours of dawn. I was sitting at the table, sipping water, unable to sleep. I heard him coming up the stairs, and our eyes met as he opened the door, dropping two large bags beside him.

"*No more, Sunny. I can't sleep without you anymore.*" Then he held out his arms, and I ran straight into them. They closed around me tightly, offering me safety, love, and comfort. He carried me to the bedroom, and we collapsed on the bed, both too exhausted to do anything but pull up the duvet and sleep. He didn't even stir when I slipped out to go to the bakery. It was as if his body knew I'd be close, so I let him rest.

He came and went as needed from Toronto but returned every night—even if it was well past midnight. He used the table in my place as a desk. He had a hundred and one projects on the go, it seemed. He was constantly on his phone, jumping into his car to head to a meeting, carrying mysterious plans rolled into cardboard containers. I had no idea what all he did, but it didn't matter. He was here with me and that was all I cared about.

And tonight was our date.

I fluffed my hair and touched up my lip balm. There was no point in applying lipstick. Linc kissed it off all the time, so I gave up. I had no idea why I was so nervous, but I was. It was Linc, for heaven's sake. We basically lived together now, sharing this cramped apartment. I was waiting for him to decide we needed more space—it made sense, but I was allowing him to make the decision. I knew that was one of our major hurdles to overcome. I was certain of our future —just not where our future resided.

A firm knock on my door made me grin. He was serious about the entire date thing. I hoped he didn't plan on playing hard to get at the end of the night. I would have to make sure I weakened his defenses.

Before I opened the door, I tugged the bows a little looser on my shoulders, letting the dress drift lower on my breasts. Linc had a thing for them. He always had.

I opened the door, my breath catching in my throat. Linc stood, tall and proud, dressed in a navy suit, fitted to his wide shoulders and trim waist perfectly. His hair had been brushed until it gleamed, and his chin held the day's stubble—just the way I liked it. His blue eyes sparkled as he looked at me, his gaze lingering, as I knew it would, on my breasts. He held a bunch of wild flowers in his hand that he held out.

"Sunny," he murmured. "You take my words away. I can't even think properly."

"You clean up pretty well yourself." I took the flowers with a smile. "Thank you."

"I picked them for you."

He followed me into the kitchen as I put them in a vase. I glanced over my shoulder. "Am I dressed okay? You never said where we were going."

He rested his hand on the small of my back, bending over my shoulder so his lips were close to my ear. "You're perfect. Absolutely perfect." He kissed my neck, making me shiver. Before I could turn and get a real kiss, he stepped away. "You may need a shawl or something for later."

I picked up my purse and shawl. "Got it."

He plucked my purse from my hand. "You won't need that."

I sighed. "It has my lip gloss in it."

With a smirk, he opened the purse, dug out the gloss and the mints I had inside and slipped them into his pocket. "Anything else?"

"No. I'm ready."

He caught me off guard as he suddenly yanked me tight and kissed me. Hard. Wet. Deep. His tongue possessed my mouth, claiming me, and stealing my breath. Then with a wide grin, he stepped back, casually wiping my gloss off his lips with a handkerchief from his pocket. "Now you are. I like your lips ready for me, Sunny. I prefer the taste of them to this fruity stuff."

He opened the door. "Shall we?"

I walked past him, shaking my head. He chuckled and followed me.

Outside, I was surprised when we didn't head to the car. Instead, he tucked my arm through his. "I want to show you something."

"Okay."

We crossed the street, and he used a key to open one of the doors. I followed him up the stairs, looking around in surprise when we entered a spacious, furnished room. A large desk sat in front of the window. In the middle of the room was a sizable conference table, monitors and notepads already on it. Across the room, another, smaller desk was set up—this one more feminine. A thick area rug was under my feet. A few pictures hung on the walls—one I recognized. It was a copy of the painting in the library. I turned, confused.

"They let me borrow it. I had it copied, reframed, and returned to them. I wanted a copy for myself. I wanted part of my mother here."

"So, this is yours?"

He nodded. "The second office of Webber Holdings Inc." He winked. "Your dining room was getting a bit tight, Sunny." He indicated the monitors. "I can hold meetings with anyone, anywhere, with the click of my mouse. I've leased out the office space in Toronto, keeping one small spot for when I need to go in. I can do everything I need to do from here, but I have a few clients that demand face-to-face."

"Linc, I don't know what to say. I know you never wanted to come back here..." My voice trailed off.

"Things have changed. I've changed. Besides—" he dropped a kiss on the end of my nose "—I don't have this view in Toronto."

I peeked out the window and laughed. He looked right down into the bakery. He stepped behind me, a warm tower of strength at my back.

"I can look across and see you anytime I want. Walk a few steps and touch you. Get the best coffee and biscuits all day long. Any client who comes here will get served items from your bakery. I guarantee they'll be stopping there before they leave town. It's a win-win for both of us, Sunny."

I didn't know what to say. Turning, I stared up at him, tears forming in my eyes. "Thank you."

He wiped away the tears that spilled over my cheeks. He bent and kissed my face, whisper-soft kisses that left a trail of heat everywhere they touched. "This is only the beginning, Sunny."

He pulled back and cupped my face. "Are you ready?"

"Ready."

We pulled up to a set of gates about six minutes outside of town. I looked around in confusion. It looked like the entrance to Gerry and Cindy's place, but it wasn't. It couldn't be. The gates were wrought iron and supported by tall brick walls. Linc punched in a code, and the gates opened smoothly. There was a smooth concrete driveway that branched into two directions. We headed to the left. I looked over my shoulder, certain the right driveway would lead to the house we had visited last month.

But why had Gerry installed gates and a new driveway? And where were we going? I glanced over at Linc, but his eyes were on the road, although a wide smile played on his lips.

A few seconds later, I gasped as we rounded a gentle bend in the road and I saw what the trees had been hiding. The other part of the old camp—or what used to be the old camp. The woods had been shaped and trimmed, leaving a wide-open area. The ground leveled. There was a clear view of the water, which was stunning. The sun was still high in the sky, shining on the water, causing hundreds of shimmering rays to bounce off the lazy rolling waves that broke along the sandy beach. I racked my brain, trying to remember if the beach had always been that sandy or if it, too, was new and spruced up.

We parked beside a catering truck that was set up by a canopied tent. Beside it was a pretty SUV. I admired the rich copper color as Linc got out and opened my door, offering his hand. I let him pull me from the car, gazing around in wonder. He led me around the tent, and we stood looking over the water.

"It's so lovely."

"It is."

I looked over, blushing when I realized he wasn't looking at the water, but at me. I swung my gaze back to the vista, getting excited when I realized exactly where we were.

"Oh, Linc, look—those are our trees!"

"I know. Our names are still there."

"You'll have to show me."

"Later," he promised.

I waved at the tent. "You did this?"

He lifted my hand to his mouth and kissed my knuckles. "I have a lot of plans I want to show you, Sunny. Lots of things I want to discuss I hope you'll be a part of."

"Including your plans for this area?"

He smiled. "I finally figured out what belonged here. Gerry and Cindy are onboard with it—in fact, they're quite excited." He tugged on my hand. "Come and have dinner, and later I'll tell you all about it."

Inside the tent was a table, set for two, complete with flowers and candles. A small serving area was off to the side. An ice bucket holding champagne was waiting. A bottle of my favorite red wine open on the table. Tiny twinkle lights were strung from the ceiling of the tent, soft music played, and the entire tent felt dreamy and special. At the back of the tent was a longer table. It held two large white boxes covering some secrets I assumed Linc would share after dinner. He had thought of everything to make this romantic and cozy.

In one corner were thick blankets piled with pillows. I met Linc's eyes, mischief dancing in them, making them sparkle under the lights.

"Pretty sure of yourself, Mr. Webber."

He wrapped a hand around my waist, pulling me close. "Pretty sure of *you*, Sunny. Don't think I didn't notice the girls on display earlier." He brushed a kiss to my ear. "Your fucking tits always turn me on. You know that, you naughty girl."

I tried to wrap my arms around his neck, but he stepped back with a shake of his head. "I have tonight all planned, Sunny. Your overwhelming lust for me is not waylaying them."

Then he stepped to the table and pulled out my chair. I didn't fail to notice the bulge in his dress pants or the low groan he made as I pressed myself against him before sitting. He sat across from me, pouring my wine. He lifted an eyebrow in warning, his eyes narrowing. "Behave."

I picked up my wine and sat forward, my dress dipping a little lower. I smiled innocently at him. "Of course."

LINC

She was trying to kill me. I had the entire evening planned out. Showing her my new office, bringing her here, unveiling my plans for the future—our future. I had visions of romance and laughter. Gentle teasing and great joy. And celebration.

I hadn't banked on that dress.

That pretty, lacy garment of torture. The colors swirled around her as she moved, the light, diaphanous fabric hinting at the curves it covered. It would have been fine except for those goddamn bows. Tempting little curls of fabric that teased, begging to be pulled open —with my teeth. My body ached knowing that, with one tug, the dress would fall from Sunny's body and she would be naked and stunning. Her full, perfect breasts on display for my eyes only. My cock was hard, pressing against my zipper, hoping I would give in and adjust my plans. Use the blanket and pillows now. Not later.

Breasts—particularly Sunny's breasts—had always been my downfall. When I was a teenager, they were endlessly on my mind, playing out in every fantasy I ever had. As an adult, I was still fascinated by them, but none affected me the way Sunny's did. Seeing her in a baggy shirt, one shoulder bare, knowing there was nothing between the fabric and her breasts, stirred something within me. When she was dressed and busy in the bakery, I thought of the pretty scraps of lace cupping her underneath her apron, wishing it were my hands instead.

And tonight. Nothing but that dress. Two bows and Sunny's knowing smile as she leaned forward, her full breasts—her amazing, round, full *tits*—swaying as she did, pressing against the pretty garment, pulling the front down little lower, teasing me without regard.

I shook my head. I was a full-grown adult. A savvy businessman who made millions with a single deal, commanded boardrooms, planned out this evening in meticulous detail.

I would not be sidetracked by a pair of breasts. No matter how spectacular they were.

I narrowed my eyes at her in warning. "Behave."

She bowed her head, leaning back, pretending to be innocent. Little minx knew exactly what she was doing to me.

I tapped out a message on my phone, and a waiter appeared. He made quick work of serving our dinner, then leaving. Luckily, Sunny was hungry, so she settled in to eat her meal.

"This smells amazing."

I lifted my glass in a toast. "To us," I stated simply.

She touched her glass to mine. "Us," she repeated.

We relaxed and ate, the filet cooked exactly the way she liked it, her favorite vegetable, asparagus with béarnaise sauce, still crisp and fresh. She exclaimed over the tiny potatoes, the ragout of root vegetables I thought she would enjoy, and finished everything on her plate. I loved knowing I had fed her, taken care of her needs. I planned to take care of every single one—tonight and for the rest of her life.

The waiter reappeared, removed our plates, and slid a tray on the table. "Dessert and coffee."

"Thank you."

He left, and a few moments later I heard the van leave. They would return much later to clear away the last of the dishes and take down the tent. They had been well paid to handle every detail.

"I think I'm too full." Sunny frowned.

I waved away her worries. "No problem. We can have it later." I felt the stirrings of anxiety building in my stomach as I stood. "I have some things to show you."

She let me take her hand, guiding her to the back of the tent. I switched on a light they'd set up and indicated the smaller of the two white boxes. "Open this one, Sunny."

She lifted the cover, gasping at what she saw. "Linc, is this..."

"Yes. The concept model for the Amanda Webber Community Center. We break ground next week."

She dropped the lid to the side, throwing her arms around my neck. She hugged me close. "Oh, Linc, this is wonderful! Show me."

I explained the outlay. "The main floor has an open area where kids can hang out. A kitchen area where kids can be taught how to cook or, if needed, be given a meal. Learning rooms—free tutoring, computers, that sort of thing. I added an art studio. There will be counseling available. Someone to talk to if they need it."

She squeezed my arm. "Linc, love, that is amazing."

I blinked. Sunny had never called me a pet name before. I rather liked it. I squeezed her hand back. "Upstairs is all library. It will hold three times the number of books the one in town does. The place is open to everyone, Sunny. Anyone who wants to walk in the doors is welcome."

I paused, looking at the concept model. "I was going to add a pool, but I was advised against it. So I'm donating the funds to enlarge and upgrade the one in town, and I'm adding a second one at The Sunny Place."

"Wow. So you, ah, have enough..." She let the words trail off.

"Remember I told you I tripled the estate?"

"Yes."

"I'm good at finance, Sunny. I keep his money away from mine. I never touch it. It will pay for this and fund it for decades the way it is structured."

"Wow."

I tilted up her face and kissed her. "Yeah. Wow."

She indicated the table. "I am so excited for the town, and for you. Thank you for sharing it with me."

I ran my finger down her cheek, my heart racing in my chest. "I have more to share."

She bit her lip, picking up on my nervousness. "What next, I wonder?" she quipped, but the tremor in her voice gave her away.

I walked behind the table, placing my hands on the lid. "The future," I said. "Our future."

26

SUNNY

Something in Linc's posture made me tense. An underlying hint of nerves in his usually calm voice set me on edge. But I wasn't prepared for what he revealed as he lifted the cover on the larger of the two boxes. I was prepared for a concept model. But not this.

It was a house. Even as a model, it took my breath away. Shaped like a U with a courtyard in front and a large secluded backyard, it was spectacular.

For a moment, I was stunned and silent. I couldn't move, Linc's words playing and replaying in my head.

"Our future."

I blinked. This was the house he wanted to build for us? A home for us to share? I tore my gaze from the model to meet his eyes. His warm, filled-with-love eyes that assured me what I was thinking was exactly what he meant.

"For us?" I questioned.

He set down the lid and leaned on the table. "For you," he replied.

I blinked at the moisture gathering in my eyes. "I-I don't know what to say."

"Let me show it to you."

"Okay," I sniffed.

He hurried around the table and pulled me into his arms. "If you hate it, I can change it all. I promise."

I shook my head. "I already love it. I'm just overwhelmed and confused."

He winked. "Let me help."

He bent over and carefully lifted off the roof. Unlike the community center, this model was fully developed inside.

"This side of the house—" he indicated the left "—is bedrooms. Our master suite, and two others. The right side has two more guest rooms or extra kid rooms and a home office for me. The center of the house has a kitchen on one side, and a huge family slash dining room on the other."

"All one floor?"

"Yes. All the front-facing rooms will have huge windows to let in the view and the light. In the front courtyard, there will be a deck with lots of seating. The backyard off the kitchen will be fenced in and private with lots of room for the kids to run around. Sliding doors that open fully on the back and front to let the breeze blow through. A pool and maybe a hot tub out back."

"Kids?"

He grinned. "Until we have them, I'll chase you. Naked."

I giggled at the image.

"There's a large laundry room on our side, and a smaller one on the other side for the guests." He winked. "They can do their own damn laundry."

"Or as the kids get older and move across the house, they can do it themselves," I stated wryly, getting into the spirit.

"Yes," he laughed. "Perfect."

"Where will you build it?"

He touched my nose. "Right here."

I gasped. "Here?"

He smiled, stroking my hair, letting a curl wrap around his finger.

"This place holds the memories that got me through those years away from you, Sunny. It was the happiest I had ever been after my mom died. It's special to me. It was the summer of us—and now I want it to be our future."

"You'd really build here?"

"Right here. This would be your view for the next several decades. Favorite trees and all. The house has been designed around them."

"You-you'd be okay with that? So close to Mission Cove?"

He sighed. "I don't mind being close to Mission Cove, I simply don't want to live *in it*. I figured it was a compromise. I wouldn't be right there all the time, but it's only a six-or seven-minute drive to the bakery for you."

"You don't mind it, then? That I still would want to work?"

He gaped at me. "I don't want to own you, Sunny. I want you to be your own person. I know what the bakery means to you. I support you one hundred percent. But one day, if you decided not to work, to sell the bakery or keep it and let someone else run it, great. Whatever you want to do. As long as you do it with me beside you."

I looked at the beautiful gift he was offering me. A life with him in this gorgeous house he had helped design. I could see how much care had gone into the details and how much this meant to him.

A memory stirred. My younger self, staring at Linc, knowing deep in my heart that we were meant to be. That the boy I loved would be the man I grew old with. I had thought that dream was gone, but it was real and it was right in front of me. I wasn't letting it go this time.

"I love it," I told him. "I don't want to change a thing about it."

His eyes lit up. "Yeah?"

I nodded. "Yeah."

He hesitated. "I have two more things to show you, Sunny."

"I'm not sure how much more I can take."

"These are much smaller. But important." He tapped another building adjacent to the house. "This is the garage." He lifted off the roof, revealing two small model cars. He lifted out the charcoal-gray Mercedes. "This is mine."

I chuckled, the sound dying in my throat as I saw the vehicle left in the model garage. A bright copper-colored SUV. One I had seen very recently—right outside this tent. He lifted it up, holding it out to me on his palm. "Yours."

I blinked. Looked at him. Turned my head in the direction I knew the SUV was sitting right now. Blinked again.

Was he serious?

He took my hand, leading me outside. Under the moonlight, the vehicle glowed, the sparkle in the paint bright. Linc opened the door, and I slid behind the wheel, shocked into silence. I ran my hand along the leather of the steering wheel. Touched the smooth dashboard. I had never owned a new car before. I drove Uncle Pete's car in Nova Scotia and all the way here. When it died, I went back to walking. The van I utilized for the bakery was old and used, but it was all I could afford.

This one was so pretty.

"Put your foot on the brake and press the start button."

The engine roared to life, the dashboard lighting up, buttons and knobs appearing in the dimness of the interior.

"My own little truck."

Linc chuckled. "SUV."

"Linc," I whispered. "I can't take this all in. I don't know what to say."

"It's all yours, Sunny. All of it. The house, the SUV, my heart, and my love. The only word you have to say is yes."

I glanced toward him, wondering why his voice had changed. As if he had moved.

He had.

He was on one knee, holding up a tiny square package. "One last box to open tonight," he said. "One last surprise."

Tears sprang to my eyes. He warned me he'd be doing this big. I'd had no idea how big.

"Marry me, Sunny. Live with me here and make a lifetime of memories with me. Give me what I want more than anything in the world. The right to call you mine. Please."

There was no hesitation. Without a thought, I flung myself from the little truck and into his arms. We fell back onto the damp earth, landing with a dull thump as I knocked the breath out of him, pressing hundreds of kisses to his face.

"Yes. Yes, yes, yes, yes, Linc."

He laughed into the open sky, wrapping his arms around me. He let me prattle on, probably because he was too shocked, or perhaps winded, to move.

Then he kissed me.

LINC

I lay on the soft, damp earth, my arms around Sunny. She babbled, laughing and crying at the same time over her pretty little truck, getting married, the house. All of it. I finally caught my breath, not having anticipated the lunge, and lifted her still-talking-mouth to mine and kissed her.

That shut her up.

I managed to get to my feet, still holding her, our mouths locked together. Blindly, I reached inside the vehicle and pressed the ignition, shutting off the SUV. I strode to the tent, setting her on her feet, and pulled away. She growled in frustration, reaching out for me, but I grabbed her hands, kissing them. "No, Sunny." I shook my head in amusement. "You haven't even looked at your ring."

"Oh. I love it. And I said yes, so back to kissing, please." She rose up on her toes, looking hopeful.

I chuckled, gently eased her back to her feet, and took the box from her hand. Only my Sunny wouldn't give a fig about the ring in the box. Most women wouldn't even agree to getting married until they checked out the stone. I was pretty damn certain she was going to be pleased. I opened the lid and let her see the ring.

Her eyes widened as she stared at the cushion cut diamond, surrounded by two rows of tinier diamonds set in platinum. It twinkled and flashed white under the lights, reflecting all around the tent in its brilliance. Her hand flew to her mouth, tapping her lip in worry. "I can't wear that in the bakery."

"Not while you're baking, no. But you can the rest of the time." I pulled the ring from its cushion and took her hand. "May I?"

She nodded in silence, and I slipped on the ring, kissing her hand when I was done. "Perfect."

She twisted her hand side to side, studying it. "It's so beautiful."

"So are you."

She bit her lip in worry.

"I have something that will make you feel better." From my pocket, I drew a set of thick platinum bands. Hers was so tiny it nestled within mine until I lifted it away. I liked the fact that my ring encircled hers. The way my love would encircle her from now on. "I want to see this with your ring, Sunny. I want you to promise once I put it on your finger, you'll never take it off. I know you have to remove the diamond for work, but not this one. Promise me."

"I promise."

"And I want to see it on your finger, soon."

She swallowed. "How soon?"

"I spoke with Hayley and Emily. They're both good to fly in next week."

"Next week?" she squeaked.

"The company that made our dinner is prepared to do it all over again for us—except on a slightly larger scale."

"How many?"

I shrugged. "That's up to you, Sunny. I only need you to be there. Gerry and Cindy, of course. Abby, Ned, and their plus ones. Whoever you want. The point is, if you're willing, then we can be married fast." I grinned at her. "I was patient and waited a month so this could all be in place. My patience is gone. I want to marry you."

"Here?"

"Yes. A larger tent, some tables. We can get married under your trees. I'll carve our names and dates in again."

She studied me, a wide smile breaking out on her face. "I don't know what to do with you, Lincoln Webber."

"I guess you'd better marry me, then."

Her smile became wider.

"Yes."

I lifted her into my arms, swinging her around. I covered her mouth with mine, kissing her with everything in me. Love and relief. Gratitude that she had made my life brighter in our youth, and that she would be there beside me until I left this world.

I vowed to do everything in my power to make her happy. To let her know every single day how important she was to me.

We swam in the sensation of our kisses, the air morphing from celebration to something else. Something far less civilized, and far more profound.

I slid my hands up her arms, my fingers lingering on those flirty little bows. I cupped her neck, continuing to kiss her as my fingers reached, tugging at the sexy ribbons. Laughing, Sunny pulled away, walking backward until she was in the corner. She winked and pulled sharply on a bow. It opened, her dress slipping down her soft skin, her breast beginning to peek out at me.

"You want to do the other?"

"No," I replied, my voice hoarse. "I'm enjoying the view."

Her gaze traveled to my crotch. My erection strained against the material. She grinned as I shrugged off my jacket, letting it fall to the floor.

"Why do I see another walk of shame coming up?" she asked, teasing the second bow.

"No shame," I disagreed. "I'm going to make love to my fiancée

until she screams my name. I'm going to be plenty proud of that fact."
I unfastened my trousers, pushing them off my legs.

"Your shirt," she insisted.

I tugged it over my head and stood before her, my chest heaving in anticipation. She tilted her head and gave a tug.

That dress, that damn sexy, teasing slip of a dress, dropped to the ground, leaving Sunny bare to my eyes except for the tiny wisp of lace between her legs.

That was going to be easily taken care of, and I didn't plan on it being there very long.

She opened her arms, and I went willingly.

———

Once she was in my embrace, the hot roar of lust dissipated, and all I wanted was to do exactly what I said—make love to her. She was mine—now and forever. Nothing would separate us again.

I wouldn't allow it.

We sank into the thick blankets and pillows I had brought here earlier, thinking we would cuddle on them after celebrating.

Instead, I lost myself to the moment. To her softness. I whispered words of love, of forever, of adoration into her ear. I kissed her as if we hadn't kissed for eons. I worshiped every inch of her, using my hands, my mouth, and my words to keep her lost with me.

She pulled on my shoulders, her voice pleading. "Linc, please. Oh please, my love."

I want her to call me that for the rest of my life. I settled between her thighs, slipping inside her heat, groaning.

"Sunny," I vowed. "I have you. I will always have you."

We moved together slowly, nothing fast or frenzied. We savored the moment, the touches, the feelings. Our bodies never separated. I rolled into her, meeting her movements in perfect synchronization. Our lips fused, our oxygen shared, neither of us needing anything more. Her hair tumbled down her back, and I fisted the soft waves, clutching at her. She buried her fingers in my hair, tugging at the strands. I felt the cold metal of her ring on my skin as I moved within her. Our eyes were open, our hearts and souls sharing the depth of the moment and the love we were finally able to live.

My climax hit me like a long, lazy wave. I increased my grip on Sunny. "Baby, come with me. Come with me," I begged as I fell. She tightened around me, riding out her own pleasure as we lived the moment. I collapsed in her arms, tugging the blanket around us, not wanting her chilled.

We lay in silence, listening to the sound of the water lapping at the shore. The night was dark, the only glow from the twinkling lights at the ceiling.

"We can listen to this every night," Sunny whispered. "Us and the sound of the waves."

"Yes."

"We'll build a life here, Linc."

I held her tighter. "Yes."

Her heart rate slowed, and my thundering pulse became steady. I raised myself up on my elbow, looking down at her. Her hair was a mess, a bright swath of color on the dark pillows. Her lips were swollen, her neck scratched. She looked thoroughly loved—and satisfied.

I brushed my mouth across hers. "You want to head back?"

"No, I'm not ready."

"Okay. Dessert and champagne?"

"That sounds decadent."

"I promise you lots of decadence, Sunny."

I pushed up to my feet, looming over her. She waggled her eyebrows playfully. "Does that include lots of this?"

I pulled her to her feet, encasing her in my arms. "Yes."

"I'll take it."

We dressed, and I helped her tie those silly, tempting little bows.

I draped my coat around her shoulders since the air was becoming chillier.

I lifted the cover on the crème brûlées—another one of her favorites. She clapped her hands when I popped the cork, and we clinked glasses, sipping the cold, bubbly liquid.

"Can we come back? While the house is being built?"

"Anytime."

"How long will it take?"

I grinned at her with a wink. "The company I hired promised double crews. A lot of it is done off site and brought here. It will be ready by Christmas."

"Really?"

"Money talks, and this time, I'm using it for personal reasons. I want to share our first Christmas together in our new home. The work they do is amazing—their technology top-notch. They're also doing the community center. I'm their number one customer right now."

"Wow."

"Until then, you can come back anytime." I winked at her. "You can drive your new SUV."

"I love my little truck."

I gave up. She could call it anything she wanted.

Silence fell, her eyelids drooped, and I stood. "Let me take you home, baby."

She let me pull her from the chair. "My trees," she insisted. "You said you'd show me my trees."

I didn't argue. Using the light on my phone, we walked across the dirt and ducked under the long branches.

I aimed the light toward the bottom. Dirty and worn, it was still there. I pointed out her name and the year I had carved it in. Then I showed her the same on the other tree, my name and date still embedded in the trunk.

"When we get married, I'll add our last name on both and a new date." I stood and brushed off my pants.

She slipped her arm around my waist. "Who knew that summer, that summer of us, would become—this."

I traced her mouth with my finger. "What is *this*, Sunny?"

"A lifetime of love."

I had to kiss her.

She was right.

EPILOGUE

LINC

Pearson Airport, as usual, was crowded. I waited by the glass doors, cart at the ready for Emily and Hayley's plane to land. I'd volunteered to pick them up. It would give us some time to catch up with one another, and I knew Sunny already had a lot on her plate. She was in Mission Cove, preparing for their arrival, working at the bakery, and overseeing the details of our wedding.

I grinned to myself thinking the words.

Our wedding.

In less than seventy-two hours, Sunny would be my wife. My body hummed in anticipation. Sunny Webber. Lincoln and Sunny Webber.

I chuckled out loud. My mind was channeling a teenage girl it seemed, writing our names with a flourish on a small notepad.

Shouts of my name drew my attention, and I glanced to the left just as two bodies collided with mine. I hugged the two women close, smiling at their enthusiasm. When Sunny had told them I was back, they had been skeptical and cautious. We had spoken several times since that first call, and I enjoyed their funny texts, feeling as if they were including me in their lives now. When I called to tell them I wanted to marry their sister, they had been enthusiastic. When Sunny informed them we were moving ahead with our plans, the squeals had been loud coming through the speaker of my phone.

I stepped back, looking at Sunny's sisters. The last time I had seen them in person, they were still kids, and now they were all grown up. FaceTime wasn't the same as seeing them in front of me. Emily was twenty-two, and Hayley was twenty. They were both small like Sunny, had the same dark eyes, but Hayley's hair was more auburn and curlier, while Emily's long, straight hair was brown. They were pretty, excited, and as happy to see me as I was to see them.

We got their luggage, both of them chatting away as we headed to the car.

"We've never flown first-class before," Hayley gushed. "What fun!"

Emily was more subdued, but her eyes danced as she nudged me with her elbow. "It was. Thanks, Linc."

"Stick with me, kid."

We got to the car, and I loaded in the luggage and we headed to Mission Cove.

"Is Sunny okay?" Emily asked.

"She's good. We're keeping things pretty simple. Vows, dinner, some nice music. Only very close friends and family."

"Why a Tuesday evening? Why not the weekend?"

I chuckled. "The bakery is busy on the weekends. Tuesday and Wednesday are the quiet days. We get married Tuesday, I get to take her away overnight, and she plans on being back in the bakery Thursday in time to prepare for the weekend rush."

Hayley glanced up, shocked, from her phone. I met her eyes in the rearview mirror. "No honeymoon?"

"In the fall."

"Why?"

"Because I know how crazy the bakery is right now, and I don't want her stressed out. All I care about is marrying her. I don't care if

I'm standing beside her on Saturday morning making coffee for customers or if we're staring at some ruins in England. As long as she's my wife and with me, I'm good."

"You make the coffee?"

"I make damn good coffee. I've even got those leaf things down pat."

Hayley shook her head, going back to her phone. Emily stared at me. "You're a good guy, Linc."

I squeezed her hand. "Thanks."

I paced the floor, anxious and uptight. Abby walked into the room, and I paused. "Wow."

She laughed, patting her hair. "I know. I'm rocking it."

Abby and Gerry were my attendants. Abby insisted on wearing a tuxedo, and she was, indeed, rocking it. Her hair was swept up, the pink streak bright against the blond. Her blouse was a pale pink, and her cummerbund and bow tie matched her hair. She was quite adorable.

Gerry and I were in more traditional colors, the cummerbund and ties in a soft green that Sunny had picked out. Our tuxes were all in a dove gray, keeping to the light colors Sunny preferred.

Gerry looked at his phone and smiled. "The girls are good. Your bride is quite anxious for this to start."

Sunny and her sisters were at her apartment, Cindy with them, making sure all was on schedule, and the limo would pick them up and bring them here. Sunny would wait in the small tent I had installed for her, and we would meet at the pretty trellis set up between our trees. Gerry offered Abby and me the use of his house so Sunny didn't have to worry I would see her beforehand.

Our gathering was small—fewer than twenty people, but it was what we wanted. Most of the town knew we were getting married

THE SUMMER OF US

and offered up congratulations and even dropped off small gifts at the bakery but allowed us our privacy.

Once we said our vows, we would have pictures taken, return to the enclosed tent for dinner, and after, there would be dancing. I didn't plan on staying around long once the dancing started. Abby would make sure the party continued without us. I was going to whisk Sunny away. I had a penthouse suite waiting in Toronto, and I didn't plan on leaving it until we returned to Mission Cove.

But I needed to make her my wife first.

I hadn't seen her since yesterday. She insisted it was romantic and would add to our wedding night. As it was, I hadn't been able to do much more than sneak in a kiss or two since her sisters arrived. They were staying in her apartment, so I went back next door to Abby's. Sunny and I barely had a moment alone and I was slowly going crazy. When she reminded me of the tradition yesterday morning when I went to get my coffee, I wasn't pleased. It seemed silly since we'd basically lived together for weeks, but the pleading look on her face forced me to smile and agree.

I kissed her and returned to my office. Abby worked for a while, then announced she was going back to the bakery. I tried not to be jealous of the fact that Abby still got to see her, but I failed. Sulking, I worked for a while, not looking up when the door opened.

"Forget something, Abby?" I asked.

"Not really."

I snapped up my head at the sound of Sunny's voice. "Aren't we breaking tradition?" I asked, then kicked myself for bringing it up.

"You looked so sad when you left, and I realized you had forgotten when we talked about it a few days before."

I sighed. "I was probably so busy trying to get you somewhere alone so I could kiss you, I would have agreed to anything."

"You have me alone now."

I held out my hand. "Get over here."

She placed a bag on my desk, and I didn't have to ask what was

*inside. It would be biscuits and jam to drown my sorrows in after she
left.*

But for now, she was here, sliding on my lap, smiling at me.

I took full advantage.

I grinned at the memory, then glanced at my watch. "We should
head down, right? The photographer wants some pictures, and I need
to be out of the way before Sunny arrives."

Gerry chuckled. "Anxious, kid?"

"You have no idea."

He smirked. "I think I do." He clapped me on the shoulder. "You
deserve this. You really do. Now let's go get some pictures taken and
get this show on the road."

"Hell yes."

<hr />

The sun was still bright, shining on the rippling water behind
me. A light breeze blew, lifting the long tendrils of the weeping
willows I stood between as I waited for Sunny. Beside me stood Abby
and Gerry. Across the flower-strewn aisle were Emily and Hayley,
both dressed in soft green. Cindy sat in the seat of honor—adoptive
mother of the groom and bride. She dabbed at her eyes constantly,
blinking even harder when I winked at her.

My anxiety was gone. All I felt was the rightness of this
moment. Knowing Sunny was close, and soon, we would say the
words and she would be mine—to have and hold for as long as we
lived.

My breath caught as she appeared, walking toward me. She
didn't rush, and I took a moment to drink her in. Her beautiful hair
was swept up, tendrils framing her face and brushing her neck. Her
dress was simple—something she'd bought on a day trip into Toronto.
Ivory, lacy, and delicate. It floated around her like a feather, and as
she grew closer, I had to smile.

There were bows at her shoulders, holding up scallops of lacy froth on her arms. Tiny, elegant bows that beckoned and teased. Exactly what she had planned.

Little minx.

I met her dark gaze, the love and happiness shining in her eyes for all to see. Unable to stop myself, I stepped forward, meeting her partway down the aisle.

She beamed as I held out my hand. "Walk with me, Sunny?"

Her grip was tight. "Always."

I tucked her hand over my arm, and we finished the walk together.

The perfect start to our life together.

A FEW MONTHS LATER

I woke, my hand instantly reaching out for Sunny. Even after being together and married for months, my first reaction in the morning was to make sure she was real.

This morning, the bed was empty, although the sheets were still warm. I sat up, looking at the clock in the unfamiliar room. It was barely past five, dawn breaking outside the windows.

Sunny stood on the small balcony of our honeymoon suite, staring at the view. I had no idea why she was awake. We arrived yesterday in England and spent the day touring to ward off jet lag. Then as tradition, I spent most of the night making love to her since it was technically the first night of our honeymoon, and that was how it should be.

She should be exhausted and curled up beside me, not outside looking at the view.

Still, I took a moment to appreciate the beautiful view of my own. Wrapped in a sheet, her profile illuminated by the rising sun, she was stunning. Her hair was bright and burnished in the morning light, her creamy skin glowing. My morning wood hardened even more at the sight before me. She grew exponentially more lovely to me every day that passed. I fell more in love with my wife with each new discovery of her sweet nature. Her caring ways, her gentleness, her teasing. She taught me to find joy in the simplest of things; she gave me the gift of peace—something I had never experienced until now.

And she was, in my opinion, too far away from me at the moment.

I slid from the bed, silently walking up behind her. I wrapped my arms around her, drawing her back to my chest. I dropped my head to her neck, scattering small kisses on her skin.

She nestled into me, fitting against me perfectly. "Hi."

"What are you doing out here?"

"Just looking. Watching the city come to life." She tilted up her head. "There is so much I want to do and see!"

"And you'll get to see and do it all. I promise."

She sighed. "I know."

"Come back to bed," I murmured in her ear, flicking my tongue over the sensitive lobe.

"In a minute. I want to watch the sun rise over the Thames."

"Fine." I rolled my hips into her. "Then I'll show you something else rising over the Thames."

She gasped, then she giggled.

"I love my honeymoon."

I tightened my arms around her. "I love you."

TWO YEARS LATER

I pulled up to the house, the sight of it never failing to put a smile on my lips. I parked the car and went into the house, not surprised to find it empty. I knew I would find my wife in one of two places—by the water or by her trees.

I stopped in the kitchen and shrugged off my suit jacket, draping it over a chair. The sun glinted off the water in the pool in the back-yard. It was still and serene-looking, but I knew this weekend, as usual, it would be full, with lots of people laughing and splashing.

I walked through the family room, the inviting colors soothing and welcoming. Sunny had decorated the entire house with a beachy, warm vibe. Lots of blues and greens with ivory and gray undertones. Comfortable, well-used furniture. Fireplaces, both inside and out, that were used year-round since she loved to watch the flames dance. Lots of pictures were scattered around—of us, our family and friends. Memories of our life together. She had all my mother's paintings on the walls, even a few we had found in secondhand shops. Each one we recovered was a treasure for me. Mementos of our travels were sprinkled throughout the house. A print from London, a sculpture from Greece, a thick tartan blanket from Scotland. All of the addi-tions made the place eclectic, warm—and us.

She made the house a home.

I walked out of the open doors, spying Sunny under her tree. I made my way over, studying her as I went. Sitting on a blanket, she rested against the trunk of the tree, her legs outstretched. She faced the water, the light breeze lifting her hair. I knew she had been to the bakery today. I had watched her come and go, resisting the urge to go find her and kiss her in the storeroom. Now that she only went in on occasion, I didn't see her as much in the daytime, and I found myself missing her.

With my gentle encouragement, Sunny had given up the day-to-day running to Mack. He still controlled the kitchen, but he had lots of help. Lori and Shannon were still there and fulltime, along with three other staff members. Sunny handled all the marketing and finance and developed many of the new products they offered. She went in from time to time and helped out during the busier tourist time, but she now had a desk in the office here at home and worked in the kitchen a lot.

I was the official guinea pig for her attempts, and I loved it.

She volunteered at the community center fairly often. We had added a day care into the plans, and she loved spending time with the little ones, as well as talking to the teenagers. She was a favorite with many at the center—both staff and kids.

I was thrilled, knowing her life was easier now. I took my job as her husband very seriously. The caveman in me wanted her at home all the time, relaxed and stress-free, but I knew she would hate that. This was a good compromise for now. The day she decided she wanted something else, I was ready.

Emily now lived in Mission Cove, teaching at the local school. She also assisted at the community center, offering her services as a tutor. She lived in Sunny's old apartment and loved to help out at the bakery. Sunny was thrilled to have her close. Hayley was in nursing school. I had paid off their student loans and financed Hayley's continuing education. As their only "brother," I felt it was the least I could do. Sunny had cried, the girls cried, but none of them objected. I was pleased to be able to look after my family, and I took my job as brother as seriously as I took my husband role.

Sunny glanced up, her smile warm and welcoming. I dropped to the blanket beside her, leaning over for a kiss hello.

"You were at the bakery," I stated, reaching for the glass of iced tea beside her. "Yet no biscuits appeared on my desk, no visit from my wife to brighten my long, lonely day."

She snorted, passing me the glass. "I saw you two hours prior, and I was in the bakery for a short time to pick up some paperwork. I had other errands to run. I hardly think you needed a visit." She shook her head. "Abby was there, so don't give me the lonely bit."

I chuckled. "She was in and out all day. Jenny had something going on at school, so Abby was busy with her."

Sunny chuckled. "She's always busy."

I had to agree. Abby and Michael had a rocky, angst-filled start, but once they both accepted the feelings they had, and Michael came to grips with the fact that he could love another woman, they had flourished. Abby adored his kids, and they, in return, soaked up that affection, giving it back to her in spades. The first time Jenny had called her "Mom," Abby had wept in my arms for over ten minutes while telling me the story. Thinking it was something she would never have—a family of her own—I knew how special that was to her. Now married, she was entrenched in their lives. They were at our place a lot, Michael and I having grown closer, and she and Sunny best of friends.

Sunny sighed quietly, leaning against the bark of her tree, closing her eyes. I studied her for a moment, suddenly noticing the lines of fatigue on her face and the fact that she was paler than normal.

"Sunny?"

She didn't open her eyes. "I feel you looking at me. I'm fine, Linc. A bit tired, but fine."

"Then you need to rest more. You do too much for too many people."

A smile tugged on her lips. She opened her eyes, the look she gave me warm and tender.

"I will." Then she picked up a small bag. "I got you something."

I took the bag, filled with curiosity. I loved buying Sunny presents and did so regularly. She deserved to be spoiled. Her gifts were rarer. She said I was hard to buy for, but the truth was, I had all I wanted. Usually her gifts came in the form of a new kind of biscuit or something lacy she would wear for me. Those, I had to confess, were my favorite gifts.

But this bag was too heavy for lacy. I reached in and pulled out a small pot, containing a plant. I frowned at the odd gesture, then looked at Sunny. Her expression was bright, her eyes luminous.

"Um, thank you?" I murmured. "For my desk?" I guessed.

She shook her head. "I want to plant it about ten feet that way." She pointed toward the house.

"Oh. Another willow?"

"Yes," she said. "A *baby* willow. I thought we could plant it in recognition of the one you planted." As she finished speaking, she bit her lip, looking nervous.

"But I haven't planted..." My voice trailed off as her words sank in. I gaped at her. A baby willow. For the baby I had planted. In her.

A tear slipped down her cheek as I stared at her. Sweet, warm, anticipating, leaning on her tree, one hand resting on her stomach as the news—the wonderful, amazing news—she had to share with me took shape in my head.

Then she was in my arms and we were laughing, crying, kissing —celebrating. I cupped her face. "We're having a baby?" I confirmed.

"Yes."

"Are you all right?"

"Aside from being tired, yes. The doctor told me to rest a little more."

"I'll make sure of it."

"I knew you would."

I kissed her again, holding her close.

"I'll plant the tree tomorrow."

She laid her head on my chest. "I thought maybe we could make a whole grove someday."

I dropped a kiss to her head. "One, two, six. Whatever we decide. Whatever we're blessed with." My voice became thick. "I already have more than I dared to dream of."

She snuggled closer. "I love you, Linc."

I held her, my mind rampant, my thoughts a mass of jumbled emotions—mostly good, but one doubt I needed her to ease.

"Will I be a good father?" I asked, allowing my fear to show. "I didn't have a good role model."

"Which is why you'll be amazing. You will give this child every-thing you didn't have. I think you'll love this child—all our children—endlessly. You're patient and kind. Caring. Generous." She sighed. "Just like your mother."

I kissed her again. She always knew what to say. I caressed her stomach with the wonder that, beneath my hand, our child was grow-ing. Still tiny and fledgling. But there. Right under my hand.

"I love you," I murmured, bending low. "I already love you." I met Sunny's tender stare. "Thank you."

Sunny covered my hand with hers. Then she smiled.

And all was right with my world.

FOUR YEARS LATER

I turned my chair, staring across the street, the stress of the last meeting melting away. Sitting at the table in the window of the bakery across the street was my daughter. The light caught her golden curls, her feet swinging furiously as she babbled away to my wife, who was seated across from her. My daughter clutched something in her hand, and I was certain it would be a biscuit, slathered in jam and butter. Like me, that was her favorite.

I grabbed my phone and texted Sunny. She read my text and leaned over the table to Amanda, no doubt giving her my message. Amanda immediately turned to the window, waving wildly. Laughing, I stood close to the window and waved back. I was about to get up and go join them when my phone rang, and with a sigh, I turned away from the window, shooting off another text before answering.

Tell her Daddy misses her and can't wait to see her.

I answered the call, wanting to finish up and head over to the bakery. My family was there, and that was where I wanted to be. I always wanted to be with them.

There were now four willow trees out in front of our house.

The day Amanda Sophie was born was one of the greatest days of my life. When her brother, Chase Gerald, followed a couple of months ago, my life was complete. The house buzzed constantly.

I had hated to return to work, although I knew it was necessary.

But I planned on working from home more. Sunny only went into the bakery now every so often. Mandy loved going and seeing all her "friends," reigning like the little princess she was from her table.

As quickly as possible, I finished up the call and turned back to the window, disappointed to see the table empty. Sunny must have made the visit a short one, and I wondered if Chase was fussy again today. He was far more vocal and demanding than Amanda had been as a baby.

I focused on my work, determined to get it done and head home. My office door opened, and I glanced up, expecting Abby, hoping to see Sunny, confused when the open door was empty. Using my finger, I hooked the edge of the laptop, pulling it down, confusion changing to delight when I saw my daughter peeking through the open door.

"Daddy!" she crowed, bursting in.

I rounded the desk and bent low as she rushed toward me. I caught her in my arms, twirling her the way she loved. Her happy laughter filled the room, making me laugh as well. She always did. She had Sunny's coloring and stature—tiny and perfect—but my blue eyes. Freckles scattered across her nose and cheeks, and I loved to kiss each one, making her giggle.

She cupped my face with her tiny hands, her eyes dancing. "Hi!"

"Hi yourself." I looked at the pass dangling from her hands. She loved to be grown up and be the one to swipe the pass to get into the building or use the key at home. Anything to prove she was capable— not only had she inherited Sunny's looks, she had also inherited Sunny's stubborn streak. Watching the two of them go head-to-head at times was vastly amusing.

Amanda had been ahead of the curve her entire life. Aware of her surroundings early in life. Walking before she should, talking in full sentences while others her age jabbered. I encouraged her all the time. She constantly amazed me.

I looked toward the open door. "Where is Mommy?"

She pointed behind me. "Da bakery."

My heart stuttered in my chest. "What? Is Abby with you?"

She furrowed her little brow. "No," she explained slowly, as if I were the child and she the adult. "I took da key and came to see you, Daddy. Mommy say you miss me. Now you not have to."

"Amanda Webber," I said in my sternest voice. "How did you get here?"

"I walked." She shook her head as if I was slow. "I waited for da little man to say it was okay, and I crossed da street and came upstairs. Just like you taught me."

I lunged for my phone, unsure whether to laugh or cry. Somehow, while Sunny was busy, no doubt with Chase, my daughter decided to slip away and simply come see me. By herself. Crossing at the crosswalk the way we taught her, waiting for the little man to appear instead of the hand that said stop. She even thought to bring the key.

She thought it out and did it. By herself. At not even four years of age.

We were toast.

My phone rang before I could dial, and I answered without looking who it was.

"She's here. With me."

Sunny's panicked voice stuttered in relief, her words rushed. "Chase needed to be changed. She was eating her biscuit, chatting to Lori. When I came out, she was gone—I thought she went to the kitchen. But she wasn't there. She took the keys, Linc! She took my keys! I couldn't find her!" Her voice rose at the end.

"And used them properly," I muttered. "I'll talk to her. She's fine, Sunny."

I heard her muffled sob.

"Sit down. I'll be there in a moment," I instructed gently. "I'll talk to her first."

"Okay."

I sat down heavily, still holding Mandy. Her wide grin faded as she looked at me. "What's wrong, Daddy?"

271

I sat her on the desk in front of me. Then I stood, needing to be the scarier *Dad* for this conversation.

"Baby, you can't leave the bakery without an adult. Ever. Do you understand?"

"But I'm a big girl. You said so."

I had. On many occasions. I praised her. Cajoled her.

"You don't need a sippy cup. You're a big girl now."

"You did that all on your own? What a big girl you are!"

"No, you don't sleep in a crib. That's for Chase. You're a big girl and a big sister."

Now those words had come back to bite me in the ass.

I improvised.

"You can't leave anywhere without an adult until you're this high." I held my hand off the floor to my shoulder. "It's the law."

Her eyes widened. "Oh." Then she pursed her lips. "Mommy isn't dat tall, and she leaves all da time!"

She was too freaking smart.

"Mommy is an adult. The law changes when you are twenty-one."

That shut her up—for a minute.

"Sometimes Jesse comes to da bakery, and he isn't dat tall."

"He's a boy. It's different."

"It always is," Sunny sighed, walking in holding Chase's carrier. I could see the lingering panic on her face. Her eyes were bright with tears and rimmed in red.

I took the carrier, and she sat in front of Amanda. "You scared Mommy," she said quietly. "You shouldn't have left the bakery alone. Even to go see Daddy."

The sight of my wife's tears did way more than my warning for Amanda. Her little face was shocked. "Mommy, why you cry?"

"Because I couldn't find you, Mandy. You have to promise me never to do that again. Ever."

"I promise." Amanda flung herself into Sunny's arms. "I promise, Mommy!"

I watched the little tableau with a lump in my throat. We knew Amanda was adventuresome and brave. And far too smart. Everyone in town knew who she was, and being off-season, the town was quiet. Which was one reason she'd skipped along undetected. I doubted she had been in much danger, but Sunny was right. She couldn't be slipping out to see me or anyone else. We needed to nip this in the bud.

"You need to be punished for this, Amanda," I said.

Her eyes grew round with worry. I'd never used that word before now. I swallowed hard.

"No dessert tonight," I proclaimed. "And no TV either for the rest of the day."

She looked at Sunny, who nodded in agreement.

"Okay."

"You go sit at Abby's desk while I talk to your mother."

She slipped off Sunny's knee and shuffled past me, gazing up in sorrow. "I sorry, Daddy."

I stroked her head. "I know, baby."

"I play with Chase?"

I took the carrier to the desk and set it beside the table. "I'll be right over there."

"Okay." She bent over, whispering to Chase. She always did that, and I often wondered what secrets she was sharing.

I pulled Sunny into my arms and held her. "You okay?"

She sighed, burrowing closer. I sat down and tucked her onto my lap. We both needed to be close.

"That hurt?" she asked. "Saying the word punishment?"

"Yeah, it did."

"Pretty lame punishment, Daddy. She got off easy."

"It was all I could come up with on the spur of the moment. It's my first time, you know. Cut me some slack."

She smirked. "I think we'll find we'll need some more, ah, guidelines."

"Christ, she's too smart. All happy and proud, walking in,

clutching your pass, coming to see me," I muttered. "Telling me how she waited for the little man before crossing the street."

Sunny covered a laugh behind her hand. "Lori said the back door buzzed, so she went to let in the supplier. She told Mandy she'd be right back. She's sat there having her snack numerous times—she's never done this before."

I sighed. "I'd never waved to her before and said I missed her. I'm sure the idea popped into her head. I think we're entering new territory here." I glanced over at Amanda and groaned. "And she'll teach Chase. She's already started."

Sunny followed my gaze. "You said no TV. She's streaming."

I put my lips close to her ear. "She'd tell us it's a computer, therefore different."

"We are so screwed," Sunny sighed.

I watched Amanda as she sat on the floor, pointing out funny things on the screen to Chase. She'd pulled Abby's laptop down with her, signing in, no doubt using the password Abby shared with her at some point.

Amanda knew she was bending the rules, and I tried not to find delight in my little rebel of a daughter. She knew I would take away the computer, and she would surrender it with no fuss, but until then, she would enjoy her time with her brother.

And the sight of it made me smile.

"We are screwed," I agreed.

"But I love them," Sunny sighed again. "Our little fusspot and the rulebreaker."

I hugged her close. I rather looked forward to seeing what they would do to keep us on our toes.

We'd certainly never be bored.

"Me too," I assured her. "Especially their mother." I kissed her. Once. Twice. Third time for luck.

She cupped my face. "Now, let's take them home," she said. "I have biscuits for you in the car. We can have them for lunch before you forget the no-dessert thing too."

I had to kiss her again. An unexpected afternoon with my family. "Perfect."

TWELVE YEARS LATER

AMANDA

I crept up the path, sliding my fingers through the wooden slats until I found the latch. It lifted noiselessly thanks to the WD-40 I had squirted on it yesterday in preparation. I had learned my lesson before—that stuff leaves a scent, and if my dad smelled it, he would know something was up.

Luckily, my parents slept at the front of the house and I had already checked their light was off. I had Damon leave me by the beach and I cut up across the sand and stood under the willow trees to make sure. I slipped from tree to tree—there were six in total. The older ones were my parents, and the younger ones were us kids. It was kind of a sentimental thing for them, but I had to admit I sorta liked it. My tree was the tallest, then Chase's. The twins—Cedric Michael and Kelsey Lynn—weren't far behind. They were born two years after Chase. I loved them all, even if they were a pain at times.

I slipped through the gate, my shoes in one hand, hoping the patio doors would be unlocked. If not, I would have to go to the front and use my key. That would wake up my parents for sure. The solar lights flickered around the pool, and the outside light glowed dimly in the darkness as I crept closer. I'd almost gotten to the house when a voice broke the stillness.

"Not so fast, young lady."

I spun on my heel.

"Oh. Hi, Daddy."

"Don't 'Hi, Daddy' me. You're an hour past your curfew."

I glanced at my phone. "An hour and a half, actually."

My dad tried not to grin. "Honest to a fault—even for a rule-breaker. Sit down."

I curled into the chair next to him.

"Your mother and I are pretty lenient with you. But you broke three rules tonight, Amanda."

"Damon and I were talking, Daddy. I forgot about the time."

He shook his head. "Four rules now."

"Four?"

He held up his fingers and counted. "You broke curfew. You didn't call and let us know you were okay. You didn't answer my call. You just lied to my face." He sat back. "I noticed the squeak is gone from the gate as well, so technically, you planned on being late, so that's five."

I blushed. I had lied. I couldn't exactly tell my dad Damon and I had been kissing on the beach and I lost track of time. I always did when we kissed. He was an artist with his tongue, and I was crazy about him. I kept my mouth shut about all that. It would send my dad off the deep end.

He grasped my hand. "Your mother and I trust you, Amanda. We know how incredibly intelligent you are. I also know, thanks to the kickboxing lessons you attend, you can take care of yourself. But our trust will waver if you pull this shit again."

"Dad, it's summer. All the other kids get to stay out later."

"Those other kids aren't my daughter," he responded.

I huffed a sigh and crossed my arms.

"Just give me my punishment." My dad's punishments were always easier to take than my mom's—she was way tougher.

He mimicked my posture and sat back. "If you want to discuss extending your curfew, then you need to sit down with Mom and me to talk to us about it. The same way you did when you wanted a bigger allowance, or to go to movies alone with your friends. I don't appreciate you sneaking around to see more of this boy."

"I'm not sneaking around, and he isn't just some boy."

My dad's eyebrows shot up. "Pardon me?"

I couldn't meet his eyes. "He's...*special*." I sighed. "You wouldn't understand."

For a moment, there was silence. When he spoke, his voice was soft and gentle. "I do understand, baby. I met your mother when I was a kid. She was my best friend, and when I was fifteen, I fell in love with her. I've loved her ever since."

He had never told me that before. "Really?"

"Yes. We went through a lot to be together."

"Like what?"

He waved his hand. "That's a story for another time. The point is, we aren't trying to keep you apart, Amanda. Bring him around. Let us meet him. Hang out here some. If he's as important as you say, we want to get to know him."

"Really?"

"Yes. No more breaking curfew. I'll speak to him man-to-man about it."

I flung myself into his arms. "Thank you, Daddy!"

"Off to bed." Then as I turned to go, he held out his hand. "Your cell phone. Give it to me."

"Why?"

"That's your punishment. No cell phone for twenty-four hours. And you stay in your room tomorrow. No leaving the house. And you don't see this boy again until he comes for dinner."

I handed him my phone. "Mom's suggestion?"

"Yes. She said no dessert tomorrow wasn't enough this time." His eyes danced in the overhead light. "I didn't remind her you had messenger on your laptop either. You owe me one. But I mean it about the dinner."

I didn't mind having Damon over for dinner. He was alone a lot because his parents worked long hours. I knew he'd enjoy the meal since my mom was such a great cook. And they would like him—I knew it.

I bent and kissed his cheek. "You're the best dad ever."

"Pretend to be mad at me tomorrow, or I'll never hear the end of it from your mother."

"Okay."

"And we are having that talk tomorrow."

"Okay."

Then he smiled. "Love you, my little rulebreaker."

"I love you, Daddy."

LINC

After I knew Amanda was safe in her room, I locked up the house, set the alarm and climbed into bed, sliding up to Sunny and wrapping my arm around her waist, tugging her back to my chest.

She made a low noise of protest in her throat at being woken up, making me grin. She sounded exactly like Amanda did on school mornings.

I kissed the side of her soft neck, teasing the skin with my tongue.

She tilted back her head, squinting at me in the dim light.

"Is she home?"

"Yes."

"How late was she?"

"About an hour. She informed me it was an hour and a half."

Sunny snorted. "At least she's honest."

"That she is."

"Did you talk to her?"

"Yes," I said proudly. "I punished her too—just like you said."

Sunny huffed out a long breath. "How'd she take it?"

"Well, actually. I think she knows it could have been worse. She's crazy for this boy, Sunny." I sighed. "Christ, she is too young."

She laughed, her breath blowing over my arm. "We were in love young too, Linc."

"I know, that's what scares me. She's so similar to you. Even to me, emotionally. She feels things so deeply."

"Then we need to watch over her."

"I told her to invite this Damon boy over for dinner. Officially. I want to talk to him."

"We did meet him. He seemed very nice. His parents are lovely people, although they both work a lot. He comes to the center at times and helps out."

"We met him casually. Like we have all her friends. He's more." I snorted. "'*Special*,' Amanda said. He's more than a crush. I can feel it, Sunny. I want to get to know him."

"Good plan."

"I think she's been seeing more of him than we know. I think at a lot of the group outings, the two of them are pairing off. It's time to take this seriously and set some rules."

"All right, Linc. We will."

I sighed. "She wants to hear our story."

Sunny was quiet for a moment.

"I think she's old enough. She knows you had a terrible relationship with your father, and by telling her, it will explain why. She has always wondered how you couldn't love your dad the way she loves you." She paused. "It might help her understand."

"Do we tell her everything?"

"You may want to gloss over a few things."

"Yeah. We only spent the night in the cabin, *talking*, before I disappeared. And we never had sex until we got married. I'll emphasize those parts."

Sunny buried her face, laughing. "Okay, Daddy. Good plan. I meant some of your later, ah, decisions when it came to your father."

I huffed out a sigh. "Yeah, we'll stick to the basics there."

"We'll tell her together."

"Good." With Sunny beside me, it would be easier.

"Just so you know, I changed the password on her laptop. She can't message at all tomorrow."

"Dammit, woman, you are tough."

"One of us has to be. I'll make her suffer until the afternoon and then let her have it back. You can do it and be the hero again."

I laughed. My kids knew I was a pushover. But they were good kids—Amanda included. Smart, funny, kind, and loving, they all had my heart.

And they knew it.

The room was silent for a moment. "Are you asleep?" I asked.

Sunny growled. "I was trying."

"Oh. I was feeling hungry."

"It's called emotional eating."

"Whatever."

"There're some biscuits in the cupboard. You know where the jam is."

"Great. You coming?"

"No."

A different hunger tugged at me. A smile grew on my face, and I tucked her closer, running my lips up her neck and kissing the sensitive spot behind her ear. "Would you like to?"

For a moment, she said nothing. Then she giggled.

I rolled her over, hovering above.

"I'm feeling like a teenager."

"Horny?"

"Yep."

She arched up, rubbing herself against my groin. "You feel like it too."

"Wanna make out a little?" I nipped at her lips. "Or a lot? I'll make it good for you."

"You always do."

"I love you, Sunny-girl."

She pulled me down to her mouth. "I guarantee you a home run, Linc. Then you can have biscuits."

I grinned.

Sunny and biscuits.

The perfect pair.

Perfect for me.

ACKNOWLEDGMENTS

As always, I have some people to thank. The ones behind the words that encourage and support. The people who make my books possible for so many reasons.

Lisa, thank you for all you do. Your comments make me giggle, and your red pen makes the words better.

Beth, Trina, Melissa, Peggy, and Deb—thank you for your feedback and support.

Karen, this journey wouldn't be the same without you. I love working with you but getting to call you friend is even better. I promise you— your wine is safe. For now.

To all the bloggers, readers, and especially my promo team. Thank you for everything you do. Shouting your love of books—of my work, posting, sharing—your recommendations keep my TBR list full, and the support you have shown me is deeply appreciated.

To my fellow authors who have shown me such kindness, thank you.
I will follow your example and pay it forward.

My reader group, Melanie's Minions—love you all.

BOOKS BY MELANIE MORELAND

Vested Interest Series

BAM - The Beginning (Prequel)

Bentley (Vested Interest #1)

Aiden (Vested Interest #2)

Maddox (Vested Interest #3)

Reid (Vested Interest #4)

Van (Vested Interest #5)

Halton (Vested Interest #6)

Sandy (Vested Interest #7)

Insta-Spark Collection

It Started with a Kiss

Christmas Sugar

An Instant Connection

An Unexpected Gift

The Contract Series

The Contract (The Contract #1)

The Baby Clause (The Contract #2)

The Amendment (The Contract #3)

Mission Cove

The Summer of Us Book 1

Standalones

Into the Storm

Beneath the Scars

Over the Fence

My Image of You (Random House/Loveswept)

ABOUT THE AUTHOR

NYT/WSJ/USAT international bestselling author Melanie Moreland, lives a happy and content life in a quiet area of Ontario with her beloved husband of thirty-one-plus years and their rescue cat, Amber. Nothing means more to her than her friends and family, and she cherishes every moment spent with them.

While seriously addicted to coffee, and highly challenged with all things computer-related and technical, she relishes baking, cooking, and trying new recipes for people to sample. She loves to throw dinner parties, and enjoys traveling, here and abroad, but finds coming home is always the best part of any trip.

Melanie loves stories, especially paired with a good wine, and enjoys skydiving (free falling over a fleck of dust) extreme snowboarding (falling down stairs) and piloting her own helicopter (tripping over her own feet.) She's learned happily ever afters, even bumpy ones, are all in how you tell the story.

Melanie is represented by Flavia Viotti at Bookcase Literary Agency. For any questions regarding subsidiary or translation rights please contact her at flavia@bookcaseagency.com

Connect with Melanie

Like reader groups? Lots of fun and giveaways! Check it out Melanie Moreland's Minions

Join my newsletter for up-to-date news, sales, book announcements and excerpts (no spam): Melanie Moreland's newsletter

Visit my website www.melaniemoreland.com

facebook.com/authormoreland

twitter.com/morelandmelanie

instagram.com/morelandmelanie

CPSIA information can be obtained
at www.ICGtesting.com
Printed in the USA
LVHW050831040520
654932LV00004B/1174

9 781988 610320